WORLD WAR II
Day by Day

WORLD WAR II
Day by Day

Antony Shaw

ZENITH PRESS

This edition first published in 2000 by Zenith Press, an imprint of MBI Publishing Company, Galtier Plaza, Suite 200, 380 Jackson Street, St Paul, MN 55101-3885 USA

© 2000, 2005 Brown Reference Group plc

MBI Publishing Company books are also available at discounts in bulk quantity for industrial or sales promotional use. For details write to Special Sales Manager at Motorbooks International Wholesalers & Distributors, Galtier Plaza, Suite 200, 380 Jackson Street, St Paul, MN 55101-3885 USA

Library of Congress Cataloging-in-Publication Data Available.

ISBN 0-7603-0939-6

Printed in China

PAGE 1: *The backbone of the Soviet Red Army – the ordinary "Ivan." He and millions like him brought about the defeat of Nazi Germany in 1945.*

PAGES 2–3: *During the Battle of Santa Cruz in October 1942, the USS Hornet is attacked by Japanese dive-bombers. It would later sink.*

THESE PAGES: *British Crusader tanks in the North African desert in August 1942. Poorly armed and armored, they were no match for the German Panzer IV.*

Editor: Peter Darman
Art Editor: Duncan Brown
Production: Matt Weyland
Cartographer: William Le Bihan
Indexer: Kay Ollerenshaw

CONTENTS

INTRODUCTION

World War I, "The War to End All Wars," was to create many of the conditions that would lead to the outbreak of an even more destructive conflict – World War II. At the end of World War I Germany was in dire straits: its population was near starvation and devoid of hope, and its army and navy were in disarray. The Treaty of Versailles of June 1919 added to Germany's woes as it removed its overseas possessions, implemented the occupation of part of the Rhineland to ensure Germany complied with provisions of the treaty, and imposed huge reparations for the damage inflicted on France and other countries during World War I.

The fact that Germany was almost bankrupt meant that it was extremely unlikely Germany would be able to pay, even less so when the world slump of 1921 arose. The next year German defaulted on reparations payments for the second year running. In retaliation, France, showing amazing shortsightedness, occupied the Ruhr, the center of German industry. This not only reduced the already slim chances of Germany paying any reparations, but also increased hostility between the two countries.

The stoppage of the Ruhr industries had a calamitous impact on the German currency, which plummeted in value. Overnight, savings were wiped out, leaving millions penniless and destitute, their careers, hopes, and finances totally destroyed.

ADOLF HITLER
In such an atmosphere people desperately searched for answers. They found them in the vitriolic oratory of an

▼ *A Nuremberg rally. Each one was designed to increase support for both Hitler and Nazism.*

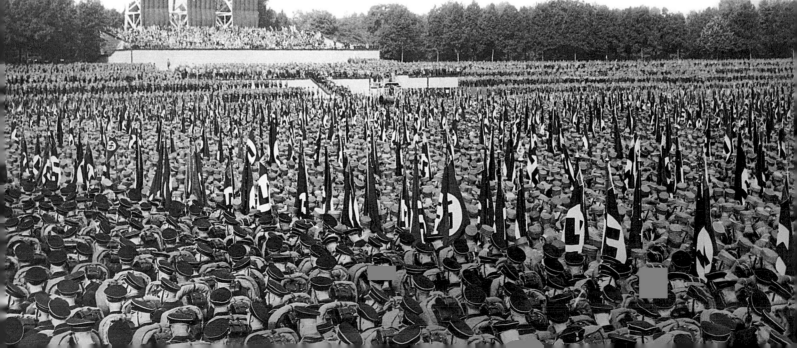

▶ German dictator Adolf Hitler, who was obsessed with the creation of German "living space" in Eastern Europe.

ex-soldier named Adolf Hitler, who belonged to the *Nationalsozialistische Deutsche Arbeiterpartei* (National Socialist German Workers' Party, or Nazi Party for short). The failure of Germany's Weimar government to cope with war debts and inflation made Hitler's claim that an alternative was needed seem sensible.

Notwithstanding his failure in the ludicrous 1923 Munich Beer Hall

▲ The 1936 Berlin Olympic Games, which provided Hitler with an opportunity to present Nazism on a world stage.

Putsch, the Nazi Party's membership continued to grow in the 1920s. The 1929 worldwide economic slump played into the Nazis' hands, for Hitler was able to blame the financial crisis on unpatriotic Jews and the conspiracies of communists – views that found receptive ears. In 1932 Hitler polled 36.9 percent of the vote, and after ingratiating himself with the World War I hero President Paul von Hindenburg, the latter invited the Nazi leader to become chancellor in 1933.

Once in power Hitler was able to establish a dictatorship. He created jobs by expelling Jews, by insisting that

women should stay at home and produce offspring, and by sending young men to labor camps (not to be confused with concentration camps). But there was a heavy price to be paid: the abolition of trade unions, and the persecution of Jews and communists. Hitler also renounced the Treaty of Versailles, began rearming, and reoccupied the Rhineland.

EXPANDING THE REICH
Having consolidated his position within Germany, Hitler now looked for *Lebensraum* ("living space") beyond its borders. His ambitions were helped by the peace treaties that followed World War I. For example, he wished to bring Czechoslovakia's Sudeten Germans back into the fold, while at the same time coveting Czechoslovakia's armaments industry.

As Austria and Czechoslovakia were absorbed into the Third Reich, the Western democracies dithered. Indeed, in both Britain and France there was a belief that the terms imposed on Germany by the Treaty of

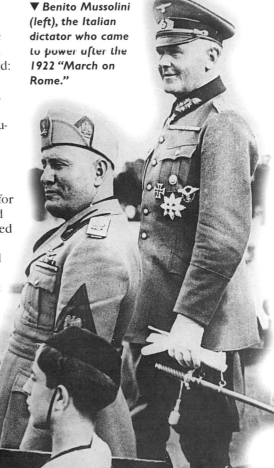

▼ Benito Mussolini (left), the Italian dictator who came to power after the 1922 "March on Rome."

KEY MOMENTS

APPEASEMENT

Appeasement has, since the end of World War II, been equated with cowardice and is held in contempt by some. In the 1930s, however, appeasement as believed in by British Prime Minister Neville Chamberlain and French leaders such as Edouard Daladier encapsulated reasonable steps that might be taken to prevent Hitler taking the law into his own hands. It was also the manifestation of a very real desire to avoid another general European war and its many associated horrors.

Appeasement had its roots in the growing feeling in the early 1930s in Britain and France that the terms of the Treaty of Versailles had been harsh on Germany. Seen in this light, Adolf Hitler's demands for a rearmed Germany and the restoration of "German" territories appeared reasonable. Thus by agreeing to these essentially "just" demands, Chamberlain believed he could lay the foundations for a lasting peace.

Unfortunately, appeasement relied on the goodwill of both parties to be a success. Thus after the Munich talks in September 1938, Chamberlain and Daladier agreed to Hitler's demands for the incorporation into the Third Reich of German-speaking Czechoslovak Sudetenland. Chamberlain proclaimed the agreement heralded "peace with honor." For his part Hitler had expected a confrontation over the issue, and Britain and France's failure to stand up to him encouraged more brinkmanship. He occupied the rest of Czechoslovakia in March 1939, signaling the end of appeasement. This guaranteed that both Britain and France would fight to defend Poland.

Versailles had been harsh, and that by appeasing Hitler by assenting to his "just" demands, a basis for a lasting European peace could be laid.

But they were both mistaken. The belief that the Munich agreement of September 1938, whereby the Sudetenland was ceded to Germany, would lead to "peace in our time" was also wrong. This was confirmed in March 1939 when Germany occupied the rest of Czechoslovakia.

MUSSOLINI'S ITALY

World War II had, for all practical purposes, begun; the more so because Hitler had similarly belligerent allies in Europe and the Far East. In Italy, for example, Benito Mussolini fancied himself as a twentieth-century Caesar. His fascist regime had achieved some notable results in the country, such as the drainage and cultivation of marshes, the construction of factories and roads, the balancing of the budget, and, probably his greatest achievement, making the trains run on time. His regime built up the army, navy, and air force, and glorified war, while Mussolini himself talked of the Mediterranean as being *Mare Nostrum* ("Our Sea").

Mussolini realized that his armed forces required modern equipment, and so he picked his opponents carefully. His attack against Ethiopia (then Abyssinia) was regarded with disgust

▼ *Danzig, on the Baltic at the mouth of the Vistula River, was designated a "free city" by the League of Nations. Hitler demanded its return to Germany, along with the so-called "Polish Corridor."*

by other European nations, as Italian warplanes dropped bombs and poison gas on spear-armed tribesmen. Nevertheless, the war confirmed the impotence of the League of Nations, which could not rally any of its members to take effective action.

THE AXIS ALLIANCE

In the Far East, Japan flexed its muscles. Having defeated Russia in 1904–05, it went on to annex Korea

◀ Italian light tanks pictured during the Spanish Civil War. Both Italian and German units participated in the conflict, picking up valuable battle experience.

Poland now became the focus of Hitler's attention. Recreated after World War I, it had been given access to the sea via a corridor of land which reached the Baltic at Danzig. It had been formerly German territory, and Hitler was determined it would be again. Danzig was, in theory, a "free city" administered by the United Nations, but in reality the Nazis had gained control of the city in 1934 and did largely what they liked. Hitler ranted that it and the strip of land that divided Germany and East Prussia should be returned to the Reich.

Few people in the West knew or cared very much what the "Polish Corridor" was - some believed it to be an underground tunnel - but in March 1939 Britain and France took the fateful step of pledging themselves to the defense of Poland, which neither of them was in a military position to do. When German armies entered Poland on September 1, 1939, they had no choice but to declare war two days later. World War II had begun, little more than two decades after the end of the first great conflict.

and overrun the whole of Manchuria, which was renamed Manchukuo. When the League of Nations protested, Japan simply resigned its membership. In 1936 it signed the anticommunist Anti-Comintern Pact with Germany and Italy. Japan was now part of the Rome-Berlin-Tokyo Axis, which was seemingly further strengthened when Hitler and Joseph Stalin, the Soviet leader, signed a nonaggression pact on August 23, 1939, in which a secret clause divided up a conquered Poland between the two dictators (Stalin did not want German troops on the frontier of the Soviet Union itself).

▼ The fruits of Nazi Germany's rearmament program – Hitler inspects a new warship at Kiel.

After months of diplomatic wrangling and "appeasement" bargaining, war erupted when Germany invaded Poland. Germany's Blitzkrieg offensive, which plunged Europe into conflict, heralded a new and dramatic style of modern warfare. Although there was no Allied advance into Germany in Western Europe, fighting flared up on the Eastern Front between the Soviet Union and neighboring Finland.

SEPTEMBER 1

EASTERN FRONT, *POLAND*

A German force of 53 divisions, supported by 1600 aircraft, crosses the German and Slovak borders into Poland in a pincer movement. Plan White, directed by General Walther von Brauchitsch, aims to totally paralyze Poland's 24 divisions by swift encirclement, thus cutting their lines of supply and communication. While Poland mobilizes its full strength, its forces in action, lacking both air and armored support, are largely placed on the country's borders. They are quickly overrun, and reinforcements often arrive too late to halt the German attacks.

SEPTEMBER 2

POLITICS, *ALLIES*

Ultimatums are delivered by Britain and France to Germany demanding its immediate withdrawal from Poland.

SEPTEMBER 3

POLITICS, *ALLIES*

Britain and France declare war on Nazi Germany after their ultimatums regarding the invasion of Poland expire. Australia and New Zealand also declare war. British Prime Minister Neville Chamberlain forms a war cabinet, which includes prominent antiappeasers First Lord of the Admiralty Winston Churchill and Secretary for the Dominions Anthony Eden.

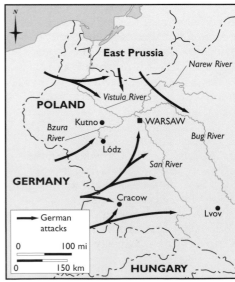

▲ *The German invasion of Poland began in September with air and ground attacks that quickly paralyzed the Polish forces.*

◄ *German troops tear down border posts as they advance into Poland.*

▲ *French citizens cheer their soldiers after mobilization orders are issued in 1939.*

SEA WAR, *ATLANTIC*
The liner *Athenia* is sunk by the *U-30* after being mistaken for a British auxiliary cruiser, claiming 112 lives.

SEPTEMBER 4

AIR WAR, *GERMANY*
Britain's Royal Air Force (RAF) Bomber Command launches its first attacks against Nazi warships in the Heligoland Bight off northwest Germany, but the government will not authorize raids on targets within Germany.

SEPTEMBER 5

POLITICS, *SOUTH AFRICA*
Prime Minister Jan Christiaan Smuts declares war on Nazi Germany following the formation of a new cabinet after political disagreements over joining the conflict.
POLITICS, *UNITED STATES*
The authorities officially proclaim their neutrality.

SEPTEMBER 6

EASTERN FRONT, *POLAND*
The Polish government and high command leave Warsaw and order

▶ *German troops make a hasty river crossing during the invasion of Poland.*

their forces to withdraw to the line of the Narew, Vistula, and San Rivers. Nazi troops make a dramatic advance that reaches beyond Lódz. They also seize Cracow in the south.

SEPTEMBER 7

WESTERN FRONT, *GERMANY*
France begins minor skirmishes across the border with Germany near Saarbrücken.

SEA WAR, *ATLANTIC*
Britain's first convoys sail across the Atlantic. The system is already operating on Britain's east coast to protect merchant ships from U-boat attacks.

SEPTEMBER 8

EASTERN FRONT, *POLAND*
The German Tenth Army led by General Walter von Reichenau reaches the outskirts of Warsaw, the capital.

SEPTEMBER 9

▲ *Polish lancers head for the front.*

General Wilhelm List's Fourteenth Army reaches the San River around Przemysl, while General Heinz Guderian's tank corps reaches the Bug River to the east of Warsaw.

SEPTEMBER 9

EASTERN FRONT, *POLAND*
A Polish counterattack is launched by 10 divisions, which gather around Kutno under General Tadeuz Kutrzeba. The attack over the Bzura River against Germany's Eighth Army is the most effective Polish offensive of the campaign, but only achieves short-term success.

▼ *A grief-striken Polish girl finds her sister has been killed during a German air attack on Warsaw.*

SEPTEMBER 10

POLITICS, *CANADA*
The government declares war on Germany.

WESTERN FRONT, *FRANCE*
Major elements of the British Expeditionary Force, led by

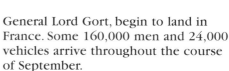

General Lord Gort, begin to land in France. Some 160,000 men and 24,000 vehicles arrive throughout the course of September.

SEPTEMBER 13

POLITICS, *FRANCE*
Prime Minister Edouard Daladier forms a war cabinet and takes additional responsibility for foreign affairs.

SEPTEMBER 16–27

EASTERN FRONT, *POLAND*
Warsaw's defenders are encircled but refuse to surrender until the 27th. Elements of Germany's Fourteenth Army west of Lvov are still locked in battle, while other units advance to join General Heinz Guderian's units in action along the Bug River.

SEPTEMBER 17

SEA WAR, *ATLANTIC*
The British aircraft carrier *Courageous* is sunk by *U-29* during an antisubmarine patrol off southwest Ireland. The aircraft carrier *Ark Royal* has managed to escape a similar attack just three days beforehand. The naval authorities act quickly and withdraw Britain's aircraft carriers from such duties to preserve these valuable vessels for other maritime roles.

◀ *Polish forces surrendering to a German officer. Despite Poland's fighting spirit, its armies were decisively defeated by Germany's Blitzkrieg attack.*

formed and many fighters escape to join the Allies. Poland is split into two zones of occupation divided by the Bug River. Germany has lost 10,572 troops and the Soviet Union has 734 men killed in the campaign. Around 50,000 Poles are killed and 750,000 captured.

SEPTEMBER 21

POLITICS, *ROMANIA*
A local fascist group, the "Iron Guard," assassinates Romanian Prime Minister Armand Calinescu.

SEPTEMBER 27

POLITICS, *GERMANY*
Adolf Hitler's senior commanders are told of his plans for a western offensive at the earliest opportunity. This announcement is met with hostility by the military, who resent Hitler assuming direct control over strategic planning and also feel unprepared for this undertaking. His plan for invading the Low Countries, formulated as Plan Yellow on October 19, is constantly aborted due to bad weather. The plan is also modified and its objectives widened before the actual offensive in 1940.

▼ *The British aircraft carrier* **Courageous** *was sunk in September 1940 by a U-boat during an antisubmarine patrol. British aircraft carriers were quickly withdrawn from such duties.*

SEPTEMBER 17–30

EASTERN FRONT, *POLAND*
In accordance with a secret clause in their 1939 pact with Germany, the Red Army invades. Little resistance is encountered on Poland's eastern border as the Polish Army is fighting for its life to the west.

SEPTEMBER 18–30

POLITICS, *POLAND*
The Polish government and high command flee to Romania, only to be interned. A government-in-exile is

STRATEGY & TACTICS

BLITZKRIEG

Blitzkrieg ("lightning war") aimed to inflict a total defeat on an enemy through a single, powerful offensive. This was to be achieved by speed, firepower, and mobility. General Heinz Guderian's book *Achtung! Panzer!* (1933) articulated the strategy, which aimed to avoid the costly and indecisive trench warfare of 1914–18.

Germany exploited the developments in tanks, mobile artillery, and aircraft in its first Blitzkrieg, the attack on Poland. Blitzkrieg always avoided strong resistance in order to sustain the momentum of the assault, which concentrated on an enemy's rear areas to break his lines of supply and communication. Once this was achieved, less-mobile forces could annihilate isolated pockets of resistance.

Blitzkrieg not only required new technology; it also needed commanders with the tactical vision and flexibility to exploit opportunities and overcome obstacles in order to sustain an attack's momentum.

The Allies, having failed to appreciate the lessons of the Blitzkrieg strike on Poland, were equally stunned by the 1940 attacks against France and the Low Countries. Germany's formidable strategy, therefore, inflicted another major defeat.

A German Heinkel He 111 attacks Warsaw during the invasion of Poland. Aircraft were a vital component of the Blitzkrieg and acted as mobile artillery for the advancing land forces during an offensive.

KEY PERSONALITIES

ADOLF HITLER

Adolf Hitler (1889–1945), the founder and leader of Nazi Germany, was born in Austria. His experiences as a failed artist in Vienna and decorated soldier in World War I helped shape his extremist political ambitions, which led to the Nazi Party's foundation.

He exploited Weimar Germany's political turbulence and social unrest to maneuver himself into power in 1933. Violence and intimidation secured his position as dictator. His Nazism fused nationalism with racism and created powerful expansionist ambitions. Hitler articulated the dream of creating an empire by destroying Germany's supposed racial and ideological enemies. His desire to realize his expansionist ambitions plunged Europe into diplomatic chaos and, ultimately, war.

Hitler's political skills centered upon his opportunistic character and mastery of propaganda. However, as Führer ("leader") Hitler also became Germany's military master. In this capacity Hitler's boldness and confidence were demonstrated in Germany's early Blitzkrieg successes.

By 1941 Hitler's skills were in decline, and his stubbornness and lack of strategic vision exacerbated the military problems. He became isolated from reality and refused to admit the war was lost.

Hitler survived an assassination attempt in 1944 but finally took his own life in 1945. Hitler's empire was finally crushed, but the destruction it wrought left the world remolded by the bloodiest war in history.

▶ Soviet forces in Finland dismantle antitank obstacles along the Mannerheim Line in the Karelian Isthmus.

SEPTEMBER 29

POLITICS, *SOVIET UNION*
After occupying Poland, the Soviet Union concentrates on extending its control over the Baltic Sea region to safeguard against any German threat. During the next few weeks it gains bases and signs "mutual assistance" agreements with Lithuania, Latvia, and Estonia. Finland, however, will not agree to the Soviet Union's territorial demands and mobilizes its armed forces in October as political dialogue fails to resolve the crisis.

OCTOBER 14

SEA WAR, *NORTH SEA*
The British battleship *Royal Oak* is sunk, with 786 lives lost, after *U-47* passes through antisubmarine defenses at Scapa Flow in the Orkneys, where the Home Fleet is anchored. Defenses are improved at the base after this dramatic attack.

NOVEMBER 4

POLITICS, *UNITED STATES*
Changes to the Neutrality Act permit belligerent states to purchase arms from private suppliers on a "cash-and-carry" basis, whereby they have to pay for any weapons and then transport them using their own vessels. Given Britain's command of the Atlantic sea-lanes, this act is clearly intended to benefit the Allied nations.

NOVEMBER 26

POLITICS, *FINLAND*
Criticism of Finland in the Soviet press and a faked border incident further sours Soviet–Finnish relations. Joseph Stalin, the Soviet leader, subsequently withdraws from the nonaggression pact with Finland and breaks off relations. Finland, lacking allies or arms, fails to anticipate the attack, believing talks will avert a conflict.

NOVEMBER 30

EASTERN FRONT, *FINLAND*
A Soviet force of over 600,000 men, backed by air and naval power, attacks Finland in support of Otto Kuusinen's newly-proclaimed Finnish People's Government, which is sponsored by the Soviet Union. As aircraft bomb the capital, Helsinki, Field Marshal Karl von Mannerheim leads the nation's defense with a mainly reservist

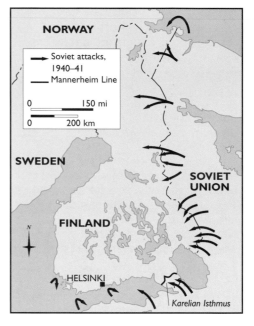

▲ The Soviet invasion of Finland comprised land, air, and amphibious attacks.

force, inferior in both numbers and arms. The main Soviet thrust through the Karelian Isthmus is obstructed by the Mannerheim Line, a 1914–18 system of fortifications that runs through rugged terrain and forest.

Other Soviet forces attack eastern and northern Finland, and also launch failed amphibious assaults on the southern coast. As the campaign progresses, highly-motivated Finnish troops exploit their familiarity with the terrain and use their ability to ski through snow-covered areas to launch hit-and-run raids on Red Army units bogged down by the weather.

DECEMBER 2

POLITICS, *FINLAND*
The League of Nations is asked by Finland to intervene in its conflict

with the Soviet Union. The League eventually agrees, but the Soviet Union opposes its involvement and is expelled from the organization on December 14.

DECEMBER 7

EASTERN FRONT, *FINLAND*

The Soviet 163rd Division approaches Suomussali village in eastern Finland. Halted by freezing conditions, its troops are targeted by the Finnish 9th Division, which severs its supply lines. The Soviet 44th Division, sent as a relief force, is blocked by Finnish attacks and both Red Army units attempt a breakout. By the end of the year these divisions have been forced to

▲ Marshal Karl von Mannerheim led Finland's determined defense against the Soviet attack on his country.

capitulate, after having 27,500 men killed by enemy action or the freezing temperatures. The Finns achieve similar successes in other engagements during the "Winter War."

DECEMBER 16

EASTERN FRONT, *FINLAND*

After advancing to the Mannerheim Line, the Soviet Seventh Army begins a major offensive. To compensate for their lack of armor and artillery, innovative sabotage techniques and improvised explosive devices ("Molotov Cocktails," named after the Soviet foreign minister) are used by Finnish ski-troops to destroy enemy tanks. The fighting will continue until February 11, 1940.

DECEMBER 13

SEA WAR, *ATLANTIC*

The British heavy cruiser *Exeter*, with light cruisers *Ajax* and *Achilles*, engage the German pocket battleship *Graf Spee* at the mouth of the Plate River, off Uruguay. The British vessels sustain severe damage as they maneuver to prevent *Graf Spee* delivering concentrated fire on a single vessel.

Graf Spee, itself damaged, withdraws to neutral Uruguay for repairs. *Ajax* and *Achilles* are later joined by the heavy cruiser *Cumberland* to await *Graf Spee*'s emergence from Montevideo port. The *Graf Spee*, however, is scuttled by its crew on the 17th.

DECEMBER 23

POLITICS, *CANADA*

The first Canadian troops, some 7500 men, arrive in Britain.

▼ Germany's pocket battleship **Graf Spee** is scuttled after being trapped by the Royal Navy in neutral Uruguay.

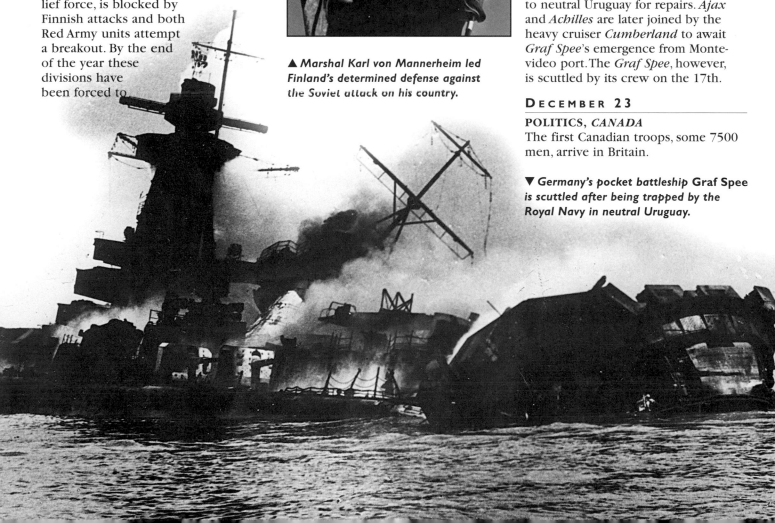

1940

The German Army conquered much of Western Europe in 1940 in a series of spectacular Blitzkrieg victories. German armor and aircraft attacked and defeated a succession of Allied armies in Scandinavia, France, and the Low Countries. Germany's defeat in an aerial battle over Britain, however, saved that nation from any invasion. Britain's survival now depended on North American aid. Meanwhile, the war widened, with Italian offensives in Africa and the Balkans.

Captured documents read by the Allies reveal an invasion plan for the 17th. For this reason, and because of poor weather, Adolf Hitler postpones the invasion until the spring.

JANUARY 14

POLITICS, *JAPAN*
Admiral Mitsumasa Yonai forms a new government in Japan after the resignation of Prime Minister Nobuyuki Abe's cabinet. Yonai's government, however, provokes opposition from the prowar military hierarchy.

FEBRUARY 5

POLITICS, *ALLIES*
The Allied Supreme War Council decides to intervene in Norway and Finland. This vague and indecisive policy relies on the cooperation of neutral Norway and Sweden. The main motivation is the Allied desire to deny Germany access to Swedish iron ore supplies, which pass through the ice-free port of Narvik in Norway.

FEBRUARY 16

SEA WAR, *NORTH SEA*
The British destroyer *Cossack* violates Norway's neutrality to rescue 299 British merchant seamen aboard the German transport *Altmark*. Germany accelerates its invasion preparations, believing that Britain is planning more military actions in Norway.

FEBRUARY 24

POLITICS, *GERMANY*
Plans for the invasion of Western Europe are revised. The main focus of

JANUARY 7–FEBRUARY 17

EASTERN FRONT, *FINLAND*
General Semyon Timoshenko assumes command of the Soviet invasion forces in the Karelian Isthmus and initiates a training program to improve service cooperation. After reorganizing and reequipping, his forces begin a determined attack on the Mannerheim Line on the 12th. The Finns complete a withdrawal to a secondary zone of defense on the line by February 17. Secret peace negotiations have already begun in late January.

JANUARY 10

WESTERN FRONT, *BELGIUM*
A lost German plane carrying two army officers lands at Mechelen.

▶ *Finnish officers discuss the battle against the Soviet invaders.*

◄ *The British destroyer Cossack, which sailed into Norwegian waters to rescue 299 British sailors imprisoned on a German vessel.*

▼ *The British destroyer Glowworm sinks after ramming the German heavy cruiser Admiral Hipper.*

the offensive is changed to the Ardennes region after a suggestion by General Erich von Manstein. The bulk of the German Army's armored units are allocated to this radical plan.

MARCH 11

EASTERN FRONT, *FINLAND*

The Treaty of Moscow between Finland and the Soviet Union is agreed after the Red Army makes hard-won gains. Although Allied help to the nation is negligible, the Finnish Army has not capitulated. Finland retains its independence but has to surrender the Karelian Isthmus and Hangö – 10 percent of its territory. Campaign losses: 200,000 Soviet troops and 25,000 Finns.

MARCH 20

POLITICS, *FRANCE*

Prime Minister Edouard Daladier resigns after criticism of his failure to take the initiative to support Finland and thereby redirect the war away from France. Paul Reynaud succeeds Daladier on March 21.

MARCH 28

POLITICS, *ALLIES*

Britain and France agree not to make any separate peace treaties. From April 5 they plan to mine Norwegian waters to force Nazi ships carrying Swedish iron ore into the open seas and expose them to naval attack. The minelaying is deferred to April 8. This is too late to prevent the Nazi invasion planned for the 9th.

APRIL 8

SEA WAR, *NORTH SEA*

The British destroyer *Glowworm* intercepts part of the German invasion fleet

◄ *Edouard Daladier, France's premier to March 1940.*

bound for Norway. It is sunk after ramming the heavy cruiser *Admiral Hipper*, but a British submarine then sinks the transport *Rio de Janiero*. However, Royal Navy vessels deployed in the North Sea have not received sufficient information about the German invading force and are unable to intercept it.

APRIL 9

WESTERN FRONT, *NORWAY/DENMARK*

A German invasion force, including surface ships, U-boats, and 1000 aircraft, attacks Denmark and Norway. Denmark is overrun immediately. The first ever airborne assault is made on Oslo and Stavanger airports in Norway, while ships land troops at six locations. Norway's six divisions have no tanks or effective artillery, while its coastal defenses and navy are generally inferior.

However, in Oslo Fiord, shore guns sink the German cruiser *Blücher*, claiming 1600 lives. This enables King Haakon to escape northward with his

APRIL 10–13

▶ Germany's Blitzkrieg on Norway and Denmark began with combined airborne and amphibious landings.

government. The British battlecruiser *Rodney* engages the battlecruisers *Scharnhorst* and *Gneisenau*, damaging the latter. The cruiser *Karlsruhe* is later sunk off Kristiansand by a British submarine.

APRIL 10–13

SEA WAR, *NORWAY*
Five British destroyers launch a surprise attack on 10 German destroyers and shore batteries to the west of Narvik. During short and confused engagements each side loses two destroyers, while eight German merchant vessels and an ammunition carrier are also sunk. The cruiser *Königsberg* becomes the first vessel to be sunk by dive-bombing during a British air attack on Bergen.

Subsequent air attacks on the *Gneisenau, Scharnhorst,* and *Admiral Hipper* by the British on the 12th fail. A British battleship and nine destroyers succeed in sinking eight German destroyers, plus a U-boat, by aerial attack in the Second Battle of Narvik on April 13.

APRIL 10–30

WESTERN FRONT, *NORWAY*
After securing their initial objectives, the Germans begin their conquest of Norway. Major General Carl Otto Ruge, Norway's new commander-in-chief, leads a stubborn defense around Lake Mjösa and the Glomma Valley.

APRIL 14–19

WESTERN FRONT, *NORWAY*
An Allied expeditionary force of over 10,000 British, French, and Polish

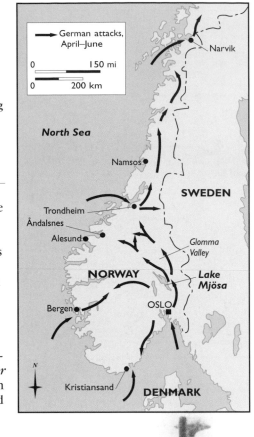

troops, first formed to assist Finland, lands at Namsos, Alesund, and Narvik. Its objective is to recapture Trondheim to secure a base in Norway, but its units

▼ German infantry arrive in Oslo, the Norwegian capital.

▲ *Norwegian ski-troops were especially useful in disrupting German lines of communication.*

coordination with the Norwegian forces is poor, but the Germans in the area eventually withdraw at the end of April.

MAY 7–10

POLITICS, *BRITAIN*
Prime Minister Neville Chamberlain is severely criticized over the Norwegian

▼ *French mountain soldiers arriving in Norway to help repel the Nazi invasion. The Allies sent a force of British, French, and Polish troops to help the country.*

▲ *The German cruiser Königsberg sinks after a British air attack.*

are ill-prepared for the campaign. There has been little liaison with the Norwegians. The various Allied units lack cohesion, training in arctic warfare, key supplies, air cover, and anti-aircraft weaponry.

APRIL 20–30

WESTERN FRONT, *NORWAY*
German troops defend Trondheim and wait for the arrival of more forces. German aircraft launch determined attacks against the Allies. British and French troops eventually evacuate Namsos and Åndalsnes on May 1–2.

APRIL 24

WESTERN FRONT, *NORWAY*
An Allied offensive on Narvik begins with a naval bombardment. Allied

◄ *Eben Emael, the key Belgium fortress captured by German paratroopers.*

campaign during a House of Commons debate. Chamberlain resigns after a significant fall in government support in a vote of confidence and the opposition Labour Party's refusal to serve under him in a coalition. Winston Churchill replaces him and forms a coalition government.

MAY 8

POLITICS, *SOVIET UNION*
General Semyon Timoshenko replaces Marshal

Kliment Voroshilov as the Soviet commissar for defense.

MAY 10

WESTERN FRONT, *LUXEMBOURG/ HOLLAND/BELGIUM*
The Germany's Army Group A, under General Gerd von Rundstedt, and Group B, commanded by General Fedor von Bock, invade after preliminary air attacks. Successful airborne landings are made against Belgium's key frontier fortress of Eben Emael,

◄ *British premier Neville Chamberlain, the appeasement advocate, who resigned after failing to save Finland and Norway.*

▼ *German troops crossing the Maas River during the invasion of Holland.*

and in Holland, to dislocate resistance. General Ritter von Leeb's Army Group C covers France's Maginot Line, the line of subterranean forts and other defensive positions running along its border with Germany.

In accordance with Allied planning, the left flank of the British and French line moves into Belgium. This decision facilitates Rundstedt's surprise Ardennes advance, which eventually divides the Allied armies in Belgium from those in France. The Allied armies advancing into Belgium up to the Dyle and Meuse Rivers above Namur, a position known as the Dyle Plan Line, are hampered by poor coordination with Dutch and Belgian forces.

MAY 11–15

WESTERN FRONT, *HOLLAND/BELGIUM*
Dutch resistance to the German attack crumbles, despite opening the flood gates and mining the Rhine River to obstruct the enemy. German forces begin to approach the Allied Dyle Line, while Belgian defenders are driven back from the Albert Canal.

Queen Wilhelmina of the Netherlands escapes with the Dutch government to Britain on May 13. The city of Rotterdam is bombed before a cease-fire is declared on the 14th, and the Dutch Army capitulates the next day.

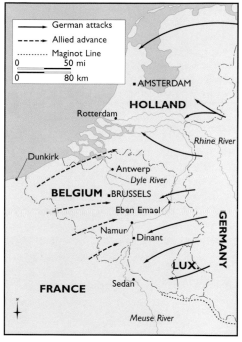

▲ A six-inch (15-cm) howitzer in action with the French Second Army during the desperate fight to save France in 1940.

◄ Germany's offensive, which began on May 10, lured the Allies into the Low Countries, while a surprise attack went into France through the Ardennes.

and Second Armies, which then mount a futile response.

MAY 15–20

WESTERN FRONT, *BELGIUM*
Germany's Sixth and Eighteenth Armies force the Allies to withdraw from the Dyle Plan Line to the Scheldt

MAY 12–14

WESTERN FRONT, *FRANCE*
German forces reach the Meuse River, the crossing of which is critical for the advance into France. Dive-bombers pound French positions and inflatable rafts are used to establish bridgeheads at Sedan and Dinant on the13th. Despite Allied air attacks, German armor advances westward rapidly, opening a 50-mile (75-km) gap in the Allied line. This drives a wedge between the French Ninth

KEY PERSONALITIES

PRIME MINISTER SIR WINSTON CHURCHILL

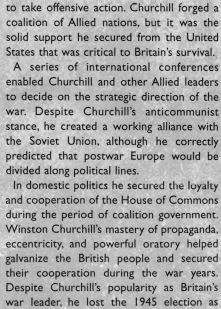

Winston Spencer Churchill (1874–1965), soldier, journalist, and statesman, had held ministerial offices but was relegated to the margins of political life in Britain during the 1930s for his anti-appeasement stance. He was propelled into power, however, as prime minister in 1940 as the Nazis appeared close to total victory.

Churchill reversed the fortunes of the nation by dismissing any sign of defeatism.

The bold but often impatient prime minister constantly urged his military commanders to take offensive action. Churchill forged a coalition of Allied nations, but it was the solid support he secured from the United States that was critical to Britain's survival.

A series of international conferences enabled Churchill and other Allied leaders to decide on the strategic direction of the war. Despite Churchill's anticommunist stance, he created a working alliance with the Soviet Union, although he correctly predicted that postwar Europe would be divided along political lines.

In domestic politics he secured the loyalty and cooperation of the House of Commons during the period of coalition government. Winston Churchill's mastery of propaganda, eccentricity, and powerful oratory helped galvanize the British people and secured their cooperation during the war years. Despite Churchill's popularity as Britain's war leader, he lost the 1945 election as many felt that a new premier was needed for the challenges of postwar Britain. Nevertheless, Churchill remains one of the twentieth century's most significant figures.

MAY 15

Line, west of Brussels, and the Dendre River. French forces have been forced to fall back from Holland, while the Belgians continue fighting between Antwerp and Brussels, finally retreating to the Escaut Canal and then to the Lys River, which is reached on the 20th.

MAY 15

AIR WAR, *GERMANY*

Britain launches its first strategic air attack on Germany with 99 aircraft hitting oil plants and railroad marshaling yards in the Ruhr region.

MAY 16–20

WESTERN FRONT, *FRANCE*

The French General Reserve and units south of the German forces are ordered to form the Sixth Army to bolster the vulnerable Allied lines, but this fails to halt the German advance. Brigadier General Charles de Gaulle's 4th Armored Division attempts to counterattack around Laon–Montcornet on May 17–19 but fails.

German tanks reach Cambrai on May 18, and finally the sea at Abbeville two days later. It now becomes critical for the Allies to cut the "corridor" made by the panzers or risk the isolation of their armies to the north from the forces in the south. The dismissal of General Maurice Gamelin, the Allied commander-in-chief, and the appointment of Maxime Weygand as his successor on the 19th further delays military decision-making, which reduces the potential for any action.

MAY 21–28

WESTERN FRONT, *FRANCE*

British tanks battle with the 7th Panzer Division at Arras until May 23. General Heinz Guderian moves toward Boulogne and Calais unaffected by the Allied "Weygand Plan," which attempts to split the tank spearhead from troops and supplies in the German "corridor." Boulogne and Calais capitulate after the naval evacuation of Allied troops.

Eager to preserve his panzers for taking Paris, Hitler halts General Gerd von Rundstedt's armor at Gravelines and allows the air force to attack the Allied "pocket" centering on

▲ *British troops surrender in Calais after trying to defend the port against attacking German armor and aircraft.*

▼ *General Maurice Gamelin, commander of the Allied armies in France, failed to halt the German Blitzkrieg.*

Dunkirk. British aircraft, however, resist the attacks, enabling the Allies to prepare for an evacuation.

MAY 25–28

WESTERN FRONT, *BELGIUM*

King Leopold of Belgium's forces are left surrounded as the Allies

Paris condemns King Leopold's surrender and assumes his powers.

MAY 26

WESTERN FRONT, *FRANCE/BELGIUM*

Operation Dynamo, the evacuation of Allied forces from the Dunkirk area, begins. A defensive perimeter established on the Aa, Scarpe, and Yser "canal line" covers the withdrawal, while an assorted rescue flotilla of pleasure boats, commercial craft, and naval vessels crosses and recrosses the English Channel.

MAY 31

POLITICS, *UNITED STATES*

President Franklin D. Roosevelt launches a "billion-dollar defense program" to bolster the armed forces.

JUNE 1–9

WESTERN FRONT, *NORWAY*

After Britain and France reveal to the Norwegians that they are to begin an evacuation, troops begin to withdraw

▼ *Plumes of smoke rise from Dunkirk's port area as troops sail back to Britain.*

withdraw to Dunkirk. Resistance seems futile and he decides to surrender on the 28th. Belgium has lost 7550 men killed. The surrender leaves the left flank of the Allied line increasingly vulnerable, and there is no hope of holding out in Belgium. The exiled Belgium government in

KEY MOMENTS

THE BATTLE OF FRANCE

Germany's sensational seizure of France and the Low Countries was the pinnacle of Blitzkrieg strategy and secured Adolf Hitler's mastery of Western Europe. The invasion that began on May 10 first struck the Low Countries, which had relied on their neutrality to save them, and were in no condition to resist the invaders.

As British and French forces rushed into Belgium in response to Germany's diversionary attack, the Nazis launched their main assault by advancing through the Ardennes forest. The Allies had dismissed this area as being unsuitable for any tank advances, which allowed the German units to move straight through against minimal opposition. This gateway into France enabled the fast-moving armored columns to advance into the Allied rear and disable communications. As the panzers raced westward to the sea, the Allied armies in the north were effectively isolated from potential reinforcements in the south. The Allies were unable to match Germany's effective exploitation of armor and aircraft or develop a credible strategy to counterattack the invaders.

As British, Belgian, and French forces completed the evacuation from Dunkirk, Germany launched the final phase of the offensive to complete the conquest. The Maginot Line, on which France's security had been entrusted, but had been completely bypassed by German forces, was eventually surrounded and penetrated.

As France's politicians floundered, the nation's high command attempted to regroup its faltering armies but resistance crumbled in the face of well-orchestrated German attacks that captured Paris on June 14. French and German officials signed an armistice agreement on June 22.

A French soldier surrenders to the German invaders.

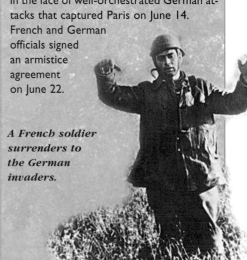

▲ *Wounded troops return to Britain after being rescued from Dunkirk.*

on June 4. King Haakon and his government leave for Britain on the 7th, and 24,500 troops are evacuated. The king finally orders the Norwegians to stop fighting on June 9, after losing 1335 men in the campaign. Entire Allied losses include 5600 men, one carrier, two cruisers, nine destroyers plus other smaller craft, and 100 aircraft. German loses total 3692 men, 19 warships, and 242 aircraft.

JUNE 3–4

WESTERN FRONT, *FRANCE*
Operation Dynamo ends. The remarkable operation has rescued

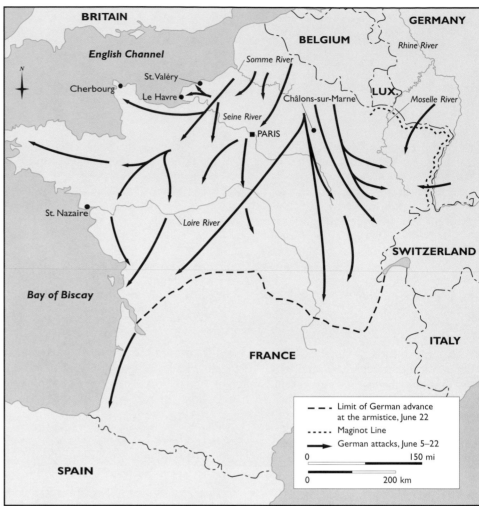

- - - Limit of German advance at the armistice, June 22
····· Maginot Line
→ German attacks, June 5–22

0 _____ 150 mi
0 _____ 200 km

▲ *Germany's conquest of France followed the Blitzkrieg principle. Armored thrusts bypassed the Maginot Line and other defensive positions. The Allied forces were then quickly isolated and defeated by air and ground attacks.*

338,226 men – two-thirds of them British – from the beaches of Dunkirk, although 243 vessels and 106 aircraft have been destroyed. General Lord Gort, the British Expeditionary Force's commander, leaves Lieutenant General Sir Harold Alexander in command after being evacuated on May 31. The Germans occupy Dunkirk on June 4 and capture 40,000 French troops.

JUNE 5–12

WESTERN FRONT, *FRANCE*
A German force of 119 divisions opens Operation Red, the conquest of France, with General Fedor von Bock's Army Group B attacking along the Somme River to reach the Seine River west of

◄ *German motorized units make rapid progress during the Battle of France.*

▶ *Triumphant German troops parade through Paris after conquering France.*

Paris by June 9. General Gerd von Rundstedt's Army Group A, moving toward the Moselle River in front of the Maginot Line, launches an offensive east of Paris. Rundstedt's tanks, reinforced by Army Group B panzers, overcome resistance from the French Fourth Army to break through at Châlons-sur-Marne on the 12th.

France's response, the Weygand Line, stretching along the Somme and Aisne Rivers, aims to protect Paris and the interior. Some of France's 65 divisions fight determined actions, but many units lack manpower and equipment. Air attacks and logistical problems also undermine General Maxime Weygand's vulnerable forces.

JUNE 8

SEA WAR, *NORTH SEA*
The German battlecruisers *Scharnhorst* and *Gneisenau* sink three empty vessels while hunting for convoys from Norway. They then sink the British carrier *Glorious* and two destroyers. These losses are blamed on the British failure to provide sufficient naval escorts for the Norway convoys.

JUNE 10

WESTERN FRONT, *FRANCE*
Some 11,000 British and other

French troops begin to evacuate from St. Valéry and Le Havre to Britain.

JUNE 10–11

POLITICS, *ITALY*
Italy declares war on France and Britain. Benito Mussolini, eager to capitalize on France's collapse, enters the war despite previous assertions that his nation will not have the capability to fight alongside Germany until 1942. Canada declares war on Italy on the 10th, as do Australia, New Zealand, and South Africa the following day.

JUNE 12–14

SEA WAR, *MEDITERRANEAN*
Britain launches a naval bombardment against the Italian base of Tobruk, Libya, on the 12th. The French Navy bombards the ports of

Genoa and Vado on the 14th. British air raids are also made on Turin and Genoa. Libyan and East African airfields are raided.

JUNE 13

POLITICS, *UNITED STATES*
President Franklin D. Roosevelt signs a $1.3 billion navy bill to improve the service. Shipments of arms also leave the country in response to Winston Churchill's request to Roosevelt for surplus weapons.

JUNE 13–25

WESTERN FRONT, *FRANCE*
Paris is declared an "open city" in order to save it from destruction and all French forces withdraw south of the capital, leaving the Maginot Line isolated. German troops enter Paris on June 14 as thousands flee the capital. Germany's Army Group C, deployed from the Maginot Line to the Swiss border, breaks through French

▼ *The German battlecruisers* **Scharnhorst** *(foreground) and* **Gneisenau,** *which attacked Allied ships evacuating troops from Norway in June 1940.*

◄ **French representatives sign articles of surrender in the railroad carriage in which Germany signed the 1918 documents.**

After Italy's armistice with France on the 24th, a cease-fire occurs on all fronts. French casualties since May 10 total more than 85,000 men, the British lose 3475 men, and German losses reach 27,074.

While Pétain's regime will collaborate with Nazi Germany, the French Army officer Brigadier General Charles de Gaulle begins broadcasting his opposition from London on the 18th with pledges to liberate the country.

JUNE 20

POLITICS, *UNITED STATES*
Democratic President Franklin D. Roosevelt appoints two anti-isolationist

defenses. German forces advance in all directions, crossing the Rhine and Loire Rivers. All of the coastal ports between Cherbourg and St. Nazaire are soon captured.

JUNE 15–25

WESTERN FRONT, *FRANCE*
The evacuation of the remaining Allied troops in northwest France begins. Operation Ariel extends this to the Biscay ports from the 16th. Some 214,000 troops are saved during the evacuation, although 3000 perish when the liner *Lancastria* is sunk on the 17th.

JUNE 16–24

POLITICS, *FRANCE*
Prime Minister Paul Reynaud fails to motivate his government to continue fighting and releases France from its agreement with Britain not to make any separate peace. France rejects a British idea to create a union between the countries.

Reynaud, after losing support, resigns and Marshal Henri-Philippe Pétain replaces him. Pétain requests Germany's armistice terms on the 17th, and the signing takes place at Compiègne, site of the World War I armistice agreement, on the 22nd. Under the terms Germany occupies two-thirds of France, including the Channel and Atlantic coastlines. The south, which becomes known as Vichy France, will have a nominal French administration and keep its colonies.

▶ **German troops enter Rouen during the offensive to conquer France.**

▲ *Italian bombers on their way to strike Allied targets. Italy's poor performance in France, North Africa, and Greece contrasted sharply with propaganda about the nation's military prowess.*

Republicans to his cabinet. Henry Stimson becomes secretary for war and Frank Knox is appointed secretary for the navy.

JUNE 20–21

WESTERN FRONT, *FRANCE*

Benito Mussolini launches attacks along the south coast. Offensives are also made along the Franco-Italian border. Italy also bombs the strategically-important island of Malta.

JUNE 26

POLITICS, *ROMANIA*

The government agrees to the Soviet occupation of Bessarabia and northern Bukovina, although Romanian troops attempt to halt the Red Army when it enters the country.

JUNE 30

WESTERN FRONT, *CHANNEL ISLANDS*

Germany invades the Channel Islands. This is the only British territory occupied during hostilities.

JULY 1

SEA WAR, *ATLANTIC*

The "Happy Time" begins for U-boat crews as their operational range is increased now that they have bases in French ports. This lasts until October. U-boat crews inflict serious losses on Allied convoys.

▶ *A German officer speaks to a British police officer in the Channel Islands, the only part of Britain occupied in the war.*

JULY 3–7

JULY 3–7

SEA WAR, *MEDITERRANEAN*
Britain, fearing that France's navy will be seized by Germany, sends two battleships, a battlecruiser, and a carrier (Force H) to neutralize French vessels at Oran and Mers-el-Kebir, Algeria. After negotiations fail, the British sink one battleship and damage two. In Britain, two French battleships, nine destroyers, and other craft are acquired with minimal force. French naval forces in Alexandria, Egypt, are disarmed on the 7th.

JULY 9–19

SEA WAR, *MEDITERRANEAN*
At the Battle of Punta Stilo, the British Mediterranean Fleet tries to separate the Italian Fleet from its base at Taranto in southern Italy. An Italian battleship and cruiser suffer damage, and Italian aircraft hit a British cruiser. On the 19th, the Australian light cruiser *Sydney* and four destroyers engage two Italian light cruisers. The Italians lose a cruiser and the *Sydney* is damaged.

JULY 10

AIR WAR, *BRITAIN*
The Battle of Britain begins. Hermann Goering, the Nazi air force chief, orders attacks on shipping and ports in the English Channel. The movement of Allied vessels in the Channel is soon restricted as a result of British naval and aircraft losses.

▲ *Barges being prepared for Operation Sealion, Germany's planned invasion of Britain that was to begin in the fall of 1940.*

▼ *British pilots rush to their Hurricanes during the Battle of Britain. The Nazis failed to destroy Britain's fighter capability in the aerial war over southern England.*

JULY 16–22

POLITICS, *GERMANY*
Adolf Hitler's Directive No. 16 reveals his military plan to invade Britain, code-named Operation Sealion. This requires control of the English Channel for transporting the invasion force and the destruction of Britain's fighter

▲ *Allied vessels under German air attack in the English Channel.*

▶ *Hermann Goering (right), the Nazi air chief, with Adolf Hitler (left).*

capability to ensure a safe crossing. The air force is made responsible for destroying the strength of the RAF and Royal Navy. Hitler's plans are further advanced after his final peace offer is rejected by the British on the 22nd.

JULY 18

POLITICS, *BRITAIN*
British Prime Minister Winston Churchill agrees to close the Burma Road to disrupt supplies to the Chinese in order to avoid a confrontation with the Japanese. The onset of the monsoon season means that the supply line would be disrupted anyway. The British will reopen the aid route in October.

JULY 21

POLITICS, *SOVIET UNION*
The authorities formally annex Lithuania, Latvia, and Estonia.

JULY 22

ESPIONAGE, *BRITAIN*
Britain establishes the Special Operations Executive (SOE) to secretly give support to resistance groups across Nazi-occupied Europe.

JULY 25

POLITICS, *UNITED STATES*
The United States introduces licensing to restrict the export of oil and metal products outside the Americas and to Britain. This measure is particularly directed toward Japan, which is heavily dependent upon imports of these

▼ *Peasants on the Burma Road, a key supply route to China during the war. Britain temporarily closed it to avoid a rift with the Japanese.*

resources. As a consequence, Japanese strategic planning devotes greater attention to the resources of the Dutch East Indies and Malaysia to relieve their raw material shortages.

AUGUST I

POLITICS, *GERMANY*
Hitler issues Directive No. 17, which states that preparations for the invasion of England are to be complete by September 15, ready for an invasion between the 19th and 26th.

AUGUST 2

▲ Air Chief Marshal Sir Hugh Dowding led the RAF's fighters to victory in the Battle of Britain.

▼ A German Heinkel bomber over the East End of London during the Luftwaffe's air offensive on Britain.

AUGUST 2

SEA WAR, *MEDITERRANEAN*
A British naval force attacks the Italian naval base on the island of Sardinia.

AUGUST 3–19

AFRICA, *BRITISH SOMALILAND*
Italian forces, superior in manpower and artillery, attack the 1475-strong garrison in British Somaliland from neighboring Ethiopia.

AUGUST 5

POLITICS, *GERMANY*
General Franz Halder, the chief-of-staff, inspects the first plans for the invasion of the Soviet Union. He proposes a two-pronged offensive, principally

▲ German pilots discuss their daring dogfight tactics during the Battle of Britain.

directed against Moscow, and a secondary attack on Kiev.

AUGUST 13–17

AIR WAR, *BRITAIN*
"Eagle Day" heralds a four-day German air offensive designed to destroy Britain's Fighter Command with raids on airfields and industrial targets. Hermann Goering, head of the Luftwaffe, postpones the early raids, however, and the later attacks are inconclusive.

AUGUST 15

AIR WAR, *BRITAIN*
Three German air fleets totaling 900 fighters and 1300 bombers launch massed daylight and night attacks on British airfields and ports to lure RAF fighters into combat. Air Chief Marshal Sir Hugh Dowding's 650 operational fighters, aided by effective radar defenses,

KEY MOMENTS

THE BATTLE OF BRITAIN

The Battle of Britain was Germany's attempt to achieve air superiority over the skies of southern England. With this achieved, it could then control the English Channel for the crossing of the invasion force, which was being prepared on the continent.

Germany's air force commander, Hermann Goering, assembled 2800 aircraft against Britain's 700 fighters. Widespread German attacks on ports, shipping, and airfields lured British fighters into action and inflicted heavy losses.

Britain's fate rested upon the bravery, determination, and skill of its fighter pilots. These men were drawn from the British Empire, North America, Czechoslovakia, Poland, and other Allied nations. The performance of the Hurricane and Spitfire fighters they flew also played a key role.

Crucially, a centralized command-and-control structure and radar network also enabled fighters to be effectively concentrated to meet enemy attacks. Germany's gravest strategical error was the decision, from September 7 onward, to concentrate on the bombing of British cities, despite eroding the capability of Fighter Command by widespread and incessant raids across southern England. This change in strategy enabled the RAF to concentrate its fighters and inflict heavier losses on the Luftwaffe. The RAF also benefitted from longer flying time as it operated over its own territory. In addition, crews who baled out were able to resume fighting, unlike their opponents who parachuted into captivity.

On October 31, after 114 days of aerial combat, Germany conceded defeat, having lost 1733 aircraft and 3893 men. The RAF, at a cost of 828 aircraft and 1007 men, had effectively saved Britain from invasion.

▼ Hurricane fighters helped Britain defeat Germany's air offensive in 1940.

are able to concentrate effectively to intercept the attackers in the coming days.

AUGUST 17

POLITICS, *GERMANY*
A total blockade of the British Isles is declared. Any Allied or neutral vessels found in British waters will be attacked on sight.

AUGUST 17–18

SEA WAR, *MEDITERRANEAN*
British naval vessels bombard Bardia and Fort Capuzzo, Libya, and shoot down 12 Italian bombers sent to attack them.

AUGUST 24–25

AIR WAR, *BRITAIN*
The Luftwaffe inflicts serious losses on the RAF during attacks on its main air bases in southeast England, straining the resources of Fighter Command to breaking point in a few days. London has also been bombed.

AUGUST 26–29

AIR WAR, *GERMANY*
The RAF launches a night raid with 81 aircraft on Berlin following a similar raid on London. Raids also take place against Düsseldorf, Essen, and other cities. The raids contribute toward a critical change in Germany's strategy, as aircraft are redirected to make retaliatory raids on London. This move relieves the pressure on Fighter Command's air bases.

SEPTEMBER 2

POLITICS, *BRITAIN*
Britain and the United States ratify a deal whereby 50 old destroyers, needed for convoy duties, are handed to

◄ Police and rescue workers frantically clear debris after a German air raid on London. The Nazi bombing offensive quickly spread to other cities in Britain.

bridgeheads on the south coast of England for an invasion force of nine divisions and 250 tanks.

SEPTEMBER 7–30

AIR WAR, *BRITAIN*

Full-scale bombing raids on London – the "Blitz" – begin with 500 bombers and 600 fighters. The RAF is initially surprised by the new German tactics, but adapts and concentrates its weakened forces against this threat. The bombing reaches its greatest intensity on the 15th, but the Luftwaffe is now suffering heavy losses, especially during its daylight raids on English cities, which are largely abandoned by the 30th. Bomber Command raids in France and the Low Countries destroy a tenth of the Nazi invasion barges on the 14th–15th.

SEPTEMBER 13–18

AFRICA, *EGYPT*

An Italian force of 250,000 men under Marshal Rodolfo Graziani advances from Libya into neighboring Egypt against the British Western Desert

◀ *Civilians prepare to spend the night safe from the bombing by sheltering in one of London's underground stations.*

▼ *Bomb damage to St. Paul's Cathedral. Nazi raids tore the City of London apart but failed to destroy public morale.*

Britain in exchange for bases in the Caribbean and Bermuda. Such exchanges will accustom the US public to aiding the Allied war effort.

SEPTEMBER 3

POLITICS, *GERMANY*

The Operation Sealion landings are postponed from September 15 to the 21st. Two airborne divisions will be used to establish three

▼ *Charles de Gaulle, the leader of the Free French forces based in Britain, opposed the puppet Vichy French regime.*

▶ *Italian forces invade Egypt from Libya. The offensive was later shattered by a British counterattack.*

Force of two divisions under General Sir Richard O'Connor. Graziani establishes fortified camps along a 50-mile (75-km) front, while the British remain 75 miles (120km) to the east. British plans to attack Graziani are delayed as units are redirected to Crete and Greece, where an Italian invasion is feared.

SEPTEMBER 15

POLITICS, *CANADA*
Men aged between 21 and 24 are to be conscripted.
POLITICS, *SOVIET UNION*
Men aged between 19 and 20 are to be conscripted.

SEPTEMBER 16-17

SEA WAR, *MEDITERRANEAN*
The British carrier *Illustrious* and battleship *Valiant* sink two Italian destroyers and two cargo ships at Benghazi, Libya.
HOME FRONT, *BRITAIN*
The Selective Service Bill permits the conscription of men aged between 21 and 35.

SEPTEMBER 17

POLITICS, *GERMANY*
Adolf Hitler decides to suspend Operation Sealion after Germany's failure to achieve aerial supremacy over southern England, while the General Staff inspects further plans for the invasion of the Soviet Union. General Friedrich von Paulus, deputy chief of the Army General Staff, suggests offensives

toward Leningrad, Kiev, and Moscow, with the latter being the main thrust.

SEPTEMBER 20-22

SEA WAR, *ATLANTIC*
German U-boats launch their first successful "Wolf Pack" operation, sinking 12 ships. In this tactic some 15–20 U-boats are deployed across the approaches to Britain. When a U-boat finds a convoy, it tracks the vessels and awaits the gathering of the entire "Wolf Pack" for a combined attack.

◀ *Marshal Rodolfo Graziani, the commander of Italian forces in Libya, who was responsible for the attack against British, Indian, and Australian forces in Egypt.*

SEPTEMBER 21

POLITICS, *AUSTRALIA*
Prime Minister Robert Menzies wins another general election for the United Australia Party, although Labor remains the largest individual party.

SEPTEMBER 22

FAR EAST, *INDOCHINA*
Japanese forces enter the French colony after the powerless Vichy French authorities finally agree to the occupation. Some Vichy French resist the Japanese, who aim to prevent China obtaining supplies through the country.

SEPTEMBER 23-25

SEA WAR, *AFRICA*
A British and Free French expedition, code-named Menace, attempts to occupy Dakar, French West Africa, with naval forces, including the British aircraft carrier *Ark Royal*, and 7900 troops. The Free French commander Charles de Gaulle fails to reach any agreement with the Vichy authorities, whose warships open fire. The Vichy French lose a destroyer and two submarines. Prime Minister Winston

DECISIVE WEAPONS

RADAR

Radar uses synchronized radio transmitters and receivers that emit radio waves and process their reflections for display. This is especially useful for detecting aircraft. Although the United States and Germany had been working on this technology since the beginning of the century, it was Britain that first established a series of radar stations in 1938 in response to the threat of German bomber raids. The stations acted as a warning system to alert fighter aircraft to the presence of approaching bombers. This was critical in the Battle of Britain as the overstretched RAF was able to concentrate its fighter forces to repel enemy attacks. Axis aircraft could be detected over 70 miles (112km) from the stations in southeast England. Sector stations (as seen above) recorded the information from the various radar sites under their control and scrambled fighters to intercept the threat.

As the accuracy of ground-based radar increased, target range and direction information provided firing data for anti-aircraft guns. Eventually, guns received a stream of accurate information as radars "locked on" and automatically tracked the targets.

Aircraft radar, introduced in 1941, initially enabled nightfighters to locate targets and eventually aided bomber navigation. U-boats that surfaced in darkness for safety could also be detected by aircraft, which then illuminated the submarines with lights before attacking them. Ground-based radar also helped bomber crews hit targets by precisely tracking and relaying information to the aircraft. In the war at sea, radar was used to detect enemy aircraft and also directed gunfire, which could be effectively employed even in complete darkness with the new technology.

Churchill cancels Operation Menace after a Free French landing fails and British vessels suffer damage from Vichy French forces.

SEPTEMBER 24–25

AIR WAR, *MEDITERRANEAN*
Vichy France launches ineffective air raids on Gibraltar in retaliation for the British attack on Dakar.

SEPTEMBER 25

POLITICS, *NORWAY*
Nazi sympathizer Vidkun Quisling, who proclaimed himself Norway's leader following the German invasion, becomes head of the government. In reality Quisling remains a German puppet with limited authority.

SEPTEMBER 27

POLITICS, *AXIS*
Germany, Italy, and Japan agree a military, political, and economic alliance that pledges each country to fight any state that declares war on an Axis nation. The Tripartite Pact specifically aims to deter intervention by the United States in Europe or Asia.

▼ *Greek troops send letters home during the war against the Italian invasion. Italy's invasion, which was launched in October 1940, met fierce Greek resistance.*

OCTOBER 7

BALKANS, *ROMANIA*
German forces enter Romania on the pretext of helping to train the army of the fascist Iron Guard government. Germany's principal motive is to occupy the Ploesti oil fields.

OCTOBER 9

POLITICS, *BRITAIN*
Winston Churchill succeeds Neville Chamberlain, the former prime minister, as Conservative Party leader. Churchill was initially an unpopular figure in the party but his war leadership has gone a long way to reverse this.

OCTOBER 12

POLITICS, *GERMANY*
Hitler postpones Operation Sealion until spring 1941.

OCTOBER 15

POLITICS, *ITALY*
The Italian war council decides to invade Greece. Italy plans not to tell its Axis partner Germany about the operation, which is scheduled to commence at the end of October.

OCTOBER 16–19

POLITICS, *JAPAN*
The Dutch East Indies agrees to supply 40 percent of its oil production to

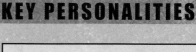

Japan for six months despite British attempts to obstruct this.

OCTOBER 18

POLITICS, *VICHY FRANCE*
The puppet Vichy regime introduces anti-Semitic laws.

OCTOBER 28

BALKANS, *GREECE*
Italy issues an ultimatum to Greece demanding the right to occupy the country for the war's duration. Before the ultimatum expires, eight divisions, led by General Sabasiano Visconti-Prasca, attack from Albania. Italy hopes for a rapid advance to rival Germany's conquests, but mountainous terrain and the absence of maps for commanders hamper the invasion. The winter weather limits air support and thousands die of cold. Greek forces, under General

▶ *Franklin D. Roosevelt was elected for a third term as US president in 1940. He prepared the nation for war and aided the Allies by expanding economic output.*

▲ *Greek troops carry brandy to the front. The ill-prepared Italian invaders lacked proper clothing and supplies to sustain their campaign during the freezing winter months in the mountains.*

Alexander Papagos, the commander-in-chief, mount stiff resistance.

OCTOBER 30–31

MEDITERRANEAN, *CRETE*
British forces occupy the Greek island.

NOVEMBER 5

POLITICS, *UNITED STATES*
President Franklin D. Roosevelt is elected for an unprecedented third term.
SEA WAR, *ATLANTIC*
The German pocket battleship *Admiral Scheer* attacks a British convoy of 37 ships escorted by the armed merchant cruiser *Jervis Bay*, which fights to save the convoy. The battleship rams and sinks *Jervis Bay*, but only five other vessels are lost. Eastbound convoys are suspended until the 17th while the Allies search for the *Admiral Scheer*.

KEY PERSONALITIES

"IL DUCE" BENITO MUSSOLINI

Benito Mussolini, journalist, soldier, and politician, exploited the instability of inter-war Italy to become the dictator of a fascist state. After rising to power in 1922, he suppressed opposition and promised the nation that a new Roman Empire would arise. Mussolini presented himself as a tough alternative to previous liberal statesmen and a patriotic enemy of communism. Fascist propaganda hid his regime's economic instability, and the conquest of Ethiopia (1935–36) and Albania (1939) attempted to divert public attention away from domestic problems.

Mussolini established close relations with Adolf Hitler, but insisted that Italy would not be ready to enter into war until 1942. After the defeat of France in June 1940, however, he was keen to capitalize on Germany's conquests and declared war on the Allies. Military blunders in France, North Africa, and Greece left Italy dependent on German military assistance. Mussolini, physically and mentally weakened, faced growing public apathy and political threats as his country faltered.

In July 1943, Mussolini was overthrown by the Fascist Grand Council. The new regime agreed to an armistice with the Allies in September. Mussolini, now imprisoned, was then rescued by the Germans. Axis-controlled Italy remained under Berlin's direction but Hitler was benevolent toward Europe's first fascist leader. Italian partisans shot Mussolini in April 1945.

NOVEMBER 10

▲ Marshal Pietro Badoglio, the Italian commander-in-chief, who resigned after the failure of the invasion of Greece.

NOVEMBER 10

POLITICS, ITALY
General Ubaldo Soddu replaces General Sabasiano Visconti-Prasca as the Italian commander-in-chief in Albania.

NOVEMBER 11–12

SEA WAR, MEDITERRANEAN
At the Battle of Taranto British torpedo aircraft from the carrier *Illustrious* destroy three Italian battleships and damage two vessels during the raid on the Italian base. *Illustrious* loses only two aircraft. When the fleet leaves for Naples and Genoa, three British cruisers sink four vessels in the Strait of Otranto. This air attack on a fleet in harbor is closely studied by other navies, especially the Japanese.

NOVEMBER 14–22

BALKANS, GREECE
Greece launches a major counter-attack and 3400 British troops, plus air support, arrive from Alexandria, Egypt. When Greek forces finally enter Koritza they capture 2000 Italians and drive almost all the invaders back into Albania by December.

NOVEMBER 14

AIR WAR, BRITAIN
Germany sends 449 bombers to bomb the city of Coventry. The raid kills 500 civilians, leaves thousands homeless, and shocks the British public.

NOVEMBER 18

TECHNOLOGY, BRITAIN
British "Air-to-Surface-Vessel" radar

▲ A German reconnaissance photograph of Coventry, the English city devastated by an air attack in November 1940.

▶ A Polish Jew in the Warsaw ghetto, which was created in November 1940.

fitted to a Sunderland flying boat locates its first U-boat during a patrol in the Atlantic.

NOVEMBER 20

POLITICS, HUNGARY
Hungary joins the Axis powers. Since the Italian invasion of Greece, the Germans have been attempting to secure their food and oil supplies from the Balkans by pressing the countries of the region to join the Tripartite Pact.

NOVEMBER 23

POLITICS, ROMANIA
Prime Minister General Ion Antonescu leads Romania into the Axis alliance.

NOVEMBER 26

FINAL SOLUTION, POLAND
The Nazis begin creating a ghetto in Warsaw for the Jews, who will eventually be kept there in intolerable conditions.

DECEMBER 18

POLITICS, *GERMANY*
Adolf Hitler issues his plan for invading the Soviet Union, code-named Operation Barbarossa. His Directive No. 21 retains a three-pronged offensive but the weight of the invasion plan has now shifted northward to Leningrad and the Baltic area, where Army Groups North and Center are to annihilate the enemy forces, before attacking and occupying Moscow.

DECEMBER 29

POLITICS, *UNITED STATES*
In President Franklin D. Roosevelt's "fireside chat" broadcast, he describes how the United States must become the "arsenal of democracy" by giving maximum assistance to Britain in its fight against the Axis powers.

◀ *General Sir Archibald Wavell (right), the British commander-in-chief in North Africa who repelled Italy's attack on Egypt in December 1940.*

▼ *British, Indian, and Australian troops in Egypt halted the Italian offensive despite the numerical superiority of the invaders. This success was only reversed after the arrival of German forces.*

NOVEMBER 30

POLITICS, *JAPAN*
Japan officially recognizes the puppet government of President Wang Ching wei in China.

DECEMBER 6

POLITICS, *ITALY*
Marshal Pietro Badoglio, Italy's commander-in-chief, resigns.

DECEMBER 9–11

AFRICA, *EGYPT*
General Sir Archibald Wavell, the commander-in-chief in the Middle East and North Africa, launches the first British offensive in the Western Desert. Major General Sir Richard O'Connor's Western Desert Force of 31,000 British and Commonwealth troops, supported by aircraft and long-range naval gunfire, is ordered to attack the fortified camps that have been established by the Italians in Egypt. Sidi Barrani is captured on the 10th and 34,000 Italians are taken prisoner as they retreat rapidly from Egypt. It is a famous victory in the face of overwhelming odds.

1941

The Allies continued fighting in North Africa, where they now faced General Erwin Rommel's Afrika Korps, and the war in the Balkans intensified with Germany conquering Yugoslavia and Greece. In the Mediterranean and Atlantic, the Allies fought a bitter campaign to defend their vital sea-lanes. The Axis powers' declarations of war on the Soviet Union and the United States proved a critical turning point. Germany undertook a bitter campaign on the Eastern Front, while Japan had to safeguard its conquests in the Pacific. The Axis powers had to face the might of the Soviet Union and the United States.

JANUARY 2

POLITICS, *UNITED STATES*
President Franklin D. Roosevelt announces a program to produce 200 freighters, called "Liberty" ships, to support the Allied Atlantic convoys.

JANUARY 3–15

AFRICA, *LIBYA*
General Sir Archibald Wavell's Middle East Force, renamed XIII Corps, with air and naval support, resumes its offensive into Cyrenaica. In Australia's first land action of the war, the Australian 6th Division leads the attack to capture Bardia, just across Libya's border with Egypt, on the 15th. Some 70,000 Italians, plus large amounts of equipment, are captured.

JANUARY 7–22

AFRICA, *LIBYA*
After the British 7th Armored Brigade encircles Tobruk, the Australian 6th Division leads

◀ *Italian troops in Tobruk. Allied and Axis forces battled for control of the strategically-important port.*

▶ *Admiral Ernest King led the US Atlantic Fleet in 1941 and rose to become a key naval commander during the war.*

the assault against the Italian defenders of the port, who eventually capitulate on the 22nd. Some 30,000 Italians, as well as port facilities, and vital supplies of fuel, food, and water, are seized. Major General Sir Richard O'Connor immediately sends forces farther west along the coast to capture the port of Benghazi.

JANUARY 19

AFRICA, *ERITREA*
British forces in the Sudan, led by General William Platt, begin attacking Italian forces, heralding the start of General Sir Archibald Wavell's campaign against Italian East Africa.

JANUARY 24

AFRICA, *LIBYA*
The British 4th Armored Brigade engages Italian tanks near Mechili. The Italian forces in Libya are now divided, with units inland positioned around Mechili, and other forces on the coast around Derna. They do not support each other and both face encirclement.

JANUARY 29

AFRICA, *ITALIAN SOMALILAND*
British forces based in Kenya led by General Sir Alan Cunningham begin attacking the Italian colony's garrison in the next stage of their campaign against Italian East Africa.

POLITICS, *UNITED STATES*
A significant advance in Anglo-US cooperation begins with staff talks in Washington. A decision, code-named ABC1, is eventually made that places Germany's defeat as the principal Allied aim in the event of the US declaring war. These talks lead to a US mission in March to visit potential sites for military bases in Britain.

FEBRUARY 1

POLITICS, *UNITED STATES*
Major organizational changes to the US Navy lead to it being divided into three fleets: Atlantic, Asiatic, and Pacific. Admiral Ernest King is to lead the new Atlantic Fleet, and US naval forces will be strengthened in this vital war theater.

SEA WAR, *ATLANTIC*
The German heavy cruiser *Admiral Hipper*, operating from Brest in France, embarks on a series of highly-destructive raids on Atlantic convoys that last until April.

▼ *A column of British tanks prepares for action against Axis forces in Libya.*

FEBRUARY 3–MARCH 22

SEA WAR, *ATLANTIC*
The German battlecruisers *Scharnhorst* and *Gneisenau* embark on commerce-destroying raids in the Atlantic. They succeed in dispersing

▼ *Prince George of Greece and Princess Bonaparte speak to Greek troops wounded while fighting the Italian invaders.*

numerous convoys and sink 22 ships before returning to the safety of French waters on March 22.

FEBRUARY 5–7

AFRICA, *LIBYA*
The Italians fail in their final attempt to escape encirclement at Beda Fomm, south of Benghazi, and surrender to the British 7th Armored Division. Meanwhile, the Australian 6th Division, advancing along the coastal roads, forces troops in Benghazi to surrender on the 7th.

This ends a two-month campaign in which the British have inflicted a complete defeat on a stronger enemy by executing a carefully-planned offensive using highly-trained troops backed by air and naval support.

FEBRUARY 14

POLITICS, *BULGARIA*
Bulgaria grants Germany access to its border with Greece. This move enables Germany to increase its power in the Balkans and provides a route for forces earmarked to invade Greece.

POLITICS, *SOVIET UNION*
General Georgi Zhukov is appointed chief of the General Staff and deputy commissar for defense. He has previously commanded the Red Army forces fighting against the Japanese in Mongolia in the summer of 1939.

AFRICA, *LIBYA*
In response to Adolf Hitler's offer to send an armored division to ensure that the Italians will not withdraw in Libya, the first detachments of General

▲ *Italian troops in action near Benghazi during the major British offensive into Cyrenaica, Libya.*

Erwin Rommel's Afrika Korps disembark at Tripoli.

FEBRUARY 19–23

POLITICS, *ALLIES*
A meeting of political and military leaders in Cairo, Egypt, decides to deploy forces to Greece. The Greek and British authorities subsequently agree to send 100,000 British troops to bolster the country's defenses.

FEBRUARY 25

AFRICA, *ITALIAN SOMALILAND*
British-led East and West African troops advance into Mogadishu, the capital. The defeated Italians begin evacuating the colony.

MARCH 1

POLITICS, *BULGARIA*
Bulgaria joins the Axis powers.
AFRICA, *LIBYA*
Free French forces from Chad seize the Italian air base and garrison at Kufra Oasis in the southeast after a 22-day siege.

▶ *General Erwin Rommel, the audacious commander of the German Afrika Korps, outlining his strategy for winning a battle against the British in North Africa.*

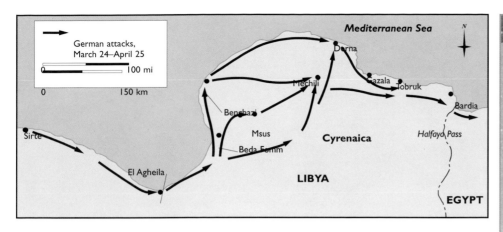

MARCH 4

WESTERN FRONT, *NORWAY*
A joint British and Norwegian commando raid and naval assault on the Lofoten Islands destroys fish-oil plants used in the production of explosives, captures 215 Germans, rescues 300 Norwegians, and sinks 10 ships.

MARCH 5

BALKANS, *GREECE*
The first contingent of British troops sails from Egypt. By April 2 some 58,000 troops will have been sent to help defend the country.

MARCH 9–25

BALKANS, *GREECE*
Italy launches a spring offensive between the Devoli and Vijosë Rivers in northwest Greece to counter the reverses it has suffered. Mussolini himself travels to Albania to supervise the deployment of

▲ *General Erwin Rommel's first offensive in the desert drove the British from Libya and threatened to seize Egypt.*

12 divisions for the attack. Greek intelligence and defensive preparations ensure that the poorly-planned Italian attacks from Albania are rebuffed.

MARCH 11

POLITICS, *UNITED STATES*
President Franklin D. Roosevelt signs the Lend-Lease Act that allows Britain to obtain supplies without having to immediately pay for them in cash. For the remainder of 1941, however, Britain is able to pay. The bill grants the president greater powers to supply military equipment to any nation he considers important to US security.

MARCH 24

AFRICA, *LIBYA*
General Erwin Rommel begins his first offensive in Libya by driving the British from El Agheila. He now begins a counteroffensive similar to the original attack by the British. While the 21st Panzer

LEND-LEASE

Following the fall of France in June 1940, US President Franklin D. Roosevelt pursued a policy of supplying Britain with the military equipment it required to carry on the fight against Nazi Germany. As dependence on these imports increased, in December 1940 the British prime minister, Winston Churchill, proposed an arrangement whereby the Allied nations could obtain essential US goods and equipment but would repay the United States after the war.

In March 1941 Congress passed the Lend-Lease Act and gave Roosevelt wide-ranging powers to supply goods and services to "any country whose defense the president deems vital to the defense of the United States." Almost $13 billion had been allocated to the Lend-Lease arrangement by November 1941.

Although Britain now had the opportunity to increase the amount of US imports, its own war production had been increasing during this period. Food and oil from the United States, however, was still crucial to its survival.

Lend-Lease was terminated by President Harry S. Truman on August 24, 1945, although Britain was still under contract to receive large quantities of US goods for which it had to pay in dollars.

Britain was not the only beneficiary of the act. The British Commonwealth, the Soviet Union, and other Allied nations also became recipients of US aid in this manner to help their respective war efforts.

US shipbuilding dramatically increased to provide vessels for the Atlantic convoys that sailed to Britain.

MARCH 25

Division races across the desert toward Tobruk, Italian forces take the longer coastal route.

MARCH 25

POLITICS, *YUGOSLAVIA*
Yugoslavia joins the Axis powers by signing the Tripartite Pact.

MARCH 27–30

POLITICS, *YUGOSLAVIA*
A coup by air force officers deposes Prince Paul's pro-Axis administration. King Peter II takes nominal charge of the country and General Dusan Simovic becomes head of government. The events alarm the Axis powers, chiefly Germany.

Adolf Hitler responds to the overthrow of Prince Paul by issuing Directive No. 25, the order for the invasion of Yugoslavia, which will commence alongside the attack on Greece, codenamed Operation Marita. Hitler approves of the army's proposals for the invasions, both of which are scheduled to begin on April 6.

MARCH 27

AFRICA, *ERITREA*
The Battle of Keren, in northeast Eritrea, ends with Italian forces being forced to retreat toward the capital Asmara. The Italians lose 3000 men compared to British fatalities of 536. Asmara falls five days later.

MARCH 28–29

SEA WAR, *AEGEAN*
The Italian fleet sails into the Aegean Sea to disrupt British convoys to Greece. A British force led by Admiral Henry Pridham-Wippell engages some Italian cruisers in a long-range bombardment. The Italians retire, fearing the presence of more enemy vessels.

▲ *British trucks carrying troops at the Battle of Keren during the campaign against the Italians in Eritrea.*

▼ *The Italian battleship* Vittorio Veneto *fires a salvo against the British in the Aegean Sea during the Battle of Cape Matapan. Torpedo-bombers hit the vessel during the action.*

KEY PERSONALITIES

FIELD MARSHAL ERWIN ROMMEL

Erwin Rommel (1891–1944) was a decorated World War I officer who commanded Hitler's bodyguard and was responsible for the Führer's personal safety during the Polish campaign. He then took command of the 7th Panzer Division for the 1940 invasion of France. His speedy advance across the Meuse River and drive to the English Channel earned him a reputation as a daring tank commander.

Following the failed Italian campaign in North Africa, he was sent there to lead the Afrika Korps in 1941. Rommel became a master of desert warfare tactics with his ability to exploit opportunities, employ unorthodox methods, and deploy his armored forces to maximum effect. After recapturing Tobruk in 1942, he pushed the Allies back to El Alamein in Egypt. The "Desert Fox" was promoted to field marshal, having led the Afrika Korps to a string of victories.

Rommel was forced to retreat into Tunisia after the British victory at El Alamein in November 1942 and the Allied Torch landings. He left North Africa in 1943. Rommel's next major appointment was in France, where he was tasked with establishing the anti-invasion program he had proposed to Hitler. He commanded Army Group B after the Allied landings in June 1944. Rommel was badly wounded during an air attack and returned to Germany. After being implicated in the failed July assassination attempt on Adolf Hitler, Rommel took poison to avoid a trial and the threatened reprisals against his family.

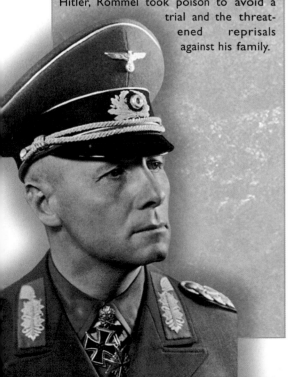

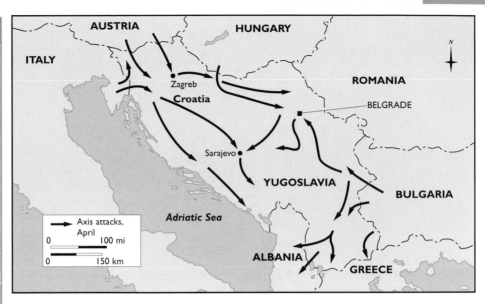

▲ *After Italy failed to seize Greece in 1940, the Germans conquered the Balkans with a successful campaign in 1941.*

Their fears are realized when the main British force, led by Admiral Sir Andrew Cunningham, sends two torpedo-bombers from the carrier *Formidable* to attack the Italian naval vessels. They damage the battleship *Vittorio Veneto* and cripple the cruiser *Pola*. Three British battleships then engage two cruisers sent to cover the *Pola*. The Battle of Cape Matapan claims five Italian ships sunk and 3000 men killed. The British lose just one aircraft in the action.

MARCH 30

POLITICS, *UNITED STATES*
The authorities confiscate 65 Axis ships, which are immediately taken into "protective custody."

APRIL 1–18

POLITICS, *IRAQ*
Nationalist politician Rashid Ali and army officers hostile to Britain depose Regent Faisal and form a pro-Axis

▼ *Prisoners-of-war captured during the invasion of Greece pass a variety of German armored vehicles.*

regime in Iraq. British troops begin arriving in Iraq on the 18th to safeguard access to key oil supplies.

APRIL 4

AFRICA, *LIBYA*
General Erwin Rommel's Axis troops are advancing across Libya in three groups. A predominantly Italian force on the coast takes Benghazi. Another group inland is advancing to Msus, while farther south a third force is also heading toward the same objective.

APRIL 6–15

BALKANS, *YUGOSLAVIA/GREECE*
Thirty-three German divisions, with Italian and Hungarian support, invade Yugoslavia from the north, east, and southeast. Aerial bombing centering on Belgrade dislocates the nation's military command and communication structure, and further undermines the ineffective mobilization of its 640,000-strong army. Major cities are quickly

▲ German tanks crossing the desert during General Erwin Rommel's first offensive in the desert war.

seized, including Zagreb, Belgrade, and Sarajevo, between the 10th and 15th.

In Greece, German forces attack the Greek Second Army on the fortified Metaxas Line along the country's northern border with Bulgaria. Air raids on Piraeus port destroy a British ammunition ship, which explodes and sinks 13 vessels. The Second Army, cut off after German forces reach the sea at Salonika on the 9th, soon surrenders. The British, after initially occupying positions between Mount Olympus and Salonika, are quickly forced back to a new defensive line just north of the mountain following the collapse of Greek forces on their left flank.

APRIL 6 – 9

AFRICA, *ETHIOPIA/ERITREA*
British General Sir Alan Cunningham, after an impressive advance of over 1000 miles (1600 km) from Kenya, captures Addis Ababa, Ethiopia's capital, and then continues to harass the retreating Italian forces. Allied

▲ Italian troops were often unprepared for crossing freezing, mountainous terrain during the invasion of Greece.

◀ Following the conquest of Yugoslavia by Axis forces, Italian troops march into the province of Slovenia.

forces in Eritrea then seize the port of Massawa on the 9th and capture 17 Axis merchant vessels and other assorted craft in the harbor.

APRIL 7

AFRICA, *LIBYA*
General Erwin Rommel captures Derna, along with British Generals Philip Neame and Sir Richard O'Connor, during his advance toward Tobruk.

APRIL 10

POLITICS, *YUGOSLAVIA*
The Ustachi political group in the province of Croatia declares the formation of an independent republic separate from Yugoslavia.

SEA WAR, *GREENLAND*

The United States begins occupying Greenland to prevent the Danish colony falling into German hands. Valuable weather-observation points for Britain are situated in Greenland.

APRIL 10–13

AFRICA, *LIBYA*

General Erwin Rommel begins the siege of Tobruk. The Allies, who repulse his first attacks, are determined to hold Tobruk as it is the only major port between Sfax in Tunisia and Alexandria in Egypt, a distance of 1000 miles (1600 km). It is therefore a strategic base for forces fighting in North Africa. Tobruk comes under constant air and ground attack, its caves providing the only real shelter, while the sea-lane to Egypt is to be its only lifeline.

APRIL 13

POLITICS, *SOVIET UNION/JAPAN*

A five-year nonaggression pact between the Soviet Union and Japan is signed, which enables the Red Army to move units from Siberia to bolster its forces preparing to meet any future German attack.

▼ *An Australian gun crew defending Tobruk. The besieged garrison and the ships supplying the defenders came under constant Axis attack.*

APRIL 17

POLITICS, *YUGOSLAVIA*

Yugoslavia signs an armistice with Germany. The country is now under military administration except for the Croatian puppet state. Immediately, guerrilla forces emerge to resist the Nazi occupation.

APRIL 18–21

BALKANS, *GREECE*

Greek positions are quickly collapsing as the German invaders advance. The British have fallen back from Mount Olympus to Thermopylae. A British evacuation appears inevitable as reinforcements from Egypt are canceled on the 18th. King George assumes temporary charge of the government after the premier, Alexander Koryzis, commits suicide. A British evacuation is finalized after General Alexander Papagos, the Greek commander-in-chief, realizing the situation is hopeless, recommends a withdrawal on the 21st. Greek forces fighting in Albania surrender on the 20th.

▼ *Yugoslavian soldiers surrender to the conquering Axis forces. Although the country was occupied, partisan forces carried on fighting to liberate the nation.*

APRIL 21-30

AIR WAR, *BRITAIN*
Two raids on the nights of the 21st–22nd and 29th–30th against Plymouth by 640 bombers claim 750 lives and leave 30,000 homeless.

APRIL 21-27

BALKANS, *GREECE*
British forces leave their lines around Thermopylae on the 24th after Greek forces in Thrace capitulate. The British evacuation operation now begins, and some 43,000 men are rescued by the Royal Navy from ports and beaches in eastern Greece, while under constant German air attack. Two destroyers and four transport ships are lost.

A German attack by paratroopers at Corinth on the 26th and an advance to Patras pose a threat to the British evacuation. German forces occupy Athens on the 27th, but the Greek government has already left for Crete. Campaign dead: Greek 15,700; Italian 13,755; German 1518; and British 900.

APRIL 25

POLITICS, *GERMANY*
Adolf Hitler issues Directive No. 28, ordering the airborne invasion of Crete, code-named Operation Mercury.

APRIL 30

AFRICA, *LIBYA*
The most intense Axis attack on Tobruk to date commences but meets determined resistance from

▲ *German parachutists engaged in street fighting with the Allies in Corinth during the invasion of Greece.*

the defenders. Four days later Axis forces secure a salient on the southwestern area of the defensive perimeter. Both sides then dig in for a lengthy campaign, with the garrison entirely dependent on supplies carried by the Royal Navy. German submarines, torpedo-boats, and medium and dive-bombers constantly

threaten the supply vessels, which are especially vulnerable when unloading.

MAY 1-17

MIDDLE EAST, *IRAQ*
Iraqi forces, totaling four divisions, commence attacks on British troops, which intensify in the following days. British forces are soon bolstered by reinforcements. Germany supports the Iraqis by launching air attacks.

MAY 3-19

AFRICA, *ETHIOPIA*
At the Battle of Amba Alagi in the mountains of northern Ethiopia, the Italians make their last major stand against the Allies in defense of their East African empire. The surrender of the Duke of Aosta and 7000 troops heralds an Allied victory in East Africa. Some 230,000 Italians have been killed or captured. The Allied victory safeguards the Suez Canal from any potential threat from East Africa and also secures control of the Red Sea for Allied shipping.

▲ *Ethiopian fighters in action against Italian troops during the British campaign to destroy Mussolini's East African empire.*

MAY 5

POLITICS, *ETHIOPIA*
Emperor Haile Selassie returns to Ethiopia after being exiled for five years by the Italians.

MAY 6-12

SEA WAR, *MEDITERRANEAN*
Operation Tiger, the first Gibraltar-to-Egypt convoy for many months, transports supplies intended for a British desert offensive. Two convoys also sail from Egypt to Gibraltar. The entire Mediterranean Fleet supports

the convoy of five transports. They suffer attacks from Italian aircraft on the 8th. One transport, carrying 57 tanks, sinks after striking a mine. The convoy, however, delivers 238 tanks and 43 Hurricane fighters.

MAY 10

POLITICS, *BRITAIN*
Rudolf Hess, deputy leader of Germany, flies to Scotland on a strange mission to ask Britain to allow Germany a "free hand" in Europe in return for the Nazis leaving the British Empire intact. Hess flies to Scotland to see the Duke of Hamilton, whom he believes to be the leader of the antiwar party in Britain. Germany does not authorize his actions and the British imprison him. Martin Bormann, national party organizer, replaces Hess and becomes a key confidant of Adolf Hitler.

MAY 10-11

AIR WAR, *BRITAIN*
In the climax to the "Blitz," London is attacked by 507 bombers. This will be the last major German air raid for three years. The aerial bombing of Britain now affects Liverpool, Bristol, Belfast, and several other cities. Since September 1940, 39,678 people have been killed and 46,119 injured by Luftwaffe raids. Civil defense, fire, police, and medical organizations help the population to cope with the attacks. Infrastructure is quickly repaired and shelters provide some protection for people. The population in general remains resilient in the face of the onslaught, despite the dislocation and the strains caused by the bombing.

MAY 15-16

AFRICA, *EGYPT*
Operation Brevity, the first British operation against the Afrika Korps, attempts to throw the Axis forces back from the Egyptian frontier. Halfaya Pass and Sollum are recaptured in the operation.

MAY 20-22

MEDITERRANEAN, *CRETE*
A German force of 23,000 men, supported by 600 aircraft, attacks Crete. The German plan is to launch an airborne assault that can then be reinforced by a seaborne force. After preparatory air attacks, the Germans launch the first major airborne operation in history.

Paratroops come under attack while landing and meet determined resistance from the 42,000 British, New Zealand, Australian, and Greek troops stationed on the island. After an Allied battalion commander holding Máleme airfield mistakenly withdraws, the Germans gain a footing for

▼ German mountain troops en route to Crete, where many would die in the bitter battle to seize the island.

◀ Rudolf Hess, the Nazi who tried to make peace with the British.

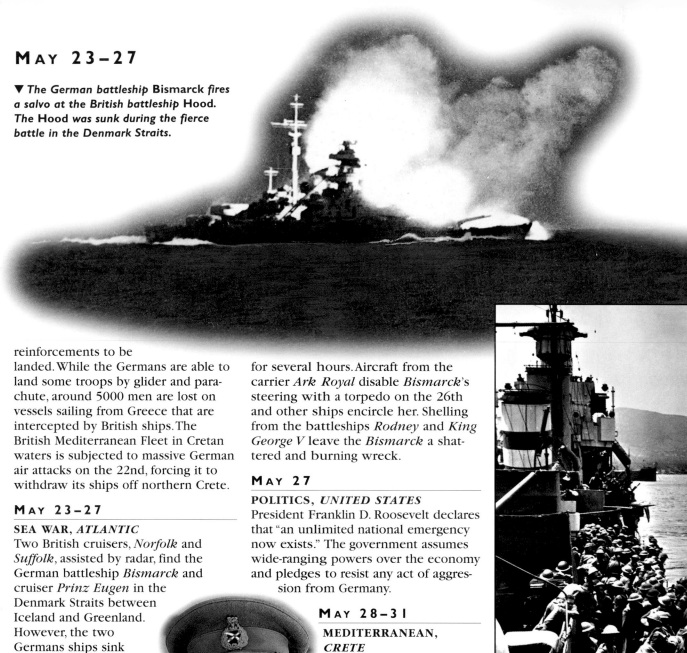

▼ *The German battleship* Bismarck *fires a salvo at the British battleship* Hood. *The* Hood *was sunk during the fierce battle in the Denmark Straits.*

reinforcements to be landed. While the Germans are able to land some troops by glider and parachute, around 5000 men are lost on vessels sailing from Greece that are intercepted by British ships. The British Mediterranean Fleet in Cretan waters is subjected to massive German air attacks on the 22nd, forcing it to withdraw its ships off northern Crete.

MAY 23-27

SEA WAR, *ATLANTIC*
Two British cruisers, *Norfolk* and *Suffolk*, assisted by radar, find the German battleship *Bismarck* and cruiser *Prinz Eugen* in the Denmark Straits between Iceland and Greenland. However, the two Germans ships sink the battlecruiser *Hood* and damage the battleship *Prince of Wales*, which have been sent to engage them. *Bismarck*'s oil tanks, however, are hit and begin leaking. That night, a torpedo-bomber hits the ship but does little damage.

The German vessels make for Brest and the British lose radar contact

▶ *Bernard Freyberg, the New Zealander who led the Allied defense of Crete.*

for several hours. Aircraft from the carrier *Ark Royal* disable *Bismarck*'s steering with a torpedo on the 26th and other ships encircle her. Shelling from the battleships *Rodney* and *King George V* leave the *Bismarck* a shattered and burning wreck.

MAY 27

POLITICS, *UNITED STATES*
President Franklin D. Roosevelt declares that "an unlimited national emergency now exists." The government assumes wide-ranging powers over the economy and pledges to resist any act of aggression from Germany.

MAY 28-31

MEDITERRANEAN, *CRETE*
Major General Bernard Freyberg, the New Zealand commander responsible for defending Crete, decides the island cannot be saved as the German offensive intensifies. His forces are already retreating toward

▲ *British and Commonwealth soldiers just off the coast of Crete during the evacuation of the island.*

Sfakia on the south coast. British losses are 1742 men, plus 2011 dead and wounded at sea, while Germany has 3985 men killed or missing. The Royal Navy's hazardous naval evacuation saves over 15,000 Allied troops but it loses nine ships in the process. Hitler suspends airborne operations on this scale in future after being informed of the devastating losses suffered by the paratroopers on Crete.

MAY 30

POLITICS, *IRAQ*

Iraq signs an armistice with Britain whereby the country agrees not to assist the Axis nations. It also agrees not to obstruct the stationing of British forces in Iraq. A pro-Allied government is subsequently installed.

MAY 31

AIR WAR, *EIRE*

The Luftwaffe mistakenly bombs the capital, Dublin, killing 28 people.

JUNE 8–21

MIDDLE EAST, *SYRIA*

An Allied force of 20,000 Free French, British, and Commonwealth troops, under General Sir Henry M. Wilson, invades Syria from Palestine and Iraq amid fears of increasing German influence in the country. They face 45,000 Vichy French troops under General Henri Dentz, plus naval forces that engage the Allies on the 9th.

In subsequent days the Allies encircle enemy units and use heavy artillery to overcome resistance. Vichy forces abandon the capital, Damascus, to the Allies on the 21st.

JUNE 13

FINAL SOLUTION, *VICHY FRANCE*

Over 12,000 Jews have been "interned" in concentration camps after being accused of disrupting relations between Vichy France and Germany. The Vichy authorities are increasingly persecuting Jews and passing legislation to deny them property rights.

JUNE 15–17

AFRICA, *LIBYA*

General Sir Archibald Wavell launches Operation Battleaxe to relieve Tobruk and break the German hold on

▶ *A soldier writes a defiant message outside a military post in Tobruk.*

▼ *A British truck pulls an antiaircraft gun across a dusty track in Syria during the Allied invasion of the country.*

Cyrenaica. An armored and infantry division crosses the Egyptian–Libyan border around Halfaya Pass, Fort Capuzzo, and Hafid Ridge. The new British tanks brought to strengthen the 7th Armored Division have suffered mechanical problems and their crews have had inadequate training. The understrength Allied divisions suffer heavily against the experienced German armor and antitank guns. Wavell halts Operation Battleaxe after losing 90 of his 190 tanks.

JUNE 17

POLITICS, *GERMANY*

Adolf Hitler decides to launch Operation Barbarossa, the invasion of the Soviet Union, on June 22. He has an extreme hatred of the Slav people and the communism that rules them. Hitler aims to enslave the "inferior" Slav peoples, exploit their resources, and occupy their lands as part of his *Lebensraum* ("living space") policy for the Aryan race.

▶ *An Italian mine-thrower crew in action during the desert campaign in Libya and Egypt against British and Commonwealth forces.*

JUNE 22

EASTERN FRONT, *SOVIET UNION*

Germany launches Operation Barbarossa, the invasion of the Soviet Union, with three million men divided into three army groups along a 2000-mile (3200-km) front. Hitler aims to achieve a speedy victory to destroy the Red Army before the summer ends and the Soviets can mobilize their immense resources. Army Group North, under Field Marshal Wilhelm Ritter von Leeb, strikes toward the Baltic and Leningrad. Army Group Center, under Field Marshal Fedor von Bock, aims to take Smolensk and then Moscow, and destroy communications. Army Group South, under General Gerd von Rundstedt, advances toward the Ukraine and the Caucasus.

Soviet forces are caught by surprise and lose a series of battles along the

▲ *Soviet soldiers surrendering to the invading German forces. Red Army units were often quickly encircled and destroyed by German tank formations.*

frontier. German air attacks quickly destroy 1800 Soviet aircraft on the ground. German forces make rapid progress in the north and center but meet stiffening resistance in the south.

JUNE 26–29

POLITICS, *FINLAND*

Finland declares war on the Soviet Union and launches an attack on the 29th. The Finns aim to recapture the territory lost to the Soviets during the Russo-Finnish War. When they finally achieve this objective, Adolf Hitler asks Marshal Karl von Mannerheim, the Finnish leader, to help Germany besiege Leningrad, but he refuses.

JUNE 26–30

EASTERN FRONT, *SOVIET UNION*

The fortress at Brest-Litovsk is taken after fierce resistance, while the important crossing of the Bug River by Army Group Center begins on the 26th. This group's initial objective is Minsk. The fast-moving panzers encircle Red Army units at Bialystok, Novogrudok, and Volkovysk, leaving them open to destruction by follow-on infantry forces. Unimaginative Soviet linear defensive tactics and weak divisions are proving vulnerable to rapid German panzer advances, especially on the flanks. In addition, Germany's total aerial superiority has led to heavy Red Army losses.

JUNE 27

POLITICS, *HUNGARY*
The government declares war on the Soviet Union.

JUNE 29

POLITICS, *SOVIET UNION*
Joseph Stalin assumes control of the federation's Defense Ministry and appoints a five-man council of defense.

▲ *A German tank drives among ruins during the invasion of the Soviet Union in the summer of 1941.*

◀ *Triumphant German troops aboard a Soviet train. Logistics were an essential element for both sides on the Eastern Front.*

JULY 1

POLITICS, *BRITAIN*
General Sir Claude Auchinleck replaces General Sir Archibald Wavell as the commander of British Middle East forces. Wavell's Middle East Command has achieved considerable success against numerically-superior Italian forces, despite supply shortages. However, subsequent commitments in Greece, Iraq, and Syria have overstretched his forces. Nevertheless, Prime Minister Winston Churchill wants a decisive offensive in the Western Desert and Wavell's failure to achieve this has led to his transfer.

JULY 1–11

EASTERN FRONT, *BELORUSSIA/UKRAINE*
The German advance continues. Army Group North crosses the Dvina River. Army Group Center moves across the Berezina River and efforts now center on bridging the Dnicpr River in order to prevent the Soviets forming any defensive line that would obstruct the Moscow advance. Army Group South overcomes Soviet fortifications on the Stalin Line and moves forward on July 10. The panzer divisions are just 10 miles (16 km) from Kiev, the Soviet Union's third-largest city, by the 11th.

Such armored units, however, are unsuitable for urban fighting and risk suffering heavy losses, especially as Kiev is strongly defended. General Gerd von Rundstedt plans to lure the Soviet units into the open steppes with the threat of encirclement. Once exposed, they might be annihilated.

JULY 3

AFRICA, *ETHIOPIA*
Italian resistance ends in the south after 7000 men surrender.

◀ *Italian troops surrender during the campaign by Allied troops to liberate Ethiopia.*

JULY 4

JOSEPH STALIN

Joseph Stalin (1879–1953), the leader of the Soviet Union, had supported the 1917 Bolshevik Revolution and then proceeded to rise through the Communist Party's ranks. After the death of Lenin in 1924, he established a dictatorship by destroying all political opposition. The development of industry and agriculture was then achieved at enormous human cost, but it made Stalin's Soviet Union a formidable power.

As Europe moved closer to war in the 1930s, Stalin feared that a German attack on the Soviet Union was inevitable and delayed this with a nonaggression pact with Hitler in 1939. His occupation of half of Poland, Finland, and the Baltic states followed, but proper preparations for the impending German attack were not implemented. Stalin was stunned by Hitler's invasion in June 1941, and it was not until the fall that he properly mobilized the human and economic resources of the Soviet Union to mount an effective defense. Stalin controlled both civil and military affairs as Chairman of the People's Commissars. In both realms he displayed a grim determination to maximize the Soviet war effort and finally stood firm when Germany reached the gates of Moscow. He even exploited nationalist sentiments to maintain morale among Russians, appealing for a "holy war" to defend "Mother Russia."

At the great conferences held by the Allies, Stalin was a forceful negotiator who constantly demanded the establishment of a "Second Front" in Europe to relieve the Soviet Union and additional supplies for his war effort. As the war progressed, Stalin often bypassed the decisions of these meetings concerning the political profile of postwar Europe, and the Allies looked nervously on as Stalin maneuvered to create a series of communist "buffer states" around the Soviet Union.

▲ Vichy French soldiers are marched into captivity after the surrender of Syria.

JULY 4

POLITICS, *YUGOSLAVIA*

Joseph Broz, known as "Tito," emerges as the leader of the Yugoslavian resistance movement, although the government-in-exile does not support him. Tito, a communist, has popular support and proposes a Yugoslavian federation that overrides ethnic and national differences.

JULY 7

SEA WAR, *ICELAND*

US troops garrison the country to protect shipping from U-boat attacks.

JULY 10

POLITICS, *SOVIET UNION*

Joseph Stalin, in an attempt to halt the advancing Germans, appoints a number of "commander-in-chiefs of direction" in three command areas (fronts – groups of armies). These are Marshal Semën Budënny (South and Southwest Front), Marshal Semyon Timoshenko (Central West Front), and Marshal Kliment Voroshilov (Northwest Front).

JULY 12

POLITICS, *ALLIES*

Britain and the Soviet Union sign a Mutual Assistance Pact, which includes a declaration that neither will make a separate peace with the Axis powers.

AIR WAR, *SOVIET UNION*

Moscow suffers its first air raid. The bombing then intensifies with three large-scale attacks this month and 73 minor raids that last until the end of the year.

JULY 14

MIDDLE EAST, *SYRIA*

General Henri Dentz defies the Vichy French authorities and surrenders Syria to the Allies. British forces begin occupying the colony and pro-Allied administrations are formed in

◄ Kliment Voroshilov, the Red Army commander of the Northwest Front.

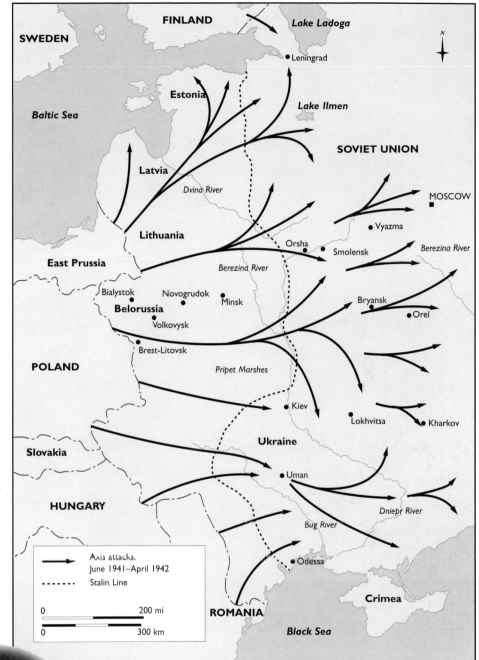

Syria and neighboring Lebanon. The Allies have sustained about 2500 casualties in the campaign, while the Vichy French forces have suffered some 3500 casualties defending their colonies in the region.

JULY 16

EASTERN FRONT, *SOVIET UNION*
Following the crossing of the Dniepr and Dvina Rivers, the encirclement of Smolensk by Germany's Army Group Center commences. The city falls after 300,000 Red Army troops and 3200 tanks are trapped in the vicinity of the city but, despite this, the surrounded Soviet forces are not finally defeated until August.

JULY 18

POLITICS, *CZECHOSLO-VAKIA*
Britain recognizes the Czech government-in-exile led by Edouard Beneš. The Czechs also make a mutual assistance agreement with the Soviet Union and promise to form an army.

▶ *Edouard Beneš, the leader of the Czech government-in-exile during the war.*

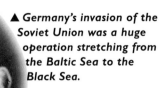

▲ *Germany's invasion of the Soviet Union was a huge operation stretching from the Baltic Sea to the Black Sea.*

JULY 19-29

EASTERN FRONT, *SOVIET UNION*
General Heinz Guderian's 2nd Panzer Group, plus supporting infantry, leading the advance toward Moscow, receives orders to swing south and help tackle the Soviet Fifth Army, which is situated in the Pripet Marshes. This Soviet force vastly outnumbers the opposing German units and poses a serious threat to Field Marshal Walther von Reichenau's southern operations. Army Group Center's remaining panzer unit, the 3rd Panzer Group, is assigned to assist Army Group North take Leningrad. Guderian and other

53

▲ Japanese industrial power relied on fuel and raw material imports. The nation's moves to war thus accelerated after vital imports of US oil ceased.

◄ Soviet fighters surrender during the German encirclement of Red Army forces in the Ukraine.

commanders are hostile to this decision and attempt to persuade Adolf Hitler not to halt the Moscow advance, but to no avail.

JULY 21

SEA WAR, *MEDITERRANEAN*
Operation Substance, the British transportation of supplies from Gibraltar to Malta, begins. Besieged Malta, a naval base, occupies a key location across the short sea and air route between North Africa and Italy.

JULY 22

EASTERN FRONT, *BALTIC*
Germany's Army Group North halts west of Lake Ilmen, south of the city of Leningrad. Troops and equipment along the entire front are suffering from the rigors of the advance and stronger Soviet resistance. During such rest periods the Soviets reinforce their lines, especially those in front of Moscow and Leningrad. The resources needed to take these two cities will be immense.

▶ Reinhard Heydrich, the infamous head of the SS secret police and architect of the "Final Solution" to destroy the entire Jewish population of Europe.

security chief and head of the SS secret police, receives orders to begin creating a draft plan for the complete destruction of the Jews, which becomes known as the "Final Solution." Heydrich will become the infamous administrator of the state apparatus that persecutes and murders millions of people.

AFRICA, *LIBYA*
General Ludwig Cruewell takes command of the Afrika Korps and General Erwin Rommel takes charge of Panzer Group Africa (one infantry and two panzer divisions).

AUGUST 1

POLITICS, *UNITED STATES*
The United States bans the export of oil except to the British Empire and western hemisphere states. Japan, which is entirely dependent on oil imports, is severely affected by this and has to choose between changing its foreign policy or seizing oil by force.

AUGUST 5

POLITICS, *VICHY FRANCE*
Admiral Jean François Darlan assumes responsibility for Vichy-controlled North Africa.

EASTERN FRONT, *UKRAINE*
Romanian and German forces begin a 73-day siege of Odessa. The Soviet high command sends reinforcements to try to help form a line on the east bank of Dniepr River. Meanwhile,

troops delay the Germans on the west bank while industrial resources are destroyed or removed to beyond the Ural Mountains, where Soviet industry is being relocated.

AUGUST 6

POLITICS, *POLAND*
Lieutenant General Wladyslaw Anders is appointed to form a Polish army in the Soviet Union. Anders eventually forms an army but will lack the supplies to fight, while the Soviets will not permit the Poles to serve on the Eastern Front.

AUGUST 12

POLITICS, *GERMANY*
Adolf Hitler's Directive No. 34 outlines revisions to Operation Barbarossa, with the advance on Moscow being halted while the advance to Leningrad is resumed. The southern wheatlands and industries of the Ukraine have also become a higher priority than the Soviet capital.

AFRICA, *LIBYA*
Australian troops, at the request of their government, leave Tobruk; 6000 Poles relieve them.

AUGUST 14

POLITICS, *BRITAIN/UNITED STATES*
A meeting between Winston Churchill and Franklin D. Roosevelt in Canada produces the Atlantic Charter. This

JULY 24

EASTERN FRONT, *UKRAINE*
Hitler orders Army Group South in the Ukraine to close the pocket around the concentration of Soviet forces based on Uman. They seal it 15 days later, isolating three Soviet armies from Red Army forces around Kiev. This leaves the Soviet South and Southwest Fronts seriously weakened, and Odessa is now only accessible by sea. The Germans trap some 100,000 men and 317 tanks in the pocket.

JULY 26–29

POLITICS, *BRITAIN/UNITED STATES*
Britain and the United States freeze Japanese assets in their countries. Japan retaliates likewise against both. Holland freezes Japanese assets in the Dutch East Indies on the 29th. As a consequence, much of Japan's foreign trade is lost.

JULY 31

POLITICS, *GERMANY*
Reinhard Heydrich, Germany's

▶ **General Heinz Guderian, the talented armored warfare tactician, inspecting his men on the Eastern Front.**

asserts liberal policies that articulate their intentions not to acquire any territories or change national borders without the support of the populations concerned. People are also to be granted self-determination regarding how they are governed, and equal access is to be given to economic resources. The United States also secretly guarantees to defend any British possessions and to commence search-and-destroy patrols to support Atlantic convoys.

AUGUST 18

EASTERN FRONT, *UKRAINE*

Soviet forces in the Ukraine begin withdrawing across the strategically-important Dniepr River to form a defensive line farther north – the Bryansk front – leaving the Thirty-fifth Army in Kiev.

Hitler plans to trap and then destroy the bulk of the Red Army before it retreats across the Dniepr. To achieve this the Germans have to make wide encirclements to trap Soviet units. This move, however, creates large gaps through which Red Army troops can escape east.

▶ *British forces move into Iran to safeguard oil supplies inside the country.*

AUGUST 21

SEA WAR, *ARCTIC*

The first trial convoy to the Soviet Union from Britain transports vital supplies to the Russian port of Archangel. The Arctic convoy reaches its destination on the 31st.

AUGUST 23

EASTERN FRONT, *UKRAINE*

The German 2nd Panzer Group and 2nd Army Group strike southward aiming to link up with Army Group South to the east of Kiev.

AUGUST 25

MIDDLE EAST, *IRAN*

Soviet and British forces begin occupying Iran following fears that Germans are operating in the country. Allied forces seize vital oil installations and encounter little resistance.

AUGUST 30

EASTERN FRONT, *UKRAINE*

The Soviet Union launches a counter-attack with the Twenty-first Army

north of Kiev, but it fails and risks defeat by the 2nd Panzergruppe.

SEPTEMBER 1

EASTERN FRONT, *BALTIC*

German forces near Leningrad are now within artillery range of the city. Soon, the city's rail and road approaches are cut off and a bitter siege commences that lasts until early 1944. Leningrad is a key industrial center and is used by the Soviet Baltic Fleet, which potentially threatens vital Swedish iron ore shipments to Germany.

SEPTEMBER 3

FINAL SOLUTION, *POLAND*

Experiments using Zyclon-B gas chambers to slaughter Jews and others deemed "undesirable" by the Nazis are carried out in Auschwitz concentration camp, Poland. The experiments are a success, and will lead to the widespread use of the gas.

SEPTEMBER 4

SEA WAR, *ATLANTIC*

A U-boat mistakes the US destroyer *Greer* for a British vessel and attacks it. This is presented as an act of aggression and US warships are ordered to "shoot on sight" in waters integral to national defense.

SEPTEMBER 6

FINAL SOLUTION, *GERMANY*

Restrictions on Jews are reinforced with an order requiring them to wear a Star of David badge. Their freedom of movement is also restricted.

◀ *The British cruiser* Sheffield *sailing with an Arctic convoy of merchant ships taking vital supplies to the Soviet Union.*

OCTOBER 6–15

EASTERN FRONT, *UKRAINE*
Germany's Second Army and Second Panzer Army encircle three Soviet armies north and south of Bryansk on the 6th. Soviet forces begin evacuating 35,000 troops by sea from the besieged port of Odessa on the 15th.

OCTOBER 7–20

EASTERN FRONT, *SOVIET UNION*
After fierce fighting, six Soviet armies are encircled around Vyazma by the 14th. German forces elsewhere cover great distances, but the onset of heavy rains on the 8th severely limits mobility as the roads to Moscow become quagmires. Until the 20th, the Second Panzer Army also has to reduce the Bryansk pocket. The encirclements at Vyazma and Bryansk trap 673,000 troops and 1242 tanks, but also preoccupy the advancing forces, giving the Red Army time to establish new defensive positions.

OCTOBER 16

POLITICS, *JAPAN*
General Hideki Tojo, defense minister and

◀ *Japanese war leader General Hideki Tojo.*

SEPTEMBER 15

EASTERN FRONT, *UKRAINE*
Guderian's 2nd Panzer Group links up with Army Group South at Lokhvitsa, 100 miles (160 km) east of Kiev, trapping four Soviet armies. This seals the fate of the Soviet Southwest Front and its 500,000 men.

SEPTEMBER 17–19

EASTERN FRONT, *UKRAINE*
Soviet forces begin a fighting withdrawal from Kiev, having been delayed in abandoning the city by Joseph Stalin's insistence on holding it. This delay enables the Germans to cut off their escape routes. The Germans seize Kiev on the 19th, killing or capturing 665,000 men after 40 days of bloody combat. This seals the fate of the western Ukraine.

SEPTEMBER 24

SEA WAR, *MEDITERRANEAN*
The first U-boat enters the Mediterranean (half the entire U-boat force will be operating there later in the year). The Operation Halberd convoy leaves Gibraltar bound for Malta. During the six-day trip, Italian warships attempt to intercept the convoy, but an Italian submarine is sunk. The British bombard Pantellaria, an Italian island situated between Sicily and Tunisia.

SEPTEMBER 29

FINAL SOLUTION, *UKRAINE*
Nazi troops kill 33,771 Jews in Kiev.

SEPTEMBER 30

EASTERN FRONT, *UKRAINE*
The 1st Panzer Group begins the offensive against the southern Ukraine

from the Dniepr and Samara Rivers, and immediately severs a vital Soviet rail line. The advance toward Rostov moves behind three Soviet armies. General Erich von Manstein's Eleventh Army then advances to trap 106,000 Soviet troops and 212 tanks between the two German forces on October 6 in a classic encirclement operation. One Soviet force, the weakened Twelfth Army, retreats northeastward.

EASTERN FRONT, *SOVIET UNION*
Operation Typhoon, the attack on Moscow, officially begins. Germany's Army Group Center's 73 divisions face 85 Soviet divisions plus 10–15 in reserve. General Heinz Guderian's Second Panzer Group thrusts toward Bryansk and Orel. Two days later, the 3rd and 4th Panzer Groups move to encircle Soviet forces around Vyazma.

leader of the militarist faction within Japan, replaces the more moderate Prince Fumimaro Konoye as prime minister. Konoye's attempts to satisfy the prowar military hierarchy and reach some form of settlement with the United States has failed. His

▲ *Female fighters march through Moscow. Thousands of Soviet women helped defend the city from attack.*

▼ *Soviet infantry in their winter clothing. German troops often lacked the kit needed for the freezing temperatures.*

successor exerts authoritarian control over the War and Home Affairs Ministries. This change signals the political ascendancy of the prowar faction in Japan and is a step closer to conflict with the United States and the Allies.

OCTOBER 19

EASTERN FRONT, *SOVIET UNION*
Joseph Stalin declares a state of siege

in Moscow. The Soviet Union is now in the process of mounting an enormous defensive operation. Reinforcements are arriving from northern and southern regions, and a formidable series of defensive lines are now being built by Moscow's citizens, who are also ready to fight in them. General Georgi Zhukov is to command the West Front responsible for defending Moscow.

Across the entire Eastern Front the Soviets are preparing strong defensive positions and mobilizing the entire population to support the war. Soviet resistance is fierce, and atrocities become commonplace on both sides. Agricultural and industrial resources are destroyed if they cannot be prevented from falling into German hands – a deliberate scorched earth policy.

OCTOBER 20–25

EASTERN FRONT, *SOVIET UNION*
Germany halts the original Typhoon offensive and sets more limited objectives, reflecting the deteriorating weather and strengthening Soviet

resistance. The Ukraine offensive has delayed the advance on Moscow. The Germans are now racing to beat the winter weather and the mobilization of Soviet men and equipment.

OCTOBER 24

EASTERN FRONT, *UKRAINE*
The German Sixteenth Army enters Kharkov, the Soviet Union's

fourth-largest city. Unlike the siege of Kiev, Joseph Stalin does not order a costly defense of the city. The Soviets' ill-equipped soldiers of the Southwest Front around Kharkov escape by making a gradual withdrawal.

OCTOBER 31

SEA WAR, *ATLANTIC*
The US destroyer *Reuben James*, part of an escort group accompanying a British convoy, is sunk by a U-boat, claiming 100 lives.

NOVEMBER 1

EASTERN FRONT, *UKRAINE*
Germany launches an offensive on Rostov, at the mouth of the Don River. The Soviet Ninth Army's deep and flexible defensive lines, together with the winter weather, obstruct the encirclement. A frontal assault from the coast on the 17th is then counter-balanced by the Soviet Thirty-seventh

▶ *A muddy German motorcyclist on the Eastern Front in the fall of 1941.*

◀ *The British aircraft carrier Ark Royal, which was hit by torpedoes and then sank after a fire broke out.*

Army's attack north of the city. The Germans capture Rostov on the 21st but the Soviets recapture it within eight days. General Gerd von Rund-stedt then resigns after defying Hitler's orders concerning a tactical with-drawal from the city.

NOVEMBER 6

POLITICS, *UNITED STATES*
A loan of US $1 billion is made to the Soviet Union for Lend-Lease purchases.

NOVEMBER 13

SEA WAR, *MEDITERRANEAN*
Two U-boats attack the British carriers *Argus* and *Ark Royal* en route to Gibraltar after flying off fighters to Malta. *Ark Royal* is badly hit. The carrier sails to within

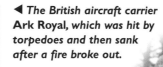

NOVEMBER 15

25 miles (40 km) of Gibraltar when a fire breaks out and the ship sinks along with 70 aircraft.

NOVEMBER 15

EASTERN FRONT, *SOVIET UNION*

The strength, mobility, morale, and logistical support of the German forces on the Eastern Front are severely affected by fierce winter weather. By the 27th, the panzer spearheads are only 20 miles (32 km) from Moscow, but the second phase of the advance is soon halted by Soviet counterattacks and freezing temperatures. Red Army troops, many newly equipped with the superb T-34 tank and Katyusha multiple rocket-launchers, are also properly clothed for winter operations. They are reinforced by partisan volunteers, whose hatred of the enemy is increased by Nazi atrocities against Soviet civilians.

NOVEMBER 18–26

AFRICA, *LIBYA*

The British Eighth Army in Egypt, under General Sir Alan Cunningham, launches Operation Crusader to relieve Tobruk by striking into Cyrenaica. British light tanks suffer serious losses (exacerbated by mechanical and tactical shortcomings) in various

▲ *Japanese Zero fighters take off from the carrier* **Akagi** *to escort bombers bound for Pearl Harbor US naval base.*

▼ *South African troops use a grenade to clear Germans from a building during Operation Crusader, the attempt to relieve Tobruk in North Africa.*

engagements with the Germans around Sidi Rezegh, southeast of Tobruk, from the 19th to the 23rd. On the 22nd, the Tobruk garrison attacks besieging Italian units in order to link up with the Eighth Army advancing to relieve it. General Erwin Rommel then strikes at the Allied flank but sustains heavy losses. He eventually retreats, relieving the pressure on Tobruk, although the fighting continues. On the 26th, General Neil Ritchie relieves Cunningham.

NOVEMBER 26

SEA WAR, *PACIFIC*

The Japanese First Air Fleet of six aircraft carriers, two battleships, three cruisers, nine destroyers, three submarines, and eight tankers leaves the Kurile Islands on a mission to destroy the US Pacific Fleet at Pearl Harbor, Hawaii. The carrier force,

under Admiral Chuichi Nagumo, sails 3400 miles (5440 km) and remains undetected by maintaining strict secrecy and radio silence. Japan's war aims are to destroy US naval power in the region, their only real threat, and then to seize territories in the Pacific and Far East. By establishing their "Greater East Asian Co-Prosperity Sphere," they can then obtain their economic resources and establish a defensive perimeter to repel attacks.

A series of diplomatic exchanges between Japanese and US officials has proved unsuccessful, and war appears inevitable. The United States mistakenly believes that Japan will launch its first offensive against the Philippines, Borneo, or the Malay Peninsula – Hawaii is not thought to be a likely target. Japan will thus take the US Pacific Fleet completely by surprise when its forces attack the naval base.

▼ *US Navy warships ablaze after the surprise Japanese air strike on Pearl Harbor, Oahu Island, Hawaii, in December 1941.*

NOVEMBER 27–28

AFRICA, *ETHIOPIA*

After an Allied attack on the city of Gondar, northwest Ethiopia, General Nasi, the local Italian commander, orders the surrender of 20,000 troops. Ethiopia's liberation by the Allies is complete.

NOVEMBER 30

SEA WAR, *ATLANTIC*

The first successful attack using Air-to-Surface-Vessel radar is made by a British bomber, which sinks *U-206* in the Bay of Biscay.

DECEMBER 6

POLITICS, *BRITAIN*

Britain declares war on Finland, Hungary, and Romania.

DECEMBER 7

AIR WAR, *PACIFIC*

A Japanese force of six carriers launches two

▲ *President Franklin D. Roosevelt stands before the US Congress and asks for a declaration of war against Japan in 1941.*

▲ *Thousands of German troops perished as winter set in and Soviet resistance hardened on the Eastern Front at the end of 1941. Many more would die during Hitler's war in the Soviet Union.*

▼ *A German supply column smashed by the Soviets. Supply problems became critical with the onset of winter.*

strikes on the US Pacific Fleet at Pearl Harbor on Oahu Island, Hawaii. Over 183 Japanese aircraft destroy six battleships and 188 aircraft, damage or sink 10 other vessels, and kill 2000 servicemen. The Japanese lose 29 aircraft. Five midget submarines are lost during a failed underwater attack. A planned third strike, intended to

destroy totally the harbor and oil reserves, is not launched for fear that the valuable Japanese aircraft carriers might be attacked by the remainder of the US Pacific Fleet. Japan then declares war on the United States and the British Commonwealth.

Despite information from Allied codebreaking operations, diplomatic

▶ Australian troops in Tobruk take shelter in a cave during one of the frequent air attacks upon the besieged garrison.

sources, and other warnings, the raid is a tactical surprise. The failure to take appropriate precautions at the base, exacerbated by failures in interservice cooperation, is severely criticized. Despite the attack's success, the US Pacific Fleet's aircraft carriers are at sea and thus survive, while the fleet itself is quickly repaired. In the United States there is outrage over the attack and popular support for declaring war.

DECEMBER 8

EASTERN FRONT, *SOVIET UNION*
Adolf Hitler reluctantly agrees to issue Directive No. 39, which suspends the advance on Moscow for the duration of the winter. Army Group Center begins withdrawing to less exposed positions farther west, much to Hitler's anger.

POLITICS, *ALLIES*
The United States, Britain, Australia, New Zealand, Holland, the Free French, several South American states, and Yugoslavia declare war on Japan in response to Pearl Harbor. China declares war on the Axis states.

DECEMBER 8

▶ *British and Commonwealth troops occupying defensive positions around the perimeter of the key port of Tobruk. The besieged garrison was finally relieved in December 1941 after the Axis forces under Rommel withdrew.*

AFRICA, *LIBYA*

General Erwin Rommel finally decides to withdraw his greatly-weakened units from around Tobruk. He falls back to Gazala by the 11th and then withdraws toward El Agheila on the 16th. The naval operation to sustain Tobruk, finally ended on the 10th, has evacuated 34,000 troops, 7000 casualties, and 7000 prisoners. Around 34,000 tons (34,544 metric tonnes) of supplies have been brought in. Some 27 Allied vessels have been sunk.

▼ *Afrika Korps motorcyclists speed across the desert. Germany's forces attempted to drive the British and Commonwealth forces from Libya and then strike Egypt.*

▲ US troops in the Philippines prepare to meet the Japanese invaders who landed on the islands in December 1941.

◄ A Filipino family flees from their home following a Japanese bombardment. Thousands of civilians were affected by the fighting in the islands.

PACIFIC, *PHILIPPINES*
Japanese air attacks destroy 100 US aircraft at Clark Field, while a small force lands on Luzon Island to build an airfield. General Douglas MacArthur, commanding the 130,000-strong US and Filipino force in the Philippines, had intended that US aircraft would strike the invading Japanese force as his troops are not capable of stopping any landing. On the 10th, Luzon is invaded and Guam Island quickly falls. The Japanese forces also attack Wake Island and capture it on the 24th – after two invasion attempts.

▲ *Japanese troops wade ashore during the invasion of the Malayan Peninsula.*

FAR EAST, *HONG KONG*

The Japanese 38th Division attacks the 12,000-strong Hong Kong garrison. After the garrison refuses the Japanese surrender demand on the 13th, it faces an intense attack followed by amphibious assaults. Hong Kong finally surrenders on the 25th.

FAR EAST, *MALAYA/THAILAND*

A Japanese force of 100,000 troops (the 5th and 18th Divisions), under General Tomoyuki Yamashita, begins landing on the northeast coast of Malaya and in Thailand after initial air attacks. Japanese units quickly move southward down both sides of the Malayan Peninsula. British forces are mainly stationed in the south, having anticipated an attack nearer Singapore. Japanese aircraft soon destroy most of the British aircraft. British reluctance to move into neutral Thailand before a Japanese attack enables General Yamashita to complete his landings. British forces finally advance into Thailand on the 10th but cannot halt the Japanese invasion. Well-equipped and experienced Japanese troops continue pushing southward, many by bicycle.

DECEMBER 10

SEA WAR, *FAR EAST*

About 90 Japanese aircraft sink the British battleship *Prince of Wales* and the battlecruiser *Repulse* while they are attempting to intercept Japanese warships off Malaya. The attack claims 730 lives and leaves the Allies without a single battleship in the theater.

DECEMBER 11

POLITICS, *AXIS*

Germany and Italy declare war on the United States. The United States then declares war on the two Axis states. Romania declares war on the United

States on the 12th. Germany's declaration now confirms US participation in the European war.

DECEMBER 13

SEA WAR, *MEDITERRANEAN*

Three British and one Dutch destroyer sink the Italian fast cruisers *Alberico da Barbiano* and *Alberto di Giussano* off Sicily. The Italian warships are carrying fuel to North Africa, and the attack claims 900 lives. Off Messina, the British submarine *Urge* sinks two Italian transports and damages the battleship *Vittorio Veneto*, which is carrying supplies to Libya.

DECEMBER 14

SEA WAR, *ATLANTIC*

A British convoy of 32 ships, including the aircraft carrier *Audacity*, leaves Gibraltar for Britain. *Audacity* is the first British escort carrier introduced to provide Allied convoys with constant air cover by intercepting enemy bombers or U-boat "Wolf Packs" when they are beyond the operational range of land-based aircraft. During the voyage, the convoy suffers attacks from 12 U-boats, but destroys five of them. The convoy loses *Audacity*, a

▲ *A British soldier is led into captivity by Japanese troops during the invasion of Malaya in December 1941.*

▼ *British troops prepare defenses in Hong Kong. Despite such measures, the colony was quickly overwhelmed.*

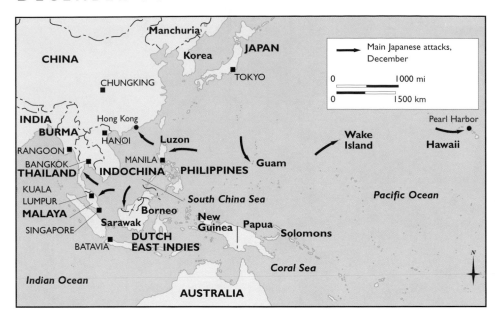

▲ Japan launched a series of attacks across Southeast Asia in 1941 to seize strategic bases and economic resources.

destroyer, and two merchant ships, before it reaches Britain on the 23rd.

DECEMBER 16

FAR EAST, *BORNEO*
The Japanese 19th Division makes three landings along the coast of Borneo. The British and Dutch forces defending the island set oil installations ablaze before retreating.

DECEMBER 17

POLITICS, *UNITED STATES*
Admiral Chester Nimitz replaces Admiral Husband Kimmel as commander of the Pacific Fleet following the attack on Pearl Harbor on December 7.

DECEMBER 18–19

SEA WAR, *MEDITERRANEAN*
The Royal Navy's Force K, operating from Malta, runs into a minefield off Tripoli. The cruiser *Neptune* and destroyer *Kandahar* are both sunk, while the remaining two cruisers are damaged. An Italian "human torpedo" attack upon the British Mediterranean Fleet in Alexandria, Egypt, sinks the battleships *Queen Elizabeth* and

Valiant. However, both vessels sink upright in shallow waters and are eventually repaired. Nevertheless, these losses severely reduce British naval power in the Mediterranean.

The "human torpedo," a midget submarine driven by two operators, is designed to enter defended harbors and clamp its warhead onto a ship's hull. The British soon develop their own version called "Chariot."

▲ *An Italian "human torpedo." These craft were used to great effect against British vessels in the Mediterranean.*

▶ *Allied convoys became increasingly vulnerable as naval forces were seriously overstretched and losses mounted.*

▼ *The British battleship* Queen Elizabeth *(front), which was sunk by an Italian "human torpedo" in Egypt.*

▲ *Adolf Hitler (center) discusses strategy with Field Marshal Walther von Brauchitsch (left) and General Franz Halder (right).*

DECEMBER 19

POLITICS, *GERMANY*
Adolf Hitler appoints himself as commander-in-chief of the army following Field Marshal Walter von Brauchitsch's resignation on the 7th. Brauchitsch resigned following a heart attack brought on by the strain of Soviet counterattacks. He was already under pressure to resign. His authority had been increasingly undermined by Hitler dominating strategic planning.

Hitler successfully keeps the Eastern Front armies in defensive positions during the winter. He develops an increasing skepticism toward the competence of his army commanders. Parallel to this is the expansion of the Waffen SS, seen by Hitler as being politically-reliable troops.

POLITICS, *UNITED STATES*
An amendment to the Selective Service Act requires all men aged 18–64 to register, and for men aged 20–44 to be liable for conscription.

DECEMBER 20–26

POLITICS, *UNITED STATES*
Admiral Ernest King becomes chief of naval operations.

PACIFIC, *PHILIPPINES*
Japanese forces invade Mindanao, the most southerly island, and Jolo. The islands offer Japan the chance to gain naval and air bases. The main invasion of Luzon commences on the 22nd. General Douglas MacArthur decides not to defend Manila, the capital, but declares it an open city in order to withdraw his forces westward to the Bataan Peninsula.

DECEMBER 22

POLITICS, *ALLIES*
US President Franklin D. Roosevelt and British Prime Minister Winston Churchill meet at the Arcadia Conference, Washington. Talks between the

▶ *African-American conscripts doing their war service with the US Army.*

▲ *Manila, the Philippines' capital, just after it was abandoned by the US and Filipino forces.*

respective political and military delegations reaffirm the "Germany First" strategic priority and establish the Combined Chiefs-of-Staff to direct Allied military action. They also agree to build up US forces in Britain in preparation for future military action against Nazi Germany and in order to continue the aerial bombing of Nazi-occupied Europe.

DECEMBER 26–28

SEA WAR, *NORTH SEA*
Britain launches Operation Archery, a commando attack against Lofoten Island, off Norway. The first force of 260 troops succeeds in destroying a fish-oil plant.

On December 27, a second landing by a further 600 troops successfully attacks fish-oil plants and radio facilities. The raids reinforce Hitler's fears that Britain is planning to invade the whole of Norway.

KEY PERSONALITIES

PRESIDENT FRANKLIN D. ROOSEVELT

Franklin D. Roosevelt, US president from 1933 to 1945, was the only person to be elected for three terms. He trained as a lawyer and subsequently pursued a political career in the Democratic Party, despite being stricken with polio. Roosevelt's peacetime administration, which began in 1932, generated popular support with its "New Deal" program to establish social and economic reconstruction during the Great Depression of the 1930s.

Once war broke out in 1939, he worked to overcome American "isolationism" and generate support for the Allied cause. Roosevelt was responsible for transforming the United States into the "arsenal of democracy" by expanding the economic capacity of the nation in order to sustain the Allies with war supplies and build up US military capability. A series of economic agreements were made with Allied states, while trade restrictions were imposed on Axis powers. Roosevelt also put the nation on a firm war-footing with military service legislation that provided the manpower for the expanding armed forces.

When the United States entered the war in 1941, Roosevelt ignored his critics and made the key decision to maintain the "Germany First" strategy rather than devoting greater effort to defeating Japan. He also took the crucial decision to demand the unconditional surrender of Japan and Germany. Roosevelt also rejected proposals by US commanders to invade Europe in 1942, and followed British plans to attack North Africa, Sicily, and Italy first.

Roosevelt adopted a conciliatory manner in inter-Allied relations, urging diplomacy between Britain and the Soviet Union to overcome the distrust that existed between these politically divergent states. This popular war leader died on April 12, 1945, three weeks before the end of the fighting in Europe.

1942

Japan's territorial conquests appeared to signal its triumph over Europe's colonial powers in the Far East. The United States, however, was now on the offensive and won crucial strategic victories at sea over the Japanese. These had serious repercussions for Japan's ability to sustain both its domestic and overseas power. In North Africa and on the Eastern Front, Axis offensives, although initially successful, were halted and then defeated by a series of Allied counterattacks. Control of the sea-lanes continued to be a crucial factor in the war.

JANUARY 1

POLITICS, *ALLIES*
At the Arcadia Conference in Washington, 26 Allied countries sign the United Nations Declaration, pledging to follow the Atlantic Charter principles. These include an agreement to direct their "full resources" against the three Axis nations and not to make any separate peace agreements or treaties. This is a key development in the formation of the United Nations Organization.

JANUARY 2–9

PACIFIC, *PHILIPPINES*
US and Filipino forces under General Douglas MacArthur prepare defensive positions on the Bataan Peninsula and the island of Corregidor as Manila falls. MacArthur realizes that Japan has air and sea superiority. He also knows that no reinforcements will be sent. His troops begin a desperate resistance against Japanese attacks across the mountainous peninsula, which begin on the 9th. For several months the 80,000 troops will resist the Japanese, despite suffering from tropical diseases and being short of supplies.

JANUARY 3

POLITICS, *ALLIES*
Following the Arcadia Conference, British General Sir Archibald Wavell takes charge of the new American, British, Dutch, and Australian (ABDA) command. He is responsible for holding the southwest Pacific. Chinese Nationalist leader Chiang Kai-shek is made commander-in-chief of the Allied forces in his country.

JANUARY 5

EASTERN FRONT, *SOVIET UNION*
Joseph Stalin orders a general offensive against the German invaders, despite warnings from General Georgi Zhukov, the Western Front commander, that the Soviet Union lacks the resources for

◀ *A Japanese tank charges through a Philippines plantation as part of the relentless Japanese offensive to capture the islands from the Americans.*

▲ *Chiang Kai-shek took charge of Allied forces in China in January 1942.*

an attack on four fronts (Leningrad, Moscow, Ukraine, and Crimea). Zhukov advocates a concentrated attack against Army Group Center, which is threatening Moscow. However, the general offensive initially makes considerable inroads and captures trains, food, and munitions. German forces offer stiff resistance and are ordered to hold their positions. They set up defensive areas ("Hedgehogs") that frustrate the Red Army's attacks.

JANUARY 5–12

FAR EAST, *MALAYA*
Following the recent landing of Japanese troops on the northeast coast, British, Indian, and Australian forces are now retreating southward toward Singapore, unable to mount any meaningful defense against the Japanese. The British have underestimated the Japanese, who are well trained and equipped. Kuala Lumpur, the capital, falls to the Japanese on the 12th.

JANUARY 9–21

EASTERN FRONT, *SOVIET UNION*
The Battle of the Valdai Hills begins in the Moscow sector. During the 12-day battle Soviet troops make a 75-mile (120-km) penetration of the German lines that captures nine towns between Smolensk and Lake Ilmen.

JANUARY 10–11

FAR EAST, *DUTCH EAST INDIES*
A Japanese force, under General Tomoyuki Yamashita and Admiral Takahashi, begins attacking the Dutch East Indies to secure the oil assets of this island-chain. The Japanese Eastern Force lands on Celebes and Amboina before taking Bali, Timor, and east Java. The Central Force lands at Tarakan and

▶ *A Japanese tank crosses an improvised bridge during the invasion of Burma.*

▼ *Japanese troops occupy Kuala Lumpur, the capital of Malaya, following the hasty retreat of British forces from the city.*

aims to take Borneo. The Western Force moves from Indochina to attack Sumatra and Java. The remaining Allied troops under ABDA command in the region, including local forces of doubtful loyalty, attempt to resist the Japanese onslaught.

JANUARY 12

POLITICS, *YUGOSLAVIA*
General Dusan Simovic resigns as prime minister of the Yugoslavian government-in-exile. Professor Yovanovic replaces him.

AFRICA, *LIBYA*
General Erwin Rommel agrees to a plan proposed by his officers to counterattack the Allies. British naval strength in the Mediterranean has been eroded, which has enabled new German supplies to arrive. At the same time, Allied forces have suffered the departure of the 7th Armored Brigade plus two Australian divisions, which have been sent to the Far East.

JANUARY 12–31

FAR EAST, *BURMA*
The Japanese Fifteenth Army's two reinforced divisions, plus air support, move northwestward into Burma from neighboring Thailand. A small group under Burmese nationalist Aung Sang

supports Japan and encourages uprisings. British, Burmese, and Indian troops around the town of Moulmein unsuccessfully engage the invaders and withdraw. Already in the previous month the Japanese have taken a key

▼ Japanese offensives to conquer Burma drove the Allies back to the Indian and Chinese borders by May 1942.

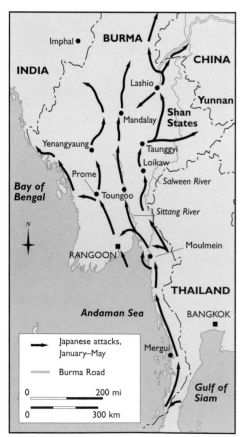

southern air base at Mergui, forming part of the air route between India and Malaya, which they have now blocked. Such airfields are then used for bombing missions. Burma has the only viable supply route to sustain the Chinese fight against Japan. The Allied possession of Burma also keeps India's northeast region secure from attack.

JANUARY 13

POLITICS, ALLIES
At a London meeting, the Allies agree to punish Axis leaders responsible for war crimes.

SEA WAR, ATLANTIC
Germany's U-boats launch attacks, code-named Operation Drum Roll, on shipping off the east coast of the United States. Approximately 20 ships are sunk in the first month of operations as a result of the US Navy's failure to take proper antisubmarine measures, despite British warnings. U-boats begin hunting in the Caribbean the following month.

JANUARY 16–19

POLITICS, GERMANY
Field Marshal Walther von Reichenau, commander of the German Army Group South on the Eastern Front, dies in a plane crash. Field Marshal Fedor von Bock replaces him on the 19th. Adolf Hitler removes Field Marshal Wilhelm von Leeb and replaces him

▶ Field Marshal Wilhelm von Leeb, one of the commanders whom Adolf Hitler blamed for failures on the Eastern Front.

▲ A female Soviet sniper in the Caucasus. Women made a valuable contribution to the Soviet war machine.

with General George von Küchler as Army Group North's commander. Since December, the Führer has removed over 30 senior officers, including two army group and two panzer group commanders, due to his impatience with their constant appeals to make withdrawals in the face of Soviet offensives.

KEY MOMENTS

WANNSEE CONFERENCE

The secret Wannsee Conference in Berlin officially launched the Nazi program to exterminate the Jewish people, who were regarded as the racial enemy of the "Aryan" Germans. The previous persecution and killing of Jews in Nazi-occupied Europe was transformed into a highly-efficient operation. European Jews were systematically herded into concentration camps in Eastern Europe, where they were worked like slaves. Millions died from maltreatment, exhaustion, disease, and starvation. In extermination camps, poison gas chambers were used to kill thousands of people. Many other people deemed "undesirable" by the Nazis, including gypsies, political opponents, and the mentally and physically disabled, also shared the same fate as the Jews.

Various efforts to save Jews were made. Some were hidden or smuggled to neutral states. Allied countries, however, were often too preoccupied with their struggle against Germany to provide any effective support, though they were aware of what was going on.

Jews who remained free were able to join resistance groups in Europe. The deportation of Jews from their ghettos in Poland for extermination led to various uprisings. In 1943, poorly-armed Warsaw Ghetto Jews resisted the Nazis for four months. The full horrors of the genocide were revealed when the first extermination camp was liberated in July 1944.

Over six million Jews were killed by the Nazis. Some of those responsible for the slaughter were tried at the Nuremberg War Crimes Trials. Thousands of others who served as guards during the "Final Solution" escaped justice, however.

The appalling sight of corpses from Buchenwald concentration camp, where many thousands died.

POLITICS, *UNITED STATES*
Donald Nelson becomes head of the new centralized War Production Board.

JANUARY 17

AFRICA, *LIBYA*
The Axis garrison of Halfaya, besieged throughout the British Operation Crusader, finally falls and 5500 Germans and Italians are captured.

SEA WAR, *ARCTIC*
U-boats make their first attack on an Allied Arctic convoy. *U-454* sinks the destroyer *Matabele* and a merchant ship from convoy PQ-8.

JANUARY 18–27

EASTERN FRONT, *UKRAINE*
Soviet South and Southwest Front forces, under Marshal Semyon Timoshenko, make an attack aiming to cross the Donets River and then swing south toward the Sea of Azov to trap units of the German Sixth and Seventeenth Armies. The Donets River is crossed by the 24th, but the Soviet advance is halted by the 27th.

JANUARY 20

FINAL SOLUTION, *GERMANY*
At the Wannsee Conference, Berlin, deputy head of the SS Reinhard Heydrich reveals his plans for the "Final Solution" to the so-called "Jewish problem." Heydrich receives permission to begin deporting all Jews in German-controlled areas to Eastern Europe to face either forced labor or

▲ *Concentration camp prisoners receive rations from an SS officer in a carefully-staged propaganda photograph.*

extermination. The killing of Jews in Eastern Europe is already commonplace. Execution by shooting, however, is proving inefficient and a strain for the troops engaged. A more efficient way of killing using poison gas will soon become widespread.

SEA WAR, *PACIFIC*
In Japan's ongoing offensive against Allied possessions in the Far East, four carriers begin air strikes on Rabaul, New Britain (soon to become a major Japanese naval base), and two submarines shell Midway Island. US and Australian warships sink a Japanese submarine off Darwin. Japanese amphibious landings are made on Borneo, New Ireland, and the Solomons on the 23rd.

JANUARY 21–29

AFRICA, *LIBYA*
General Erwin Rommel begins his second desert offensive in North Africa, moving from El Aghelia to Agedabia on the 22nd. The British Eighth Army is caught unawares and the Germans capitalize on

JANUARY 22

this by driving it back. Benghazi falls on the 29th.

JANUARY 22

EASTERN FRONT, *SOVIET UNION*
The besieged city of Leningrad evacuates 440,000 citizens over 50 days. Thousands are dying of starvation, typhus, and other diseases due to inadequate supplies reaching the city and the German shelling and bombing.

JANUARY 23–24

PACIFIC, *PHILIPPINES*
US and Filipino forces on Bataan begin withdrawing to a line running from Bagac in the east to Orion in the west.

SEA WAR, *FAR EAST*
At the Battle of Macassar Strait, four US destroyers, Dutch bombers, and a submarine attack a Japanese convoy off Borneo. Four Japanese transports are lost.

JANUARY 25

POLITICS, *THAILAND*
The government declares war on Britain and the United States.

▲ *Desert fighters from Germany's Afrika Korps make use of a captured truck during Rommel's second offensive against the British Eighth Army.*

▼*T-34 tanks in Leningrad. Thousands of people were evacuated to escape the hardships of the besieged city.*

JANUARY 26

WESTERN FRONT, *BRITAIN*
The first US troop convoy of the war reaches Britain.

SEA WAR, *FAR EAST*
Several Japanese troopships off Malaya are struck by 68 British aircraft, of which 13 are lost. That night, the British increase their attacks. The destroyer *Thanet* and the Australian destroyer

Vampire are sunk while attacking the Japanese convoy.

JANUARY 29

POLITICS, *UNITED STATES*

Major General Millard Harmon succeeds General Carl Spaatz as United States Army Air Force chief-of-staff. Spaatz takes over the Air Force Combat Command.

JANUARY 30

FAR EAST, *SINGAPORE*

Retreating British and Commonwealth troops cross the Johore Strait, separating Singapore from the mainland, and partly destroy the connecting causeway. They abandon the rest of the Malayan Peninsula, where mobile Japanese units have constantly outwitted them. Singapore is designed to repel a naval attack. Its great guns have no suitable shells for bombarding land forces as the British believe that a land invasion through dense jungle is impossible, although the RAF has asked for more aircraft to meet a land attack from the north.

FEBRUARY 1

POLITICS, *NORWAY*

Nazi collaborator Vidkun Quisling becomes prime minister, although he will be controlled by Berlin.

SEA WAR, *ATLANTIC*

Germany adopts a new radio code for

▼ *Filipino troops prepare to fight alongside US forces in Bataan.*

▲ *Japanese troops cautiously scale a hill during their advance to Singapore. The British were shocked that the Japanese could move through dense jungle.*

U-boat communications in the Atlantic. Although the British are unable to crack the code until the end of the year, the detection of U-boats is made easier by photoreconnaissance and radio direction-finding technology.

SEA WAR, *PACIFIC*

The US Navy carriers *Enterprise* and *Yorktown*, together with the cruisers *Northampton* and *Salt Lake City*, attack the Marshall and Gilbert Islands.

FEBRUARY 4

AFRICA, *LIBYA*

Axis forces have overextended their lines of communication and a stalemate is developing in the desert. Allied forces are establishing a fortified line from Gazala on the coast to Bir Hacheim farther inland. Both sides are building up their forces for a new offensive.

FAR EAST, *SINGAPORE*

Britain rejects Japanese demands for Singapore to surrender. Reinforcements are being sent to help defend the base, which is believed to be impregnable.

FEBRUARY 5

POLITICS, *UNITED STATES*

The US government declares war on Thailand.

FEBRUARY 8

▶ *Victorious Japanese soldiers celebrate their conquest of Singapore. The British had totally underestimated the military capability of the Japanese Army.*

FEBRUARY 8

POLITICS, *PHILIPPINES*
President Manuel Quezon proposes to the United States that his country should become independent, that both Japanese and US forces should withdraw, and Filipino units be disbanded. The United States rejects the proposal.

FEBRUARY 8–14

FAR EAST, *SINGAPORE*
Two Japanese divisions, supported by artillery and air bombardment, land on the northwest of the island, quickly followed by a third. Repairs to the Johore causeway enable tanks and 30,000 troops to advance, while in the air the Japanese achieve supremacy. Confused orders often result in the defenders making unnecessary withdrawals and much equipment is lost. Lieutenant General Arthur Percival, the Singapore commander, is forced to surrender on February 14 as the water supply for Singapore's residents and the 85,000-strong garrison is cut. Japan has fewer than 10,000 casualties in Malaya. British and Commonwealth forces have lost 138,000 men, and thousands more will die in captivity. The campaign is one of Britain's greatest defeats.

FEBRUARY 10

SEA WAR, *ATLANTIC*
Britain offers the United States 34 antisubmarine vessels with crews to battle the U-boats.

FEBRUARY 11–12

SEA WAR, *NORTH SEA*
The German battlecruisers *Gneisenau* and *Scharnhorst*, and the heavy cruiser *Prinz Eugen*, supported by destroyers and air cover, leave Brest and sail through the English Channel. RAF and Royal Navy strikes against the German ships are total failures, and 42 aircraft are downed. During the "Channel Dash" to the North Sea, both battlecruisers hit mines and need repairs. British operations to contain the threat of these

▼ *Lieutenant General Sir Arthur Percival's surrender of Singapore was a military disaster.*

commerce-raiders are easier while the vessels are in port. *Gneisenau* subsequently has to be rebuilt after being hit during an air raid against Kiel on February 26, but the project is never completed before the war's end.

FEBRUARY 13

POLITICS, *GERMANY*
Adolf Hitler finally abandons the invasion of Britain, Operation Sealion.

FEBRUARY 14

AIR WAR, *GERMANY*
Britain issues the "Area Bombing Directive," which outlines the strategic objectives of RAF Bomber Command. Bombing will now aim to destroy the psychological will of the German people as well as the country's war industry. Air raids will now aim to destroy residential areas to erode civilian morale.

FEBRUARY 18–23

FAR EAST, *BURMA*
Japanese forces are in constant pursuit of British forces. At the Battle of the Sittang River, the

British are withdrawing across a single bridge over the river when Japanese troops make a sudden crossing elsewhere. The British quickly blow up the bridge, losing much of their equipment with their forces only partially across; those left behind have to use boats. The Sittang River is the only major physical obstacle in the path of the Japanese forces moving toward Rangoon, the capital.

FEBRUARY 19

POLITICS, *UNITED STATES*
The virtually unknown General Dwight D. Eisenhower becomes head of the US Army General Staff War Plans Division. In this capacity he will advocate the intensification of Operation Bolero, the buildup of US forces in Britain, and press for the development of Operation Sledgehammer, a cross-Channel invasion of Europe from Britain.

◀ *General Dwight D. Eisenhower, who became a key figure in US strategic planning and commanded the North African landings in 1942.*

▼ *The German heavy cruiser Prinz Eugen, one of the commerce-raiders that evaded the British and sailed from France into the North Sea.*

KEY PERSONALITIES

AIR CHIEF MARSHAL SIR ARTHUR HARRIS

Arthur Harris (1892–1984) served as British Deputy Chief of Air Staff (1940–41) before taking charge of Bomber Command in 1942. He believed precision bombing was ineffective and favored area bombing against Germany, and he secured Prime Minister Winston Churchill's support to expand Bomber Command's size. Great bomber fleets therefore saturated districts with high explosives and incendiaries to destroy both industry and public morale.

The determination and inspiration shown by Harris encouraged his aircrews to undertake hazardous bombing missions. Raids increased in intensity, more night attacks were flown to avoid hazardous daylight missions, and photoreconnaissance improved bombing accuracy. Despite Harris's initiatives, though, there is still doubt over the success of his strategy.

The impact on Germany's civilians and economy have led some to question the morality of "Bomber" Harris's strategy. Harris himself, however, defended his strategy, claiming it saved many British lives by shortening the war.

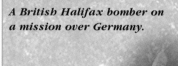

A British Halifax bomber on a mission over Germany.

▲ *Scenes of devastation in Darwin after a Japanese air attack on the port. This attack on the Australian mainland shocked the population.*

SEA WAR, *FAR EAST*
At the Battle of Lombok Strait, east of Bali, Dutch and US vessels fight several actions with the Japanese. A Dutch cruiser and a destroyer are sunk, while one Japanese destroyer is damaged.

AIR WAR, *AUSTRALIA*
Japanese carrier aircraft and land-based bombers attack Darwin, northern Australia. The raid sinks or damages 16 vessels, claims 172 lives, and causes widespread panic.

HOME FRONT, *UNITED STATES*
President Franklin D. Roosevelt signs Executive Order 9066 giving the secretary of war powers to exclude persons from military areas. This legislation is directed at the nation's Japanese-American population, which has faced growing public hostility since Pearl Harbor. The US Army subsequently removes 11,000 Japanese-Americans from the Pacific coast to camps in Arkansas and Texas for the war's duration (there are fears that they may aid a Japanese attack on the West Coast, which is regarded by many as a real possibility). Not a single Japanese-American, however, is convicted of spying for Tokyo during the war. Others go on to serve with distinction in the US armed forces, winning many awards for gallantry.

FEBRUARY 20

POLITICS, *VICHY FRANCE*
Political leaders of the Third Republic are tried by the Vichy Supreme Court, charged with being responsible for France's humiliating 1940 defeat. Former premiers Léon Blum, Paul Reynaud, and Edouard Daladier all defend their records with great skill. The trial, which quickly becomes a public joke, is never completed.

FEBRUARY 22

POLITICS, *BRITAIN*
Air Chief Marshal Sir Arthur Harris takes over Bomber Command.

FEBRUARY 23

POLITICS, *ALLIES*
Britain, Australia, the United States, and New Zealand ratify the Mutual Aid Agreement.

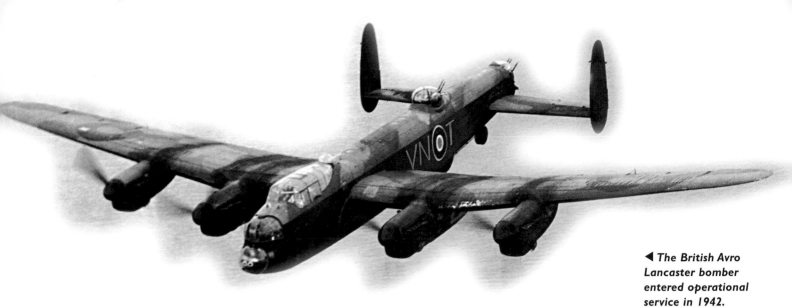

◄ *The British Avro Lancaster bomber entered operational service in 1942.*

FEBRUARY 24

SEA WAR, *PACIFIC*
The US aircraft carrier *Enterprise* leads a task force to attack the Japanese on Wake Island.

FEBRUARY 25

POLITICS, *ALLIES*
ABDA is disbanded and its commander, British General Sir Archibald Wavell, becomes commander-in-chief in India.
HOME FRONT, *UNITED STATES*
An air raid scare in Los Angeles results in a heavy antiaircraft barrage being fired.

FEBRUARY 27–29

SEA WAR, *FAR EAST*
Under the command of Dutch Rear Admiral Karel Doorman, five cruisers and nine destroyers from four Allied nations engage a Japanese force of four cruisers and 13 destroyers in the Java Sea. Following an inconclusive opening engagement, the Japanese inflict severe losses using their faster "Long Lance" torpedoes. Five Allied cruisers and five destroyers are sunk. Doorman is killed. Japan loses two transports, one cruiser is sunk, and six destroyers are damaged.

FEBRUARY 28

WESTERN FRONT, *FRANCE*
A British parachute assault destroys a German radar station at Bruneval near Le Havre. The force then escapes by sea with captured equipment.

MARCH 1–7

SEA WAR, *FAR EAST*
Two Japanese task forces, including four aircraft carriers, inflict serious losses on Allied shipping while sailing to Java in the Dutch East Indies. The Japanese surround the Allies and sink nine warships and 10 merchant vessels with close-range fire.

MARCH 2

POLITICS, *AUSTRALIA*
All Australian adult civilians become liable for war service.

MARCH 3

AIR WAR, *GERMANY*
The British Lancaster bomber undertakes its first operation by dropping mines in the Heligoland Bight in the North Sea.

MARCH 5

POLITICS, *BRITAIN*
General Sir Alan Brooke replaces Admiral Sir Dudley Pound as chairman of the Chiefs-of-Staff Committee responsible for the daily running of the war and future planning. Britain also extends conscription to men aged 41–45.

MARCH 5–7

FAR EAST, *BURMA*
Lieutenant General Sir Harold Alexander replaces Lieutenant General Thomas Hutton as British commander

◄ *Chinese troops crossing the Sittang River during the campaign to save their vital supply road through Burma.*

81

MARCH 9

in Burma. Two British divisions have been trying to resist Japanese advances toward Rangoon. Its port is the main point of entry for British supplies and troops. Alexander, however, evacuates Rangoon after realizing his dispersed forces cannot hold it. He himself narrowly escapes before the Japanese seize it on the 7th.

MARCH 9

POLITICS, *UNITED STATES*
Admiral Harold Stark replaces Vice Admiral Robert Ghormley as US naval commander in European waters. Admiral Ernest King assumes Stark's position as Chief of Naval Operations on the 26th.

FAR EAST, *DUTCH EAST INDIES*
Japan gains possession of its "Southern Resources Area" with the surrender of Allied

combatants in the Dutch East Indies. The capture of this resource-rich area and Malaya allows Japan to consider offensives against India and Australia.

MARCH 11

PACIFIC, *PHILIPPINES*
General Douglas MacArthur leaves his Far East command to become commander-in-chief of US forces in Australia. On leaving, he famously declares: "I shall return!"

FAR EAST, *BURMA*
US General Joseph Stilwell assumes command of the Chinese Fifth and Sixth Armies around the eastern Shan States and city of Mandalay. Their aim is to protect the Burma Road into China. The Allied ground forces are supported by one RAF squadron and up to 30 "Flying Tiger" aircraft flown by an all-volunteer force of US pilots. They face over 200 enemy aircraft.

MARCH 12

PACIFIC, *NEW CALEDONIA*
US Forces, including the first operational deployment of "Seabee" engineers, begin establishing a base in Noumea on New Caledonia in the southwest Pacific.

MARCH 13–30

FAR EAST, *BURMA*
Lieutenant General Sir Harold Alexander forms an Allied line below the central towns of Prome, Toungoo,

◀ *General Douglas MacArthur, the US commander in the Philippines, who directed the defense of the islands.*

and Loikaw near the Salween River and then eastward. Major General William Slim assumes command of the Burma Corps, the main elements of the British forces there on March 19. Japanese attacks begin on the 21st, directed at Chinese forces at Toungoo and the British at Prome.

MARCH 14

POLITICS, *AUSTRALIA*
Large numbers of US troops begin arriving in Australia.

MARCH 22–23

SEA WAR, *MEDITERRANEAN*
A superior Italian force engages a British convoy sailing from Alexandria to Malta. A relatively small escort of five light cruisers and 17 destroyers initially resists an attack led by the battleship *Littorio* at the Battle of Sirte. A storm, however, results in the loss of two Italian destroyers. The convoy subsequently faces air attacks and only 5000 of the original 25,000 tons (25,400 metric tonnes) of supplies arrive. British naval losses and commitments in the Mediterranean have reduced the number of ships available for convoy escorts.

MARCH 27

POLITICS, *BRITAIN*
Admiral Sir James Somerville assumes command of the Far East Fleet in Ceylon (modern Sri Lanka).

POLITICS, *AUSTRALIA*
Australian General Sir Thomas Blamey becomes commander-in-chief of the Australian forces and commander

◄ Japanese troops pass a destroyed railroad bridge as they enter Burma from neighboring Thailand.

of Allied Land Forces in Australia, under the supreme command of US General Douglas MacArthur.

MARCH 28–29

AIR WAR, GERMANY
RAF bombers, including the new Lancaster, attack Lübeck on the Baltic coast. The raid on the historic, timber-built houses of the town signals a change in Bomber Command's strategy, which is now concentrating on the civilian population.

SEA WAR, BAY OF BISCAY
Britain's Combined Operations launches an operation to destroy the St. Nazaire dry-dock in France with a force of 611 men. The objective is to prevent the German battleship *Tirpitz* (currently in Norway) being able to use the only dock large enough to enable it to mount commerce-destroying operations in the Atlantic. An old destroyer, *Campbeltown*, is filled with explosives and destroys the lock gates after ramming them. A commando force attacks St. Nazaire's dock facilities, but 144 men die and over half are captured.

MARCH 29

POLITICS, BRITAIN/INDIA
Britain announces its proposals to grant India semi-independent status when the war ends.

APRIL 2–8

SEA WAR, FAR EAST
Japan's First Air Fleet attacks British air and sea bases in Trincomalee and Colombo, Ceylon. It fails to hit the

main fleet, though, which is at sea. A British air attack against the Japanese force fails. Over several days, Japanese aircraft destroy the carrier *Hermes*, two heavy cruisers, an Australian destroyer, and several merchant ships.

APRIL 3–9

PACIFIC, PHILIPPINES
Japan launches its final offensive on Bataan, beginning with air and artillery bombardments. The US line is penetrated on the 4th. Major General Jonathan Wainright, commanding the US and Filipino forces, cannot mount an effective counterattack with his decimated units. Following the surrender on the 9th, some 78,000 US and Filipino troops are forced to make a 65-mile (104-km) march without sustenance, and are constantly beaten. Many die along the way. Wainright escapes with 2000 men to Corregidor Island off Bataan.

APRIL 10–23

FAR EAST, BURMA
Japan begins an offensive after reinforcements arrive. Lieutenant General

▲ Japanese troops establish control in the Dutch East Indies following their conquest of the resource-rich islands.

▼ US troops captured by the Japanese following the capitulation of US and Filipino forces on Bataan, the Philippines.

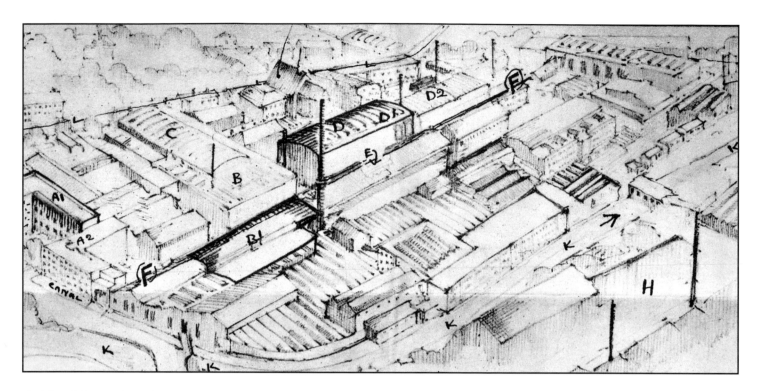

▲ A hand-drawn plan of the Augsburg diesel engine factory prepared for crew briefings before the raid to destroy it.

▶ James Doolittle, the pilot who led the first US air attack on Tokyo, presents awards to other airmen of the US Army Air Force.

William Slim fails to prevent the Japanese advancing on the oil fields at Yenangyaung in the south and sets large amounts of crude oil ablaze. The Chinese Sixty-fifth Army enters Burma to bolster the faltering defense against the Japanese. Around the central towns of Loikaw and Taunggyi, the Japanese 56th Division overwhelms the Chinese Sixth Army by the 23rd.

APRIL 17

AIR WAR, *GERMANY*
The RAF launch one of the war's most hazardous bomber raids, attacking a diesel engine factory in Augsburg. Seven of the 12 Lancaster bombers assigned to the daylight attack are lost and the other five sustain damage.

APRIL 18

POLITICS, *VICHY FRANCE*
Pierre Laval returns to head the government; Henri-Philippe Pétain continues as head of state. Laval is eager to enhance Franco-German relations and undermines the more hesitant approach advocated by Pétain.

AIR WAR, *JAPAN*
Lieutenant Colonel James Doolittle leads 16 B-25 bombers, launched from the aircraft carrier *Hornet,* on a daring mission to strike targets in Japan, including the capital Tokyo. The damage inflicted by the daylight raid is secondary to the impact on Japan's leaders, who are alarmed that US aircraft can strike at the heart of their homeland. This reinforces a decision to seek a decisive engagement to destroy US naval power in the Pacific.

APRIL 23

SEA WAR, *ATLANTIC*
The first "milch cow" submarine (*U-459*) delivers fuel and supplies to Germany's U-boats. This supply vessel doubles the operational range of the U-boats, which are no longer restricted by having to return to base for refueling.

APRIL 24

AIR WAR, *BRITAIN*
Germany bombs Exeter at the start of an air campaign against historic towns

and cities, following the British attack on Lübeck. Hitler has ordered raids against every English city featured in the famous Baedeker tourist books.

APRIL 29

FAR EAST, *BURMA*
The Japanese cut the Burma Road after seizing the town of Lashio, where the route ends. Chinese Nationalists are now almost wholly dependent on supply by air. The Japanese, being reinforced through the port at Rangoon, are advancing up the river valleys and plan to encircle the Allies in the Mandalay area. The Allies will then have to fight with their backs to the Irrawaddy River. The Burma Corps aims to fall back to India, whose defense is the main priority. Rapid Japanese advances, however, force the British to make a hurried (and potentially disastrous) retreat rather than an organized withdrawal.

APRIL 30

POLITICS, *SOVIET UNION*
Premier Joseph Stalin declares that the USSR has no territorial ambitions except to wrest its own lost lands from Nazi control.

▲ A U-boat in port. The "milch cow" supply submarines enabled U-boats to receive supplies at sea and thereby operate for long periods away from base.

▼ The German bombing of Bath damaged many fine buildings. This was one of the targets in the "Baedeker Raids" on historic English towns and cities.

MAY I

FAR EAST, *BURMA*

The city of Mandalay falls to the Japanese. The Allies are now retreating, with the Chinese Sixth Army heading for the Chinese province of Yunnan. Units of the Fifth and Sixty-sixth Armies withdraw to Yunnan or northern Burma. General Joseph Stilwell leads a 100-strong group on a 400-mile (600-km) journey to Imphal, India. Heavy rain hampers the Allied retreat.

▲ *General Joseph Stilwell (right), the US commander of Chinese forces, leads his staff on a epic journey from Burma to India to escape the advancing Japanese troops.*

HOME FRONT, *SOVIET UNION*

A six-month evacuation commences, which is intended to move the besieged citizens of Leningrad to safety across Lake Ladoga. Around 448,700 people are taken out of the city.

MAY 2

SEA WAR, *PACIFIC*

Japan deploys a large carrier force to surprise the US Pacific Fleet in the Coral Sea as part of its plan to establish greater control of the Solomon Islands. A key aim is to seize Port Moresby on the southwest Pacific

▼ *The Japanese Navy's forces gather for the battle against the US Pacific Fleet in the Coral Sea.*

▲ *Major General Jonathan Wainright broadcasts the surrender of US and Filipino forces on Corregidor, the Philippines.*

island of Papua New Guinea, which would facilitate bomber attacks on Australia and help sever its communications with the United States. The Japanese have a Carrier Striking Force containing the carriers *Shokaku* and *Zuikaku* under Vice Admiral Takeo Takagi. They also have a Covering Group that includes the carrier *Shoho,* plus four heavy cruisers under Rear Admiral Aritomo Goto. There is also the Port Moresby Invasion Group and a support force. US codebreaking enables Admiral Chester Nimitz, the US Pacific Fleet commander, to prepare his forces. He deliberately withdraws from Tulagi in the Solomons before a Japanese attack in order to reinforce their belief that only one US carrier is operating in the area.

MAY 3

SEA WAR, *PACIFIC*
US Rear Admiral Frank Fletcher's Task Force 17, including the

▶ *British Royal Marines prepare to land on Madagascar in the Indian Ocean.*

carrier *Yorktown*, damages a Japanese destroyer, three minesweepers, and five aircraft off Tulagi during the Coral Sea engagement.

MAY 5–7

AFRICA, *MADAGASCAR*
Britain launches Operation Ironclad, the invasion of Vichy French Madagascar, with a battleship and two aircraft carriers carrying a landing force. The occupation is intended to deny Axis forces access to the island. An armed Vichy merchant cruiser and submarine are lost. A British

vessel is mined. The Diego Suarez naval base surrenders on the 7th.

MAY 5–10

PACIFIC, *PHILIPPINES*
US and Filipino forces on Corregidor finally surrender after a Japanese landing on the island. Some 12,495 US and Filipino troops (including Major Generals Jonathan Wainright and Edward King) are captured. The Philippines campaign has claimed 140,000 US and Filipino lives, plus 4000 Japanese dead.

◀ Canadian troops in Ontario. Thousands of men became liable for military service after full conscription was introduced.

US destroyer *Sims*, and the tanker *Neosho* (which is mistaken for a carrier) is scuttled. US forces successfully destroy the *Shoho* and 21 aircraft that attempt to engage the US carriers.

MAY 8

SEA WAR, *PACIFIC*

US aircraft damage the *Shokaku*, while *Zuikaku*'s aircraft losses are very serious in the Battle of the Coral Sea. Japanese aircraft hit the *Lexington*, which is later scuttled, and damage the *Yorktown*. This is the first ever battle fought exclusively with carrier aircraft. The US Navy loses a carrier but repairs to the *Yorktown* are speedy. Japan loses a smaller carrier while the other two Coral Sea carriers will be unfit for action in the approaching battle at Midway. Large numbers of Japanese aircraft and experienced pilots have also been lost. The abandonment of the Port Moresby landing is the first major blow to Japanese expansionism.

MAY 8–15

EASTERN FRONT, *CRIMEA*

The German Eleventh Army launches its attack against the Soviet Crimean Front. The Soviets resume their attempt to surround German units against the Sea of Azov in a battle around Kharkov. Germany's Eleventh Army captures the Crimean Kerch Peninsula on the 15th and continues to fight along the Donets River.

MAY 11

POLITICS, *CANADA*

Full conscription is introduced following a referendum on the issue, the only significant opposition being in Quebec province.

FAR EAST, *BURMA*

British and Commonwealth troops fight a last, bitter battle at Kalewa before the remaining forces in Burma finally enter the border region with

MAY 6–7

SEA WAR, *PACIFIC*

Although the opposing Japanese and US carrier groups are only 70 miles (112 km) apart, their reconnaissance flights fail to locate each other. Australian and US cruisers in Task Force 44, under British Rear Admiral Sir John Crace, are then sent to find the Port Moresby Invasion Group. Although poor weather prevents an attack, the unfolding battle leads the group to turn back to its Rabaul base on the 7th. Japanese aircraft sink the

▲ A German armored unit during Rommel's offensive against the British Eighth Army in Libya during 1942.

▼ US sailors abandon the Lexington during the Battle of the Coral Sea.

India and eventually reach Imphal. Japan now has control over some 80 percent of Burma.

SEA WAR, *MEDITERRANEAN*
A special German bomber force locates and sinks the British destroyers *Kipling*, *Lively*, and *Jackal* to the west of Alexandria, Egypt.

MAY 14

ESPIONAGE, *UNITED STATES*
US codebreakers deciphering Japanese radio messages obtain their first intelligence about the impending Japanese operation to destroy the US Pacific Fleet in the central Pacific Ocean by drawing into battle around Midway.

MAY 15

FAR EAST, *INDIA*
British and Commonwealth forces retreating from Burma begin to arrive in India. Some 13,463 British, Indian, and Burmese troops have been killed in the Burma campaign thus far.

The 95,000-strong Chinese force has been decimated, while Japan has suffered an estimated 5000–8000 casualties to date.

MAY 18

POLITICS, *BRITAIN*
Admiral Harwood assumes command of the British Mediterranean Fleet.

MAY 22

POLITICS, *MEXICO*
The Mexican government declares war on Germany, Italy, and Japan.

MAY 25

POLITICS, *AUSTRALIA*
Three people are arrested for conspiring to establish a fascist government to negotiate peace terms with Japan.

MAY 26–31

AFRICA, *LIBYA*
General Erwin Rommel attacks the Gazala Line in Libya. Italian armor strikes at Bir Hacheim, 40 miles (60 km) from the coast,

▲ *A view of the Germany city of Cologne after the British "1000 Bomber" raid.*

but is repulsed by Free French troops. Axis tanks try to outflank the Allied lines beyond Bir Hacheim. Although the British Eighth Army has 850 tanks (plus 150 in reserve), the Axis forces deploy their 630 tanks more effectively, and their antitank guns present a serious threat. British armor and aircraft engage Axis tanks at the Knightsbridge crossroads, behind the Gazala Line. Axis armor suffers serious fuel problems until the Italians penetrate the Gazala Line to bring up fresh supplies on the 31st.

MAY 27

HOME FRONT, *CZECHOSLOVAKIA*
British-trained Czech agents attack Reinhard Heydrich, the deputy chief of the SS, who has been appointed deputy governor of occupied Czechoslovakia. Heydrich is traveling in an open-top car without an escort when the agents strike.

MAY 30

AIR WAR, *GERMANY*
Britain launches its first "1000 Bomber" raid. The target is Cologne. Over 59,000 people are made homeless. The British lose 40 aircraft.

MAY 31

AIR WAR, *GERMANY*
British Mosquito bombers, constructed from wood, make the first of many raids over Germany.

US dive-bombers in action against the Japanese during the decisive Battle of Midway.

the US base at Midway and then destroy the US Pacific Fleet commanded by Admiral Chester Nimitz. Japan deploys 165 vessels, including eight carriers, but they are too widely dispersed to provide mutual support. US code-breakers are able to warn the Pacific Fleet, which then converges to repel the Midway attack and is not diverted by a raid on the Aleutian Islands. The US Navy has a smaller force but has managed to gather three carriers.

The reconnaissance operation by Japan's 29 large cruiser submarines fails to establish the movements of the Pacific Fleet. Nagumo has no idea of US deployments when he first strikes Midway. Japan's I Carrier Striking Force

JUNE 1

AIR WAR, *GERMANY*
Britain launches a "1000 Bomber" raid against Essen and the Ruhr industrial area.

JUNE 4

SEA WAR, *PACIFIC*
The Battle of Midway begins. Japan's Admiral Chuichi Nagumo aims to seize

▼ A German woman collects water from a street tap. Water, gas, and electricity supplies were all disrupted by bombing.

▲ *The Japanese cruiser Mogami after sustaining an attack by US aircraft during the Battle of Midway.*

is decimated by US aircraft and three heavy carriers are lost. Japan's fourth carrier, *Hiryu*, then cripples the US carrier *Yorktown* before herself being fatally hit. Japan's attempt to destroy the enemy with its superior forces by luring it into a surface battle has failed. The loss of half of its carrier strength, plus 275 aircraft, puts Japan on the defensive in the Pacific.

JUNE 7

EASTERN FRONT, *UKRAINE*
The siege of Sebastopol intensifies with massive assaults by Germany's Eleventh Army. Sebastopol is under heavy shelling from German siege artillery, which includes the *Dora* gun, the world's largest mortar. The Soviet defenders continue to hold out, despite the intense bombardment.

JUNE 10

HOME FRONT, *CZECHOSLOVAKIA*
Reinhard Heydrich, the deputy governor of occupied Czechoslovakia and architect of the Nazi genocide program, dies after an attack by Czech agents on May 27. In retaliation, over 1000 Czechs accused of anti-Nazi activities are murdered, 3000 Czech Jews are deported for extermination,

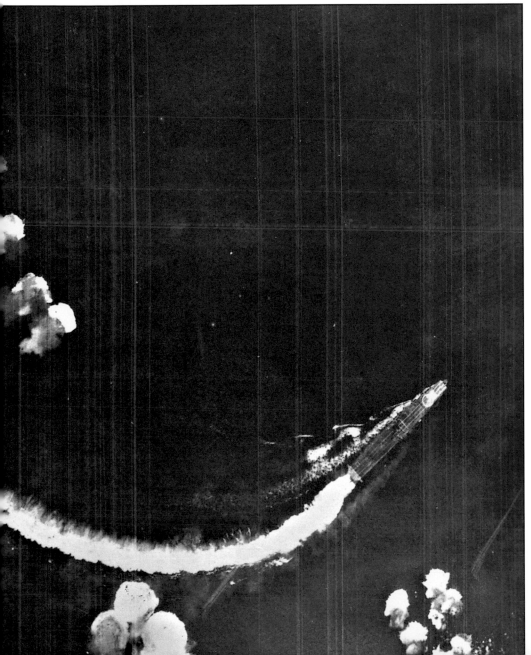

◀ *An aerial photograph of the Japanese carrier Hiryu during the Battle of Midway. The ship was set ablaze by a US air attack and subsequently scuttled.*

91

and 150 Berlin Jews are killed. The Czech village of Lidice is leveled. Its men are executed; its women and children are sent to concentration camps.

JUNE 10–13

AFRICA, *LIBYA*
Axis forces have created a fortified area ("the Cauldron") inside the Allied lines. Following the Free French withdrawal from Bir Hacheim on the 10th–11th, Axis armor advances east from the Cauldron to threaten the entire Eighth Army. British commander General Neil Ritchie orders a withdrawal on the 13th.

JUNE 18

POLITICS, *ALLIES*
At the Second Washington Conference in the United States, British Prime Minister Winston Churchill and US President Franklin D. Roosevelt try to agree a strategy in Europe for 1942–43. Conditions appear unsuitable for a "Second Front" in France, so Churchill proposes a North African invasion. In July, Roosevelt accepts that Europe cannot yet be attacked and agrees to Churchill's North African option, later code-named Operation Torch. Cooperation in nuclear research is also agreed on.

▲ *British troops surrender to the Afrika Korps after the fall of Tobruk.*

AIR WAR, *GERMANY*
Britain launches a "1000 Bomber" raid on Bremen.

JUNE 21

AFRICA, *LIBYA*
Following the Allied withdrawal into Egypt, the Tobruk garrison suddenly falls following German land and air attacks. Some 30,000 men, rations, and fuel are seized. Newly-promoted Field Marshal Erwin Rommel continues chasing the retreating Allies, taking

▼ *Soviet reinforcements being sent to Sebastopol. Despite fierce resistance, the port was captured by the Germans.*

Mersa Matruh on the 28th. General Sir Claude Auchinleck, British Middle East commander, takes personal charge of the Eighth Army and establishes a fortified line. This runs inland for 40 miles (64 km) from El Alamein on the coast to the impassable Quattara Depression. Rommel fails to penetrate the position, and the front stabilizes as his lines of supply in the Mediterranean are being strained by British air and sea attacks, assisted by intelligence from codebreaking.

JUNE 25

POLITICS, *UNITED STATES*
Major General Dwight D. Eisenhower assumes command of US forces in Europe.

JUNE 28

EASTERN FRONT, *UKRAINE*
Germany launches its summer offensive, with its Army Group South attacking east from Kursk toward Voronezh, which falls nine days later.

JULY 4–10

EASTERN FRONT, *CRIMEA*
The siege of Sebastopol ends with the Germans capturing 90,000 troops.

SEA WAR, *ARCTIC*
British Admiral of the Fleet Sir Dudley Pound gives a disastrous order for the PQ-17 convoy to disperse after air and U-boat attacks. The escorts therefore withdraw, leaving the convoy's isolated merchant ships vulnerable. PQ-17 loses 23 vessels out of 33 and enormous amounts of supplies during renewed German attacks.

JULY 13

EASTERN FRONT, *CAUCASUS*
Adolf Hitler orders simultaneous attacks on Stalingrad and the Caucasus, despite the strain this causes to his armies. Army Group B's advance toward Stalingrad is slowed after Hitler redeploys the Fourth Panzer Army to Army Group A's Caucasus drive. He believes Army Group A will not be able to cross the Don River without reinforcements. Field Marshal Fedor von Bock, leading Army Group B, is later dismissed for opposing this. The divergence of the two groups creates a gap through which Soviet forces are able to escape.

▲ *A British vessel from the PQ-17 Arctic convoy sinks after being torpedoed by a U-boat. The decision to scatter the convoy led to it suffering severe losses.*

JULY 21

POLITICS, *UNITED STATES*
Admiral William Leahy becomes the president's personal chief-of-staff. In this role he is closely involved in key military decisions.

JULY 23

EASTERN FRONT, *UKRAINE*
The city of Rostov is taken by

AUGUST 1

Germany's Army Group A, which then crosses the Don River and makes a broad advance into the Caucasus.

AUGUST 1

EASTERN FRONT, *UKRAINE*
Adolf Hitler moves the Fourth Panzer Army back to Stalingrad to accelerate the German advance. The Eleventh Army receives similar orders. This seriously strains the Caucasus advance.

AUGUST 7–21

PACIFIC, *SOLOMONS*
The US 1st Marine Division lands on Guadalcanal Island to overwhelm the 2200 Japanese garrison and capture the partly-built airfield that would enable bombers to strike Allied sea-lanes. Tulagi is also taken. US naval forces are subjected to air attacks and eventually withdraw. The Marines suffer supply shortages but are later relieved by air and sea. Japan sinks four cruisers on the 9th and starts landing forces by night to harass the Marines. US forces destroy the first major Japanese attacks on the Tenaru River on the 9th. Fighting now centers on the airstrip known as Henderson Field.

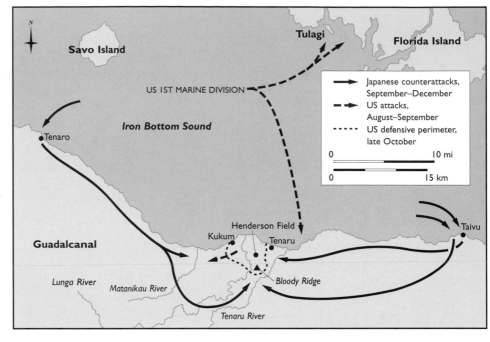

AUGUST 9

SEA WAR, *PACIFIC*
At the Battle of Savo Island, between Guadalcanal and Tulagi, the US Navy suffers one of its most serious defeats. A Japanese cruiser squadron, aiming to attack transports unloading off Guadalcanal, surprises five US and Australian cruisers. Superior night-fighting and gunnery skills enable the Japanese to sink four cruisers and damage the remaining one. The Japanese retire, fearing an air attack, while the US transports withdraw leaving the troops on Guadalcanal with serious supply problems.

AUGUST 10–15

SEA WAR, *MEDITERRANEAN*
Operation Pedestal, a 14-ship, Gibraltar-to-Malta

▼ *A German soldier leaps into action near Stalingrad.*

▲ *The fighting on Guadalcanal was among the most savage of the Pacific War, especially near Henderson Field.*

convoy, is devastated by enemy surface vessel, U-boat, and air attacks. Only four vessels reach Malta, but they enable the besieged island to survive.

AUGUST 12

POLITICS, *ALLIES*
Winston Churchill meets Joseph Stalin for the first time in talks that focus mainly on the decision to delay forming a "Second Front" in Europe.

AUGUST 13

POLITICS, *BRITAIN*
Lieutenant General Bernard Montgomery replaces General Neil Ritchie as Eighth Army commander. General Sir Harold Alexander replaces General Sir Claude Auchinleck as Middle East commander on the 18th.

AUGUST 17

AIR WAR, *FRANCE*
The first wholly US bomber raid over Europe strikes targets in France.

AUGUST 19

WESTERN FRONT, *FRANCE*
A force of 5000 Canadian, 1000 British, and 50 US troops attacks the port of Dieppe. It is a "reconnaissance in force" to gain experience and intelligence for landing a force on the continent. The assault is disastrous. Allied losses include almost 4000 men killed or captured.

▲ American ground crew prepare an aircraft for action during US offensives against the Japanese on Guadalcanal.

AUGUST 19–24

EASTERN FRONT, *SOVIET UNION*
Determined drives toward Stalingrad by Germany's Army Group B eventually reach the Volga River. Fierce resistance by the Soviet forces begins within a 30-mile (45-km) range of the city of Stalingrad.

AUGUST 22

POLITICS, *BRAZIL*
The government declares war on Germany and Italy.

AUGUST 22–25

SEA WAR, *PACIFIC*
In the Battle of the Eastern Solomons, Admiral Frank Fletcher's three-carrier task force engages a Japanese convoy bound for Guadalcanal, plus three other carriers operating in two separate groups. The Japanese light carrier *Ryujo*, a destroyer, plus 90 aircraft are lost. The US carrier *Enterprise* is damaged and 17 US aircraft downed.

AUGUST 23

AIR WAR, *SOVIET UNION*
A raid by 600 German bombers on Stalingrad claims thousands of lives.

AUGUST 30

AFRICA, *EGYPT*
Germany's tanks try to outflank the Allied line at El Alamein, but meet dense minefields and fierce resistance. The offense disintegrates under air attack and supply problems.

SEPTEMBER 2

FINAL SOLUTION, *POLAND*
The Nazis are "clearing" the Jewish Warsaw Ghetto. Over 50,000 Jews have been killed by poison gas or sent to concentration camps. The SS (*Schutzstaffel* – protection squad), a fanatical Nazi military and security organization, is chiefly responsible for Nazi persecution of the Jews and others deemed to be ideological or racial enemies of the Third Reich.

SEPTEMBER 9

POLITICS, *GERMANY*
Adolf Hitler dismisses Field Marshal Wilhelm List, commander of Army Group A laying siege to Stalingrad, for criticizing his Eastern Front strategy. General Paul von Kleist replaces him.

SEPTEMBER 12

SEA WAR, *ATLANTIC*
The liner *Laconia*, carrying 1800 Italian prisoners and Allied service

DECISIVE WEAPONS

CONVOYS

Convoys provided protective escorts for merchant vessels against enemy surface, submerged, or air attack. Allied convoys, often containing over 50 vessels, sailed in columns and weaved their way across the sea-lanes. In the Atlantic and Arctic, the atrocious weather reduced visibility, froze the crews, and created great waves that left vessels vulnerable to collision.

The main threat to Allied convoys were the U-boats, which inflicted critical losses on shipping. Antisubmarine measures gradually improved, however, with enhanced air and sea coordination, new tactics, and scientific innovations. Shipbuilding was also increased to replace lost vessels. The interception of German radio transmissions, centimetric radar, escort carriers, U-boat-detection technology (asdic and sonar), improved depth-charges, and launchers all helped protect convoys.

Germany's campaign to destroy Allied control of the Atlantic sea-lanes was especially critical as Britain came to rely upon North American aid. In the North Atlantic alone, some 2232 vessels were sunk, but the destruction of 785 U-boats secured Allied command of the sea-lanes.

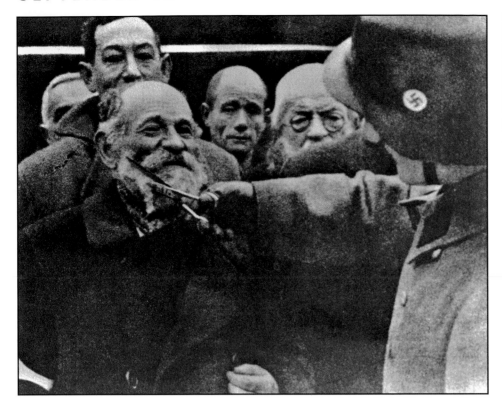

families, is sunk by *U-156*. A US bomber attacks *U-156* while it tries to aid the survivors. As a result, German navy chief Admiral Karl Doenitz instructs *U-156* to cancel the rescue. In future, no lifesaving attempts will be made by U-boats after an attack.

SEPTEMBER 13

PACIFIC, *SOLOMONS*
At the Battle of Bloody Ridge, 6000 Japanese try to seize Henderson Field, Guadalcanal, but are repulsed.

SEPTEMBER 15

SEA WAR, *PACIFIC*
Two Japanese submarines intercept a carrier force escorting troop transports to Guadalcanal. The US carrier *Wasp* and a destroyer are lost, but the troop transports arrive safely.

SEPTEMBER 24

POLITICS, *GERMANY*
General Franz Halder, chief of the General Staff, is replaced by General Kurt Zeitzler. Halder has made the mistake of criticizing Adolf Hitler's Eastern Front strategy, which demands that German troops should not retreat.

OCTOBER 18

POLITICS, *UNITED STATES*
Vice Admiral William Halsey replaces Vice Admiral Robert Ghormley as South Pacific Area commander.

▲ *A German soldier removes the beard of a Jewish man inside the Warsaw Ghetto. The abuse and terrorizing of Jews across Europe was Nazi policy.*

OCTOBER 22

AIR WAR, *ITALY*
Britain launches a series of raids on the industrial areas around Turin, Milan, and Genoa.

OCTOBER 23

AFRICA, *EGYPT*
The Battle of El Alamein begins. General Bernard Montgomery's carefully-prepared attack by 195,000 Allied troops against 104,000 Axis men begins with an enormous artillery bombardment and numerous deception measures. Massive mine-clearance operations enable Allied armor formations to push forward and leave the infantry to widen the gaps. Field Marshal Erwin Rommel is in Germany, but immediately returns after the temporary commander, General Georg Stumme, dies suddenly. First reports confirm that the Allies have made an excellent start, although Axis resistance is fierce.

OCTOBER 26

SEA WAR, *PACIFIC*
At the Battle of Santa Cruz, Japanese carriers approach Guadalcanal and fatally damage the US carrier *Hornet*

FIELD MARSHAL SIR BERNARD MONTGOMERY

Bernard Montgomery (1887–1976) began World War II leading a British division to France in 1939. After Dunkirk, he became a corps commander before Prime Minister Winston Churchill appointed him to lead the Eighth Army in the Western Desert.

Montgomery, exploiting the arrival of more men and supplies, halted Germany's drive into Egypt in 1942. Using careful planning and his ability to inspire confidence in his men, Montgomery inflicted the first British defeat on the German Army at El Alamein. This raised public morale and bolstered his reputation. After the landing of Allied armies in North Africa he helped secure the defeat of Axis forces in the desert.

After commanding the British Eighth Army in the 1943 invasions of Sicily and Italy, he was recalled to Britain in January 1944. Montgomery now had the task of helping prepare the enormous operation to invade northwest Europe. During the June 1944 D-Day landings he was commander of ground forces under US General Dwight D. Eisenhower's supreme command. From August, he became 21st Army Group commander. His relationship with US commanders was not always harmonious. He particularly disagreed with Eisenhower over the strategy for defeating Germany, favoring an all-out thrust rather than the more cautious "broad front" plan that was adopted. At the Battle of the Bulge in December 1944 Montgomery temporarily commanded two US armies, but then returned to 21st Army Group for the Rhine crossings to seal the defeat of Germany in 1945.

(leaving the US Pacific Fleet with one carrier). The Japanese cruiser *Yura* is sunk and the carrier *Shokaku* rendered ineffective by aircraft strikes.

NOVEMBER 2–24

AFRICA, *EGYPT/LIBYA*
Field Marshal Erwin Rommel, severely lacking supplies, decides to withdraw from El Alamein. He delays this for 48 hours, after Adolf Hitler's order to stand firm, but then continues following further Allied attacks. The Allies push him back to Tobruk, Benghazi, and then El Agheila by the 24th. Germany and Italy have lost 59,000 men killed, wounded, or captured. The Allies have suffered 13,000 killed, wounded, or missing. General Bernard Montgomery's victory saves the Suez Canal and raises Allied morale. Alamein is the first major defeat of German forces during the war.

NOVEMBER 5

AFRICA, *MADAGASCAR*
Vichy French forces in control of the island surrender.

NOVEMBER 8–11

AFRICA, *MOROCCO/ALGERIA*
Three Allied Task Forces, including five carriers, land 34,000 US troops near Casablanca, 39,000 US and British

▶ *Gurkhas of the British Eighth Army go on the attack during the Battle of El Alamein.*

▲ *A Japanese bomber in action against US warships during the Battle of Santa Cruz.*

troops near Oran (accompanied by a parachute assault), and 33,000 troops near Algiers. US General Dwight D. Eisenhower, the supreme commander, aims to seize Vichy French North Africa as a springboard for future operations to clear the whole of North Africa of Axis forces. Admiral Jean François Darlan, Vichy commissioner in Africa, causes

diplomatic turbulence by arranging a cease-fire and agreeing to support the Allies. The surprise invasion is a product of successful interservice planning, and Rommel is now fighting on two fronts.

NOVEMBER 11

WESTERN FRONT, *VICHY FRANCE*
German and Italian forces occupy Vichy France to prevent an Allied invasion from the former Vichy French territories in North Africa.

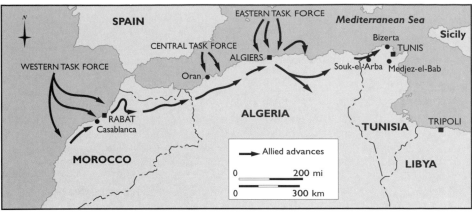

PACIFIC, *SOLOMONS*

A US cruiser-destroyer squadron inflicts serious losses on a Japanese naval force of 18 warships attempting to bombard Guadalcanal's Henderson Field, and also lands 11,000 troops.

NOVEMBER 17-28

AFRICA, *TUNISIA*

British paratroopers land at Souk-el-Arba and join a limited Allied advance toward Bizerta. Thousands of German reinforcements are arriving daily, and the Allies are not yet ready for a large offensive. By the 28th, they are within 20 miles (32 km) of Tunis but are halted by Axis counterattacks. Allied reinforcements from Algiers are slowed by rain and mud. A stalemate develops across much of Tunisia.

NOVEMBER 19

EASTERN FRONT, *UKRAINE*

General Georgi Zhukov launches a Soviet counteroffensive at Stalingrad with 10 armies, 900 tanks, and 1100 aircraft, to be carried out along a front of 260 miles (416 km). Soviet forces

▲ The Allied landings in North Africa precipitated the surrender of the Vichy French forces stationed there.

▶ German troops trapped outside Stalingrad search the skies for the arrival of supplies being brought by aircraft.

north and south of Stalingrad are to trap the Germans in a pincer movement. The attack is made during the frost, which assists tank mobility. It also coincides with the Allied North African landings, which divert Germany's attention. Allied supplies have equipped the Soviet forces for the advance. The German front buckles.

NOVEMBER 25

EASTERN FRONT, *UKRAINE*

The airlift to supply the German Sixth Army trapped around Stalingrad commences with 320 aircraft. The operation, which eventually requires 500 aircraft, lasts until February 1943.

NOVEMBER 27

SEA WAR, *MEDITERRANEAN*

Vichy French naval forces in Toulon are scuttled with the loss of 72

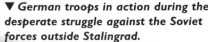

▼ German troops in action during the desperate struggle against the Soviet forces outside Stalingrad.

for postwar Britain that aim to provide a state pension and health care for everyone. This reflects aspirations for social justice to tackle society's problems.

DECEMBER 2

TECHNOLOGY, *UNITED STATES*

The first successful controlled nuclear "chain reaction" is made. It is a key step in making an atomic bomb. In this reaction, neutrons from the splitting of uranium atoms split other uranium atoms, releasing enormous energy rapidly in the form of a massive explosion.

DECEMBER 6–9

AFRICA, *TUNISIA*

Two German tank columns try to retake Medjez-el-Bab, 35 miles (40 km) southwest of Tunis. However, Allied armor and aircraft block one column as it advances, while artillery fire stops the second.

▼ *A German Junkers Ju 52 transport aircraft is refueled during the airlift that attempted to sustain the trapped Army inside the city of Stalingrad.*

DECEMBER 9

POLITICS, *UNITED STATES*

General Alexander Patch succeeds Lieutenant General Alexander Vandegrift as commander of operations on Guadalcanal. The 1st Marine Division is replaced by the US XIV Corps.

DECEMBER 10

PACIFIC, *SOLOMONS*

The Japanese are establishing a well-defended front some six miles (9 km) west of Henderson Field, Guadalcanal. Japan has a 20,000-strong force, however, while there are 58,000 US troops who are better equipped and supplied on the island. Japanese prospects are poor.

DECEMBER 11

SEA WAR, *FRANCE*

A British commando force of 10 men canoes up the Gironde River and disables six vessels in Bordeaux harbor with mines in a daring raid.

DECEMBER 19

EASTERN FRONT, *UKRAINE*

Field Marshal Erich von Manstein's attempt to relieve the German Sixth

vessels, including three battleships, before the Germans can seize them.

NOVEMBER 30

SEA WAR, *PACIFIC*

At the Battle of Tassafaronga, five US heavy cruisers and seven destroyers attack a Japanese convoy of eight destroyers bound for Guadalcanal. Japan loses one destroyer; the US four cruisers.

DECEMBER 1

POLITICS, *BRITAIN*

A report by Liberal economist Sir William Beveridge outlines proposals

DECEMBER 19

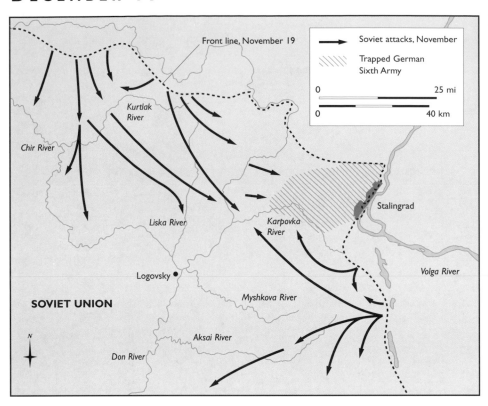

▲ Dead Japanese troops lying in a river bed on Guadalcanal. Thousands of Japanese soldiers died on the island.

▲ The Red Army completely surrounded the German Sixth Army outside Stalingrad. A German counteroffensive failed to break the Soviet grip.

▼ Soviet troops battle their way forward in the ruins of Stalingrad as the Red Army tightens its grip on the city. The damaged buildings indicate the savage fighting.

Army with an attack by Army Group Don (13 divisions formed from Army Group A in the north) advances to within 35 miles (56 km) of Stalingrad in the face of heavy resistance. Despite Manstein's pleas for General Friedrich von Paulus' Sixth Army to launch a break-out, Adolf Hitler orders him not to retreat, but fuel shortages limit

any possible action anyway. The year ends with Soviet offensives pushing the German relief force westward. In Stalingrad, German troops are suffering severe hardships, chiefly due to the weather and supply shortages.

DECEMBER 24

POLITICS, *VICHY FRANCE*
Admiral Jean François Darlan, high commissioner in North Africa, is shot dead by a young Frenchman who accuses him of betraying the Vichy regime.

DECEMBER 30–31

SEA WAR, *ARCTIC*
At the Battle of the Barents Sea, the German pocket battleship *Lützow*, heavy cruiser *Admiral Hipper*, and six destroyers attempt to destroy the Allied Arctic convoy JW-51B. Although outnumbered, the British use superior tactics and exploit the German caution arising from orders not to sustain serious damage. Germany has one destroyer sunk, while the British also lose a destroyer and have one badly damaged. The battle outrages Adolf Hitler, who believes that the German

▲ *Henri-Philippe Pétain (left) with Admiral François Darlan, who ordered Vichy French forces in North Africa to surrender after the Allied invasion.*

fleet is tying down a huge amount of manpower and resources for very little result. Indeed, the Battle of the Barents Sea will lead to the end of significant sorties by major German surface vessels for the rest of the war.

1943

A llied successes in Papua New Guinea and the Solomon Islands, together with hard-won British and Chinese advances in Burma, forced the Japanese onto the defensive in the Pacific and Far East. Allied forces also triumphed in North Africa and went on to invade Italy, triggering the fall of Mussolini, while in the Soviet Union the clash of armor at Kursk resulted in a key German defeat.

JANUARY 1–3

EASTERN FRONT, *CAUCASUS*
Soviet troops launch offensives to encircle the German forces in the north of the region. Since August 1942 the Germans have been attempting to conquer the resource-rich area and reach the oil supplies of the Near and Middle East. The Soviet South Front moves toward Rostov and the Terek River, from where the Germans withdraw on the 3rd.

JANUARY 2

PACIFIC, *PAPUA NEW GUINEA*
US forces meet stubborn Japanese resistance after assaulting Buna on the east coast.

JANUARY 3

SEA WAR, *MEDITERRANEAN*
British Chariot "human torpedoes" damage the Italian cruiser *Ulpio* and a tanker in Palermo harbor, Sicily.

JANUARY 3–9

SEA WAR, *ATLANTIC*
U-boats destroy seven of nine tankers,

▼ US Marine Corps pilots scramble to attack Japanese forces on Guadalcanal.

JANUARY 9
POLITICS, *CHINA*
The Japanese puppet government declares war on both Britain and the United States.

JANUARY 10
EASTERN FRONT, *CAUCASUS*
Soviet attacks from the north, south, and east of Stalingrad split Germany's Sixth Army into pockets and isolate them from any sort of relief. Axis forces across southern Russia are under intense pressure.

JANUARY 10–31
PACIFIC, *GUADALCANAL*
A force of 50,000 US troops launches a westward offensive to destroy strong Japanese jungle positions. A disease-ridden and starving force of 15,000 Japanese troops mounts fierce resistance and fights a rearguard action at Tassafaronga Point. The Japanese have decided to evacuate Guadalcanal.

JANUARY 13
PACIFIC, *PAPUA NEW GUINEA*
The Japanese in New Guinea finally lose control of the Kokoda Trail – a major route across the Owen Stanley Range to Port Moresby, which they intended to use as an air base. Fighting between General Douglas MacArthur's Australian and US troops and the Japanese has been going on since March 1942.

carrying 100,000 tons (90,720 metric tonnes) of oil in the TM-1 convoy, which is sailing from the Caribbean to the Mediterranean.

JANUARY 5
AFRICA, *TUNISIA*
The US Fifth Army is formed under Lieutenant General Mark Clark. Allied forces form a line from Cape Serrat on the Mediterranean to Gafsa in the south. A stalemate arises in Tunisia until Field Marshal Erwin Rommel's offensive in February.

JANUARY 6
POLITICS, *GERMANY*
Admiral Erich Raeder resigns as commander-in-chief of naval forces following the blunders made at the Battle of the Barents Sea in December. Admiral Karl Doenitz replaces him.

JANUARY 6–9
SEA WAR, *PACIFIC*
At the Battle of Huon Gulf, the Allies gather aircraft from across the south-west Pacific to launch repeated attacks on Japanese convoys carrying troops to Papua New Guinea. Three transports and some 80 Japanese aircraft are lost. Allied casualties during the action are comparatively light.

▲ *A German U-boat undergoes routine maintenance while on the lookout for Allied shipping in the Mediterranean.*

▼ *Admiral Karl Doenitz (third from left), replaced Erich Raeder as commander-in-chief of German naval forces.*

JANUARY 14-23

POLITICS, *ALLIES*

British Prime Minister Winston Churchill and US President Franklin D. Roosevelt meet at Casablanca, Morocco. The conference highlights differences between them regarding the defeat of Hitler.

The British want to keep fighting in the Mediterranean before the main attack on Europe via the English Channel. They propose invasions of Sicily and Italy as a means of drawing German reserves away from France and the Low Countries, which will precipitate the fall of Mussolini; and establishing air bases in Italy, from where German armaments factories and Romanian oil-producing facilities can be bombed.

The Americans believe this will only dissipate resources for the cross-Channel invasion, and tie down forces in a sideshow. They believe the quickest way to defeat Hitler is an invasion of northern France. However, as a cross-Channel invasion is not possible in 1943, they grudgingly accept the invasion of Sicily (though no invasion of Italy is planned).

A further source of disagreement is Roosevelt's "unconditional surrender" call. Churchill wants to split the Axis by treating Italy differently, but is persuaded to go along with the US view after considering that a more lenient treatment of Italy will only antagonize Greece and Yugoslavia.

JANUARY 15-22

AFRICA, *LIBYA*

The British Eighth Army attacks Field Marshal Erwin Rommel's forces at Buerat and pursues them to the Homs and Tarhuna area, approximately 100 miles (150 km) from Tripoli, the capital. British forces reach Homs on the 19th, and Rommel resumes his

▲ *Jewish fighters reinforce a strongpoint in the Warsaw Ghetto at the beginning of their uprising against the Germans.*

retreat toward Tunisia. Although Rommel has been ordered to defend Tripoli, he decides to save his troops and abandons the city on the 22nd to make a stand around Mareth.

▼ *Prime Minister Churchill and President Roosevelt at the Casablanca Conference, where differences of strategy arose between Great Britain and the United States.*

JANUARY 16–17

EASTERN FRONT, *CAUCASUS*
The Soviet Fifty-sixth Army begins an attack to take the town of Krasnador. Southern Front forces are halted by German resistance between the northern Donets and Manych Rivers.

JANUARY 18

EASTERN FRONT, *POLAND*
Jewish fighters in the Warsaw Ghetto begin attacking German troops. Resistance was triggered by the resumption of deportations to extermination camps, which has been suspended since October 1942.

JANUARY 21

PACIFIC, *PAPUA NEW GUINEA*
After capturing Sanananda in New Guinea, the Allies prepare to advance northwestward to clear the Japanese from Salamua and Lae. Allied control of the sea and air around Papua New Guinea will force the Japanese finally to abandon the island.

JANUARY 29

PACIFIC, *PAPUA NEW GUINEA*
Allied troops force the Japanese to withdraw from Wau at the start of the Bulldog Track, the second route used by the Japanese for their offensive against Port Moresby.

JANUARY 30

AIR WAR, *GERMANY*
In the escalating Allied air offensive, British bombers make the first daylight bombing raid over Berlin.

KEY PERSONALITIES

GENERAL DOUGLAS MACARTHUR

Douglas MacArthur (1880–1964) was appointed commander of US troops in the Far East in July 1941. After the Japanese declared war in December, he directed the defense of the Philippines from the islands. He finally left for Australia in March 1942 to assume command of the whole of the Southwest Pacific theater.

MacArthur then led a campaign to free Papua New Guinea before commanding the Pacific "island-hopping" operations that finally reached the Philippines in October 1944. In April 1945, MacArthur became commander of the US Army in the Pacific and then Supreme Allied Commander for the occupation of Japan. In this role he accepted the Japanese surrender.

This flamboyant general always appeared to achieve his objectives yet maintain low casualty rates. His self-publicity has, however, led some historians to scrutinize the claims he made about his campaigns.

FEBRUARY 1–9

PACIFIC, *GUADALCANAL*
Japanese Navy warships evacuate 13,000 troops in night operations from the island. Their abandonment of Guadalcanal marks the first major land defeat of Japan. The Japanese have lost 10,000 men killed; the Americans some 1600.

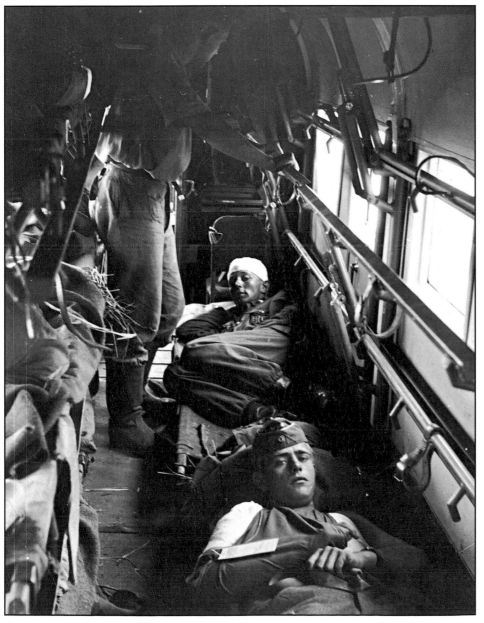

◀ *Some of the lucky ones: German casualties evacuated out of Stalingrad before the defeat of the Sixth Army.*

FEBRUARY 2

▶ *British Avro Lancaster heavy bombers were used against German U-boats in the Bay of Biscay.*

FEBRUARY 2

EASTERN FRONT, *CAUCASUS*
The siege of Stalingrad ends: Field Marshal Friedrich von Paulus and 93,000 German troops surrender. The Sixth Army has finally collapsed under the strain of supply shortages and constant attacks masterminded by Marshal Georgi Zhukov.

FEBRUARY 4

AIR WAR, *FRANCE*
British and US bombers launch Operation Gondola with a series of raids aimed at destroying U-boats in the Bay of Biscay. Bombers use immensely powerful searchlights to illuminate submarines during attacks.

▼ *Some of Orde Wingate's Chindits who operated behind Japanese lines in Burma in February 1943.*

FEBRUARY 8

EASTERN FRONT, *UKRAINE*
In their continuing offensive Soviet forces take the city of Kursk, which will be the site of a major battle.

FEBRUARY 9

SEA WAR, *MEDITERRANEAN*
An Axis convoy carrying reinforcements to Tunisia leaves Italy. Malta-based Allied aircraft sink 10 vessels between February 9 and March 22. Minefields and British submarines also destroy several of the ships.

FEBRUARY 12–14

EASTERN FRONT, *CAUCASUS*
The Soviets capture Krasnodar on the 12th and Rostov on the Don River two days later.

FEBRUARY 14–22

AFRICA, *TUNISIA*
Field Marshal Erwin Rommel launches an attack northwest from his fortified zone at Mareth to break through Allied forces between the Axis front and Bône on the coast. In the Battle of Kasserine Pass his forces strike the US II Corps and cause panic among the ranks.

US forces are 100 miles (160 km) from Gabès, a key part of Germany's Mareth Line because of its crossroads, port, and airfield. German troops exploit poor US command, land and air coordination, unit dispositions, and the inexperience of some troops. Attacks reach Thala until they lose momentum and Rommel orders a withdrawal. He loses 2000 men; the Americans 10,000.

FEBRUARY 15

EASTERN FRONT, *UKRAINE*
Kharkov and other cities are liberated as Soviet forces reoccupy territory held by the Germans. Stalin has begun to think of total victory in 1943.

FEBRUARY 16–21

HOME FRONT, *GERMANY*

Student demonstrations against Hitler's regime take place in Munich. Protests in other university cities in Germany and Austria then occur. Hans and Sophie Scholl, leaders of the anti-Nazi White Rose student group at the University of Munich, are beheaded on the 21st.

FEBRUARY 18

FAR EAST, *BURMA*

Brigadier Orde Wingate launches the first British Chindit mission. This 3000-strong, long-range penetration force aims to operate behind Japanese lines and disrupt communications. The Chindits are to be supplied by air. The six-week mission has limited military success but Prime Minister Winston Churchill is impressed by Wingate's unorthodox methods. As a result, further Chindit operations in Burma will be sanctioned.

▲ *An Allied merchant ship caught in heavy seas as a convoy makes its way across the Atlantic Ocean.*

FEBRUARY 18-27

EASTERN FRONT, *UKRAINE*

Field Marshal Erich von Manstein, commander of Army Group Don, launches a counteroffensive against the Red Army to crush the enemy thrust to the Dniepr River. Using four panzer corps, he isolates three Soviet armies, inflicting severe losses on the Red Army.

FEBRUARY 20–25

SEA WAR, *ATLANTIC*

During U-boat attacks, Allied convoy ON-166 loses 15 of its 49 ships. Only one German submarine is sunk.

FEBRUARY 21

PACIFIC, *SOLOMONS*

US forces land on Russell Island. This is their first move in the campaign to capture the island chain. The operation, code-named Cartwheel, eventually aims to seal off the key Japanese air and sea base at Rabaul in New Britain. The US Pacific commanders Admiral Chester Nimitz and General Douglas MacArthur have devised an "island-hopping" strategy whereby certain

◄ *Letters from home bring a smile to the faces of these two German soldiers of Army Group Don on the Eastern Front.*

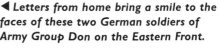

107

selected islands are retaken, while heavily-defended Japanese positions are bypassed. Allied aircraft and sea power will then isolate these strong-points, preventing them from being a threat. They will "wither on the vine."

FEBRUARY 23–24

SEA WAR, *ATLANTIC*
Seven tankers from the UC-1 Allied convoy are sunk by a U-boat group.

FEBRUARY 26–28

AFRICA, *TUNISIA*
Colonel General Jürgen von Arnim's Fifth Tank Army in northeast Tunisia finally launches a counterattack from

▼ A Japanese transport is bombed during the Battle of the Bismarck Sea.

the Mareth Line that should have been made during the previous series of attacks. It is unsuccessful.

FEBRUARY 28

POLITICS, *GERMANY*
General Heinz Guderian is appointed "Inspector-General of Armored Troops" and is given wide-ranging powers to strengthen Germany's tank arm.
WESTERN FRONT, *NORWAY*
Nine Norwegian paratroopers from Great Britain sabotage the Norsk Hydro power station where "heavy water" is made for atomic research.

MARCH 2–5

SEA WAR, *PACIFIC*
At the Battle of the Bismarck Sea eight Japanese transports and eight destroyers are attacked while sailing from Rabaul to Lae in New Guinea. US

◀ *German troops and armor await orders to advance against Kharkov in February 1943.*

nine, south of the Mareth Line. They attack across a broad front but fail to concentrate and are decisively thrown back. Field Marshal Rommel, whose morale and health are both deteriorating, leaves North Africa.

MARCH 6–20

SEA WAR, *ATLANTIC*
Two Atlantic convoys (HX-229 and SC-122) fight a running battle with 20 U-boats of a "Wolf Pack" in the Atlantic.

KEY PERSONALITIES

ADMIRAL CHESTER NIMITZ

Admiral Chester Nimitz (1885–1966) was appointed commander of the US Pacific Fleet just after the Pearl Harbor attack in December 1941. From April 1942, he was made commander of all naval, sea, and air forces in the Pacific Ocean Area.

Aided by US codebreaking efforts, he was able to anticipate and defeat Japanese plans at the Battles of the Coral Sea in May and Midway in June. These actions secured US naval superiority in the Pacific by inflicting decisive defeats on Japan's carrier capability. Nimitz then went on to lead a series of strikes against the Japanese Navy and supported the "island-hopping" operations to establish Allied control over the Pacific region. He was a strong advocate of this amphibious strategy, which pushed the Japanese back across the ocean to Japan. He was made a Fleet Admiral in 1944 and was present at the Japanese surrender in 1945. One of his strengths was being able to achieve his goals without antagonizing his colleagues.

▲ *Kharkov's battle-scarred Red Square following Manstein's brilliant capture of the city in March 1943.*

and Australian aircraft and torpedo-boats sink all the transports and four destroyers. The Allies lose six aircraft; the Japanese 25. This is the last Japanese attempt to reinforce their presence in New Guinea.

MARCH 5

AIR WAR, *GERMANY*
The British launch a four-month offensive against the Ruhr industrial area. A force of 367 bombers strikes the Krupp Works at Essen in the first attack; 14 aircraft are lost.

MARCH 6–9

AFRICA, *TUNISIA*
The Germans attempt to disrupt General Bernard Montgomery's preparations for a final offensive at Mede-

Although 21 ships are sunk, only one U-boat is lost. The Allies cannot afford such attrition.

MARCH 13

HOME FRONT, *GERMANY*
An unsuccessful assassination attempt is made on Adolf Hitler by army officers. They place a bomb in his aircraft but it fails to explode.

MARCH 14

EASTERN FRONT, *UKRAINE*
After his spearheads reached the Donets River, Manstein's forces have trapped and destroyed the Soviet Third Tank Army. In all, the Red Army has abandoned nearly 6,000 square miles (9,600 sq km) of newly-won ground in the face of Manstein's brilliant armored counteroffensive, which has stabilized the German front in southern Russia. Manstein has averted a total Axis collapse.

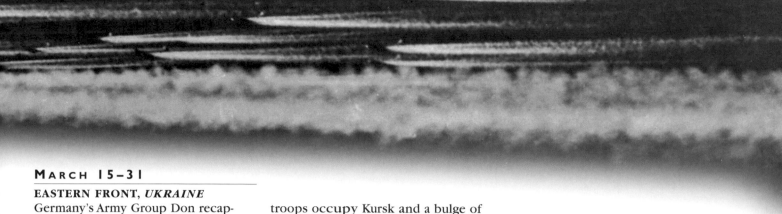

MARCH 15–31

EASTERN FRONT, *UKRAINE*

Germany's Army Group Don recaptures Kharkov, and Belgorod three days later. By the end of the month the Soviet Voronezh Front is back on the east bank of the northern Donets. The final phase of Manstein's offensive – a combined attack with Army Group Center's Second Panzer Army heading south from Orel toward Kursk – is halted by the spring thaw.

This victory encourages the German high command to launch Operation Citadel, an ambitious plan to destroy the Soviet Central and Voronezh Fronts in the Kursk salient to the north of Kharkov. Over 500,000 Red Army

▼ *Italian troops on the Mareth Line.*

troops occupy Kursk and a bulge of land stretching 100 miles (160 km) westward from the Soviet line.

MARCH 20–28

AFRICA, *TUNISIA*

Allied forces under General Bernard Montgomery launch a carefully-planned attack against the Mareth Line. The line's principal defenses along the banks of the Wadi Zigzaou are penetrated on the 21st–22nd but the 15th Panzer Division successfully counterattacks. Montgomery, however, develops an outflanking move into a major offensive, and by the 26th the Axis forces have retreated northward to the El Hamma Plain. The weakened German forces fall back to Wadi Akarit by the 28th, while many of their Italians allies surrender.

MARCH 26

SEA WAR, *PACIFIC*

At the Battle of the Kommandorsky Islands in the Bering Sea, two US cruisers and four destroyers engage four Japanese cruisers and five destroyers. The Japanese abandon the action just before they can exploit their numerical superiority. Both sides have a cruiser badly damaged.

MARCH 27

AFRICA, *TUNISIA*

General Sir Harold Alexander sends the US 34th Infantry Division to seize the Foundouk Pass but heavy artillery fire halts its advance.

MARCH 30

SEA WAR, *ARCTIC*

Britain suspends the Arctic convoys to the Soviet Union because it cannot provide enough escorts to guard against the increasing number of German warships in Norway.

APRIL 5–6

AFRICA, *TUNISIA*

The British Eighth Army attacks the Wadi Akarit Line, a defensive position situated across the route into Tunisia. The line cannot be outflanked. While

▲ *Trailing vapor, US B-17s Flying Fortresses bomb the German city of Dresden in daylight.*

the assault is successful, the British fail to exploit their breakthrough and Axis forces are able to regroup.

APRIL 7–10

AFRICA, *TUNISIA*

The British IX Corps, which includes the US 34th Infantry Division, attacks the Foundouk Pass but the Axis forces

▼ *Members of the Polish Commission look at evidence of the Katyn Forest massacre.*

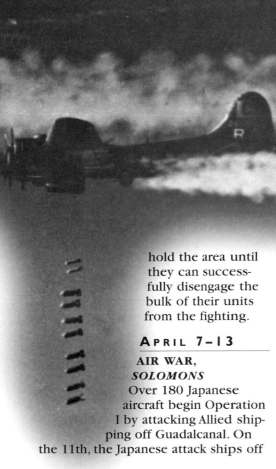

hold the area until they can successfully disengage the bulk of their units from the fighting.

APRIL 7–13

AIR WAR, SOLOMONS
Over 180 Japanese aircraft begin Operation I by attacking Allied shipping off Guadalcanal. On the 11th, the Japanese attack ships off New Guinea and raid Port Moresby airfield on the 12th, and British at Milne Bay the following day. They sink a destroyer, one corvette, one tanker, two cargo ships, and destroy some 20 aircraft. The massive aerial operation against shipping and airfields, however, does not achieve the scale of success that the Japanese anticipated.

APRIL 8

POLITICS, JAPAN
General Kawbe succeeds General Iida as commander of Japanese forces operating in Burma.

APRIL 10–12

AFRICA, TUNISIA
British troops enter Sfax, one of the ports vital for reducing the long supply lines from Tripoli, and finally halt at Enfidaville, southeast of Tunis. Axis forces are now established in their final defensive line running from Cape Serrat on the Mediterranean to Enfidaville. Defeat for the Axis forces is inevitable. Allied sea and air control denies them any reinforcements. They are determined to fight on, however, in order to delay the Allied plan to invade Italy until the fall, when deteriorating weather is likely to disrupt any Allied landings.

APRIL 12

HOME FRONT, POLAND
The German authorities announce that they have found a mass grave in Katyn Forest. They claim that it contains the bodies of some 10,000 Polish officers executed by the Soviet secret police in 1939. The Soviets claim that this is deliberate German propaganda aimed at discrediting them. Subsequent investigations reveal the Soviets were indeed responsible for the massacre of 4500 officers at Katyn Forest.

APRIL 17

AIR WAR, GERMANY
The US 8th Army Air Force attacks Bremen's aircraft factories from its bases in eastern England. It is one of its largest raids to date. Sixteen of the 115 B-17 Flying Fortress bombers from the raid are lost.

▶ A Jewish fighter surrenders in the Warsaw Ghetto as the SS fights its way through the city street by street.

▲ *Admiral Minichi Koga, commander of the Japanese Combined Fleet.*

APRIL 18

AIR WAR, *TUNISIA*
An operation by 100 German transport aircraft to fly supplies to the Axis forces in North Africa suffers a devastating attack by US fighters. Over half the transport aircraft and 10 fighters are shot down.

APRIL 19–22

AFRICA, *TUNISIA*
General Bernard Montgomery, eager for his Eighth Army to seal victory in Tunisia, launches an offensive toward Enfidaville. The attack gains little ground and casualties are heavy.

APRIL 19

EASTERN FRONT, *POLAND*
The destruction of the Warsaw Ghetto begins with German SS troops making a large-scale attack. The Jewish fighters construct a network of hiding places and fight with small-arms or improvised weapons. Up to 310,000 Jews have already been deported from the ghetto, to be executed or imprisoned in labor camps.

APRIL 21

POLITICS, *JAPAN*
Admiral Minichi Koga succeeds Admiral Isoroku Yamamoto as commander-in-chief of the Combined Fleet. US codebreakers had learned that Yamamoto was visiting bases in the southwest Pacific and aircraft were deployed to intercept the fleet. The admiral was killed after his aircraft was destroyed by US fighters on the 18th.

APRIL 22

AFRICA, *TUNISIA*
The British First Army and US II Corps prepare to breach the series

▼ *Guns and vehicles of the British Royal Artillery Regiment on the road to Tunis during the last phase of the war in Africa.*

of interlocking strongpoints across the high ground above the approaches to Tunis. The First Army attacks between Medjez-el-Bab and Bou Arada while the US II Corps farther north strikes toward Mateur and Bizerta. The main thrust is made by the First Army's V Corps along a direct line toward Tunis from Medjez-el-Bab. To achieve this, they have to capture two major Axis positions on the high ground at Peter's Corner and Longstop Hill along the Medjerda River.

APRIL 26–30

AFRICA, *TUNISIA*
The First Army's V Corps captures Longstop Hill and reaches Djebel Bou Aoukaz. From April 28–30 the Germans counterattack and take Djebel Bou Aoukaz. Meanwhile, the US II Corps fights a bitter battle to capture Hill 609. The First Army's advance is being blocked by protracted engagements against strong Axis positions. To achieve a breakthrough across the Medjerda Valley, the Eighth Army sends two divisions and a brigade to bolster the offensive.

APRIL 28

SEA WAR, *ATLANTIC*
The Allied convoy ONS-5 begins a seven-day running battle against 51 U-boats. The convoy achieves considerable success despite the limited air

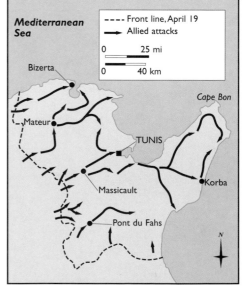

▲ *The final Allied victory in Tunisia brought an end to the North African campaign. Total Axis losses were 620,000 men, a third of them German. The Third Reich could not afford such wastage.*

support it receives. Seven U-boats are sunk and 17 damaged. The convoy loses 13 of its 42 ships.

APRIL 30

ESPIONAGE, *BRITAIN*
The British release a corpse, dressed as an officer and carrying false documents, into the Mediterranean Sea as part of a deception operation to divert German attention from Allied plans to invade Sicily. The corpse is recovered by the Germans, who find the false documents containing details of an Allied attack on Greece and Sardinia. As a result German reinforcements are sent to these areas.

MAY 3

POLITICS, *UNITED STATES*
General Frank Andrews, US commander in the European theater, is killed in an air crash. General Jacob Devers is named as his replacement.

MAY 5-7

AFRICA, *TUNISIA*
Reinforcements sent by the Eighth Army help the First Army recapture Djebel Bou Aoukaz and enable the British 7th Armored Division to advance into open "tank country." General Sir Harold Alexander can now exploit the numerical and material superiority of his armies against the

Axis forces defending Tunis. Massicault is reached on the 6th, and tanks enter Tunis on the 7th. The US III Corps reaches Bizerta the same day. The Axis forces in North Africa are facing imminent defeat, with no chance of escaping the Allies.

MAY 11-29

PACIFIC, *ALEUTIANS*
A US 12,000-man amphibious force attacks Attu Island, one of Japan's fortified positions in the northern Pacific. During the bitter offensive, only 29 of the 2500 Japanese survive. US forces sustain 561 fatalities and have 1136 men wounded.

▲ *Water gushes from the damaged Möhne dam following the successful raid by the British Royal Air Force.*

MAY 12-25

POLITICS, *ALLIES*
The Allied Trident Conference is held in Washington. Churchill and Roosevelt reinforce the "Germany First" strategy by agreeing to intensify bombing raids in Europe. A date is set for the cross-Channel invasion (May 1, 1944) and Britain urges that the Sicilian attack is extended to the Italian mainland. The British feel that the United States is committing increasing resources to the Pacific at the expense of European military operations.

MAY 13

AFRICA, *TUNISIA*
Axis forces officially surrender. Some 620,000 casualties and prisoners have been sustained by Germany and Italy. Allied campaign losses: French 20,000; British 19,000; and US 18,500.

MAY 16-17

AIR WAR, *GERMANY*
The dams on the Möhne and Eder Rivers are attacked by 19 British Lancaster aircraft, which are carrying

◄ *A happy Eisenhower (center) and General Montgomery after the Allied victory in Africa.*

◄ A German fireman struggles to douse the flames after a heavy British raid on Dortmund in late May.

MAY 23–29

AIR WAR, *GERMANY*

A massive British raid is made on Dortmund. Another offensive against Wuppertal on the 29th kills 2450 people. British bombers are intensifying their large-scale night attacks against industrial centers.

MAY 26

BALKANS, *YUGOSLAVIA*

An Axis force of 120,000 men attacks 16,000 communist partisans in Montenegro. A British military mission arrives on the 27th to meet partisan leader Joseph Tito, who confirms their intelligence reports that the rival Chetnik resistance group now supports the Axis forces. Since the fall of 1941, Tito has led a full-scale campaign in the province of Serbia but has since endured several major attacks from the Axis occupiers. Partisan forces have been preserved by withdrawing to the mountains and are now to be strengthened by large quantities of Allied aid.

JUNE 1–11

AIR WAR, *ITALY*

A round-the-clock naval and air bombardment of Pantellaria Island forces it to surrender on the 11th. Italian propaganda had falsely hailed it as an impregnable fortress and, consequently, the Allies had considered it an obstacle blocking their plans to invade Sicily and the mainland.

specially-designed "bouncing bombs." The dams generate electricity and supply water to the Ruhr region. The squadron led by Wing Commander Guy Gibson loses eight aircraft. The raid causes some disruption to industry, and boosts morale in Great Britain. German casualties are high, particularly among forced foreign workers.

MAY 16

HOME FRONT, *POLAND*

The Warsaw Ghetto uprising ends. Some 14,000 Jews have been killed, 22,000 sent to concentration camps, and 20,000 to labor camps.

MAY 22

SEA WAR, *ATLANTIC*

Admiral Karl Doenitz suspends patrols in the northern Atlantic. Some 56 submarines have been destroyed since April alone in a campaign of attrition the Germans cannot afford.

▶ *Communist partisans on the move in Montenegro as an Axis force of 120,000 men launches a campaign to wipe them out. The offensive failed.*

Escalating losses of both vessels and experienced crews force him to redeploy his remaining forces to less hazardous Caribbean waters and the Azores. Improved tactics, radar, code-breaking, air cover, and the increased building of escorts have combined to strengthen convoy defenses.

◄ *Operation Pointblank in action: the ruins of a German fighter factory after being bombed by the Allies.*

Claude Auchinleck succeeds him as commander-in-chief of India although a new East Asia Command will reduce his importance. Churchill has made these appointments as he has lost confidence in their capabilities and wishes to limit their military roles.

JUNE 20–24

AIR WAR, *GERMANY/ITALY*

The Allies launch their first "shuttle" raid. British bombers attack Friedrichshafen in Germany and then fly on to refuel in North Africa. On their return flight to Britain, they attack La Spezia naval base in Italy.

JUNE 21

PACIFIC, *SOLOMONS*

US forces begin an offensive against the New Georgia Island group. Munda airfield is the first major objective. The Solomon offensives are aided by vital reconnaissance information provided by Allied "coastwatchers" based on these little-known islands and equipped with high-powered radios. New Georgia airfields sustain air and sea bombardments while US warships mine the surrounding seas to destroy ships bringing reinforcements and supplies.

JULY 5

POLITICS, *POLAND*

General Wladyslaw Raczkiewicz, prime minister

JUNE 3

POLITICS, *FREE FRENCH*

Rival leaders General Charles de Gaulle and General Henri Giraud agree to share the presidency of the Committee of National Liberation.

JUNE 10

AIR WAR, *GERMANY*

Operation Pointblank is launched. The offensive by British and US bomber forces will last until the 1944 cross-Channel invasion. US strategy concentrates on daylight precision raids to destroy Germany's aircraft industry and its air force. British attacks focus on

▶ *The blazing hull of a Japanese ship hit by US aircraft off the Solomon Islands.*

night saturation bombing to undermine Germany's economy and civilian morale. Aircrews are assisted by the "Pathfinder" system, whereby targets are fixed by radar and marked by flares.

JUNE 18

POLITICS, *BRITAIN*

Field Marshal Sir Archibald Wavell becomes Viceroy of India. General Sir

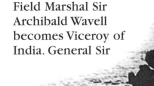
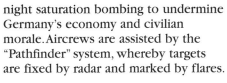

JULY 5–6

▶ *Both sides lost heavily at Kursk. This Soviet tank crew fell foul of a German antitank gun and panzergrenadiers.*

of the Polish government-in-exile, is killed in an air crash. His deputy, Stanislaw Mikolajczyk, replaces him.

JULY 5–6

PACIFIC, *SOLOMONS*
The US 43rd Infantry Division leads the main landing on New Georgia. That night US and Japanese destroyers clash at the Battle of Kula Gulf. One Japanese destroyer is sunk.

JULY 6

EASTERN FRONT, *UKRAINE*
Soviet intelligence has uncovered the plans for the offensive by 900,000 German troops against Kursk. The Germans believe that a victory on the Eastern Front will bolster domestic morale and preserve the Axis coalition, while also demonstrating to the Allies that the Nazis can still achieve victory.

From March to July, they gather 900,000 troops but the Red Army succeeds in establishing numerical superiority in men (1.3 million) and equipment. Consequently, German units are exposed to aerial and land bombardment while the Red Army prepares for the attack.

The German Army Group Center's Ninth Army, south of Orel, and Field Marshal Erich von Manstein's Fourth Panzer Army, north of Kharkov, open Operation Citadel with an offensive

against the salient. The Ninth Army under Field Marshal Gunther von Kluge only penetrates six miles (9 km) and loses 250,000 men. Over 6000 German and Soviet tanks and assault guns take part in the war's greatest armored battle. Special attention is given by the Soviets to antitank guns and obstacles. The Germans deploy 200 aircraft for the operation and the Soviets 2400.

JULY 6–9

EASTERN FRONT, *UKRAINE*
Increasing numbers of German troops reinforce the Kursk offensive but the

▼ *Polish President Wladyslaw Raczkiewicz, seen here reviewing sailors, was killed in a plane crash on July 5.*

Red Army stands firm. The Soviets counter the Germans with a deep defensive network while heavily-armed antitank units deliver concentrated fire against German armor. The Soviets quickly gain air superiority and fighters provide valuable tactical support. These measures combine to prevent the German attacks penetrating the Soviet defenses.

JULY 7–13

PACIFIC, *PAPUA NEW GUINEA*
The Japanese strongpoint at Mumbo, 10 miles (16 km) inland from Salamaua, is seized by the Australians. US and Australian forces are battling to dislodge the Japanese from the high ground they have retreated to.

▼ *The Royal Navy brings troops ashore as Allied units push farther inland on Sicily.*

Allied reinforcements are to be landed in order to clear the Japanese from northeast New Guinea.

JULY 9

MEDITERRANEAN, *SICILY*

Chaotic US and British airborne landings begin the attack on Sicily. Preparatory bomber attacks have already hit air bases on Sicily, Sardinia, and on the mainland. Mussolini expects the Allied attack to be against Sardinia. The main strategic objectives are to clear the Mediterranean sea-lanes, divert Axis forces from the Eastern Front, and possibly apply pressure on Italy to accelerate its capitulation.

JULY 10

MEDITERRANEAN, *SICILY*

An invasion fleet of 2500 vessels carries General Bernard Montgomery's Eighth Army and General George Patton's Seventh Army

▲ *German armored personnel carriers and assault guns (note armored skirts) rumble forward at the Battle of Kursk.*

to southern Sicily. The Italians are surprised as they did not expect an attack during stormy weather. The Allies will eventually land 160,000 men to fight General Guzzoni's Sixth Army (230,000 Italian and 40,000 German troops). Landings are assisted by a new amphibious truck – the DUKW.

JULY 11–12

MEDITERRANEAN, *SICILY*

The German *Hermann Goering* Panzer Division almost reaches US forces on the coast near Gela and Licata but the counterattack is obstructed by US paratroopers. General Sir Harold Alexander, overall commander of the operation, expects the Eighth Army to advance up the east coast toward the key bases at

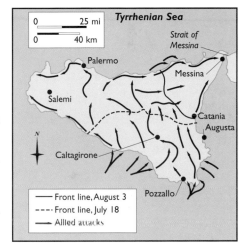

▲ *The Allied invasion of Sicily involved the largest seaborne assault mounted to date. During the initial assault seven divisions, one armored combat team, two commandos, and an assault brigade were put ashore against an enemy almost equal in numbers.*

Catania and Messina. The less experienced Seventh Army is to protect the British flank and rear.

JULY 12–13

EASTERN FRONT, *UKRAINE*

At Kursk, the Soviets launch a counteroffensive around Prokhorovka and an enormous tank battle develops. Field Marshal von Manstein's Fourth Panzer Army advances 25 miles (40 km) but loses 10,000 men and 350 tanks. Farther north, the Soviet Bryansk and West Fronts begin an offensive around Orel. Adolf Hitler calls off Operation

Citadel on the 13th. The last major German offensive on the Eastern Front has been a costly failure with the loss of over 550 tanks and 500,000 men killed, wounded, or missing. It is a major disaster for Germany, not least because the carefully-gathered strategic armored reserves have been wiped out in the fighting.

KEY PERSONALITIES

FIELD MARSHAL ERICH VON MANSTEIN

Erich von Manstein (1887–1973) was chief of staff to General Gerd von Rundstedt in 1939 before being demoted for challenging the high command's strategy for the invasion of France in 1940. He advocated a surprise thrust through the Ardennes, and when Hitler adopted this plan, his fortunes changed. Manstein led an infantry corps with distinction during the invasion of France and then took command of an armored Corps, which he led at the start of Operation Barbarossa.

By September 1941, he had risen to command the Eleventh Army on the Eastern Front. His conquest of the Crimea earned him a reputation as a top field commander and he became a field marshal in 1942. Manstein's use of armor to seize Kharkov in February 1943, when he yielded ground in the face of Soviet numerical superiority before counterattacking with his panzer corps when the enemy was suffering attrition and at the end of his supply lines, was the greatest German counteroffensive of the war.

His appreciation of the need for a flexible defensive strategy brought him into conflict with Hitler. The Führer's narrow strategic view of the Eastern Front was based on holding ground. The field marshal's plans were thus considered an abandonment of Germany's front. As a result of this conflict over strategy, Manstein was dismissed in 1944.

▲ Troops of the British Eighth Army in Catania, Sicily, in July 1943. Palermo, the capital, fell at the end of the month.

SEA WAR, *PACIFIC*
At the Battle of Kolombangara, off New Georgia, a Japanese squadron led by Admiral Izaki engages three US light cruisers and 10 destroyers. One US destroyer is sunk and one New Zealand and two US cruisers are damaged. The Japanese lose a cruiser.

JULY 15–23

MEDITERRANEAN, *SICILY*
The US Seventh Army advances westward aiming to seize the capital Palermo with an armored thrust.

JULY 17

EASTERN FRONT, *UKRAINE*
The Soviet Voronezh Front, just to the south of Kursk, and the Steppe Front, to the west of Kharkov, begin pursuing the German forces, which are now retreating in some confusion.

JULY 17–18

MEDITERRANEAN, *SICILY*
The British Eighth Army strikes northward toward the Axis stronghold at Catania but meets determined resistance from the *Hermann Goering* Division on the plain beneath Mount Etna. The British therefore decide to go around Catania toward Mount Etna, while the US Seventh Army moves along the north coast toward Messina.

JULY 19

POLITICS, *AXIS*
Benito Mussolini and Adolf Hitler meet at Fletre in northern Italy. The Italian dictator fails to tell Hitler that his country is to cease fighting and instead endorses the proposal for Germany to

assume military control in Italy. The first major Allied air raid is made on the Italian capital, Rome, by US bombers on the same day.

JULY 23

MEDITERRANEAN, *SICILY*

The US Seventh Army enters Palermo and the west coast ports of Trapani and Marsala.

JULY 23–24

EASTERN FRONT, *UKRAINE*

The German armies have now withdrawn to the lines held at the start of Operation Citadel at Kursk.

JULY 23–30

MEDITERRANEAN, *SICILY*

The Allies drive to Messina while German forces try to save the Sicilian bridgehead and the airfields around Catania. US forces move along the north coast and Highway 120 inland.

JULY 24

POLITICS, *ITALY*

The Fascist Grand Council, the key constitutional body for debating government and party decisions, meets for the first time since 1939. Dino Grandi, former minister of justice, proposes that military authority should be given to the king and not Mussolini. His motion is approved.

JULY 24–AUGUST 2

AIR WAR, *GERMANY*

A series of massive British raids are made on Hamburg. The attacks are made over four nights and last until August 2. The dropping of foil strips to confuse German radar equipment (the "Window" system) helps the bombers. Around 50,000 people are killed and 800,000 are made homeless. The attack on the 27th–28th creates a firestorm, which blazes so intensely that the flames suck oxygen from the area nearby. This creates a "hurricane" effect that feeds the flames, which travel at great speed.

JULY 25

POLITICS, *ITALY*

The king of Italy relieves Benito Mussolini of his office. Mussolini is arrested and Marshal Pietro Badoglio forms a new government that lasts only six weeks. The government deters Germany from occupying the entire country by promising to fight on. Badoglio hopes, however, that the

Allies will land and occupy most of Italy quickly and therefore confine any fighting to the north.

JULY 26

EASTERN FRONT, *UKRAINE*

The German high command orders forces around Orel to withdraw to the previously-prepared Hagen Line, just to the east of Bryansk.

AUGUST 1

AIR WAR, *ROMANIA*

A US force of 178 bombers make a 1000-mile (1500-km) flight from Libya to attack the Ploesti oil fields, which provide essential supplies to Axis forces. The low-level attack is met by fierce antiaircraft fire and 54 aircraft are lost. Damage to the oil fields is

superficial but increases Hitler's fears over the area's susceptibility to air raids or ground attack.

AUGUST 2

EASTERN FRONT, *UKRAINE*

Adolf Hitler orders Field Marshal Erich von Manstein to hold the line firmly around Kharkov. Hitler is keen to prevent the Eastern Front being pushed farther westward by the likely Soviet summer offensive. However, German forces in the region lack the manpower, tanks, and artillery to halt the Red Army permanently.

▼ *The aftermath of the raids on the city of Hamburg. The bombing and firestorms killed an estimated 50,000 people.*

AUGUST 3

AUGUST 3

POLITICS, *ITALY*
The Italian regime puts out peace-feelers to the Allies. In reply, the Allies lay down the following conditions for an armistice: the handing over of the fleet; all Italian territories to be made available to the Allies for military operations; Allied prisoners in Italy to be freed and not be allowed to fall into German hands; and the disarming of all ground and air forces.

AUGUST 3–16

MEDITERRANEAN, *SICILY*
Italian forces withdraw from Sicily. Catania surrenders to the British on the 5th.

AUGUST 4–11

EASTERN FRONT, *UKRAINE*
Red Army units retake Orel and Belgorod by the 5th. The Voronezh and Steppe Fronts are near Kharkov.

AUGUST 5–22

PACIFIC, *SOLOMONS*
US forces capture the important Munda airfield on New Georgia Island. Japanese resistance on the island disintegrates and the defenders are not to be reinforced. A sea evacuation is made from the north of the island to neighboring Kolombangara on the 22nd.

AUGUST 6

MEDITERRANEAN, *ITALY*
German reinforcements begin arriving in Italy. Hitler orders four operations: the rescue of Mussolini from imprisonment by the new Italian government, the formation of a strong Italian defense line, the revival of fascism, and the seizure of the Italian fleet. Hitler also wishes to occupy as much of Italy as possible, using it as a bastion to keep the war as far away from Germany as possible.

AUGUST 6–7

SEA WAR, *PACIFIC*
Four Japanese destroyers carrying troops and supplies to Kolombangara in New Georgia fight a night action against six US destroyers at the Battle of Vela Gulf. Torpedo strikes sink three Japanese destroyers and claim 1210 lives. No US vessels are damaged.

AUGUST 8–17

MEDITERRANEAN, *SICILY*
US forces advancing along the coast are assisted by amphibious landings east of San Stefano. British, Canadian, and Free French Moroccan troops

▲ *The Quebec Conference, where a British plan for a cross-Channel invasion of Europe in mid-1944 was agreed.*

have fought a series of bitter actions to overcome determined German resistance to the southwest of Mount Etna. The Germans finally start withdrawing on the 11th and evacuate 100,000 Axis troops before US forces enter Messina on the 17th.

Around 10,000 Germans have been killed or captured during the campaign. The Italians have lost 132,000 men, mainly prisoners. The British and US forces have suffered 7000 fatalities and 15,000 men have been wounded. The capture of Sicily means the Allies have a springboard for the invasion of Italy.

▼ *US bombers on their way to hit the Romanian Ploesti oil fields at the beginning of August.*

AUGUST 13–24

POLITICS, *ALLIES*
British Prime Minister Winston Churchill and US President Franklin D. Roosevelt attend the First Quebec Conference in Canada. Britain reaffirms US control over the Pacific theater, where it is intensifying operations. Further Chindit operations are proposed for Burma and aid to Chiang-Kai-shek in China will continue. Vice Admiral Lord Louis Mountbatten takes charge of Southeast Asia Command.

Fighting in Italy will intensify to capitalize on Mussolini's downfall. They adopt British General Sir Frederick Morgan's plan for the cross-Channel invasion, Operation Overlord, scheduled for May 1, 1944. Floating artificial ports (Mulberry Harbors) are to be built in Britain and towed to the French beaches. The supreme commander for the invasion will be a US senior general.

AUGUST 15

PACIFIC, *ALEUTIANS*
A US and Canadian amphibious assault on Kiska Island finds that the Japanese garrison has been evacuated.

AUGUST 17–18

AIR WAR, *GERMANY*
The rocket research center at Peenemünde on the Baltic Sea is attacked by 597 British bombers. The center has been developing a remote-controlled, pulse-jet-powered "Flying Bomb" (V1) and a faster, liquid-fuel model (V2) as terror weapons to undermine the morale of enemy populations. The raid kills 732 people and delays V2 testing. The British lose 40 aircraft. A raid by 230 US bombers is made on ball-bearing works at Schweinfurt and Regensburg. Around 20 percent of the bombers are destroyed.

AUGUST 19

PACIFIC, *PAPUA NEW GUINEA*
Allied forces finally take the Japanese strongpoint of Mount Tambu. Japanese troops are now wedged between Salamaua and the Francisco River.

AUGUST 22–23

EASTERN FRONT, *UKRAINE*
Kharkov is retaken by the Red Army. The Soviets now seriously threaten the southern area of the German front in Ukraine and are well placed for advancing to the Dniepr River. The Soviets have

won victories at Kursk, Orel, and Kharkov by exhausting the enemy with fierce defensive actions followed by decisive counterattacks.

AUGUST 26

EASTERN FRONT, *UKRAINE*
Soviet forces begin their offensive to seize the eastern Ukraine and cross the Dniepr River. The river forms a key part of the German defenses established to halt Red Army advances.

AUGUST 28

POLITICS, *DENMARK*
The Danish government resigns after refusing a German demand for the repression of "saboteurs." The Danish authorities have tried to avoid collaboration with Germany. Martial law is declared on the 29th, the army is disarmed but many Danish warships are scuttled or sent to Sweden before the Germans can seize them.

SEPTEMBER 3

MEDITERRANEAN, *ITALY*
General Bernard Montgomery's Eighth Army crosses from Sicily to seize a bridgehead in Calabria. The British encounter little opposition as the Germans in southern Italy have orders to withdraw.

SEPTEMBER 4–5

PACIFIC, *PAPUA NEW GUINEA*
An Allied offensive is launched to capture the major settlement and airfield at Lae. Amphibious landings are made

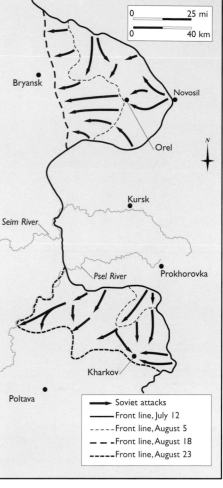

▲ The Red Army quickly recaptured Kharkov following the collapse of Germany's Citadel attack.

▶ Red Army artillery pounds German units outside Kharkov in the Soviet advance to the Dniepr River.

SEPTEMBER 8

STRATEGY & TACTICS

STRATEGIC BOMBING

Strategic bombing – air offensives against an enemy's industrial centers and population – using fleets of bombers had been considered a war-winning formula by its prewar proponents. After Germany began its first major raids against Britain in 1940, however, its limitations were exposed.

Although attacks were highly destructive, they failed to paralyze the economy or undermine morale; indeed, the opposite seemed the case as the population steeled itself for the onslaught. The effect of Allied raids on Germany met with similar results, especially as they sustained heavy losses during daylight raids, in which they were easily targeted, and were forced to make less-accurate night raids. Britain's answer was to use saturation bombing to destroy homes and factories across wide areas.

US bombers began operations over Europe in 1942 and were primarily trained for daylight, high-level precision attacks. They soon found that enemy fighters and poor weather seriously undermined the effectiveness of their missions. Fighter, flak, and radar defenses combined to make bomber raids increasingly hazardous. The Allies countered this with a series of technological innovations to enhance navigation and bomb aiming. The defensive firepower of bombers and fighter escort cover was also improved. Nevertheless, aircrew losses were often heavy and Britain's Bomber Command lost 55,573 men while the US 8th Army Air Force (based in Britain) had 43,742 airmen killed.

While the Allied bombing of Germany's oil industry and transport system did play a key role toward the end of the war, the bombers were never capable of completely defeating the enemy alone as its prewar proponents had often predicted (Germany industrial output actually increased during the Allied bomber offensive).

Raids against Japan began in 1944. Although the attacks against 65 cities succeeded in undermining the faltering economy, the nation did not capitulate until the nuclear strikes in 1945. Although the earlier bombing raids did not force Japan to surrender, they did reduce whole cities to ashes and killed many thousands.

The questionable impact such raids had on the economic and psychological capacity of a population to continue fighting, and the moral concerns over civilian deaths, subsequently led many to question this method of waging war.

► Free French troops catch their first glimpse of Corsica as they arrive off the island on an Allied troopship.

around 20 miles (30 km) east of Lae on the 4th. US paratroopers land at Nadzeb on the 5th and begin securing the Markham River valley.

SEPTEMBER 8

POLITICS, *ITALY*
The surrender of Italy is officially announced by the Allies. German forces take over the north of the country and occupy coastal defenses in anticipation of a major Allied invasion. They disarm Italian ground units but the navy succeeds in sending 24 warships to Malta.

SEPTEMBER 9

MEDITERRANEAN, *ITALY*
Lieutenant General Mark Clark's US Fifth Army, plus the British X Corps, lands in the Gulf of Salerno.

SEPTEMBER 10–11

MEDITERRANEAN, *SARDINIA/CORSICA*
The Germans withdraws 25,000 men from Sardinia to Italy, via Corsica. A 7000-strong French and US force leaves Algeria to occupy Corsica at the beginning of October.

SEPTEMBER 11–15

PACIFIC, *PAPUA NEW GUINEA*
Salamaua is captured on the 11th and Lae four days later. These victories deny the Japanese a key port and airfield. The Japanese are now left occupying the Finschhafen fort. The fort has to be taken to clear the peninsula, which is adjacent to the sea approaches to New Britain – the next Allied objective.

SEPTEMBER 12

POLITICS, *ITALY*
German airborne troops led by Lieutenant Colonel Otto Skorzeny rescue Mussolini from imprisonment in Gran Sasso in the Abruzzi Mountains. Mussolini, however, will now be under Germany's control.

SEPTEMBER 12–18

MEDITERRANEAN, *ITALY*
German forces fiercely counterattack the Allies around Salerno and threaten the entire bridgehead. Only massive aerial and artillery support saves the besieged Allied units.

SEPTEMBER 15

MEDITERRANEAN, *AEGEAN SEA*
British forces land on the island of Kos in the Dodecanese. The islands, off southwest Turkey, are a potential approach to southeast Europe and a base for air operations against German communications and oil resources in Romania. A victory here might also persuade Turkey to support the Allied cause as the threat of German air raids from Rhodes would be eliminated. Kos is to be a springboard for an assault against the German stronghold on Rhodes. By the end of September,

▲ *German troops on their way to the Dodecanese following the landing of British forces on the islands.*

▼ *Jubilant German paratroopers photographed after their rescue of Mussolini from the Gran Sasso hotel.*

British forces make contact with cooperative Italian troops on most of the neighboring islands.

SEPTEMBER 17

EASTERN FRONT, *SOVIET UNION*
The Red Army capture Bryansk.

SEPTEMBER 19–23

SEA WAR, *ATLANTIC*
The German U-boat packs resume operations against Allied convoys. They are now equipped with electronic monitoring devices, improved anti-aircraft guns, and acoustic torpedoes. Twenty U-boats inflict serious losses on warships and merchant vessels in convoys ON-202 and ONS-28 from the 18th to the 23rd.

SEPTEMBER 21

SEA WAR, *FAR EAST*
Australian commandos sink two Japanese transports after canoeing into Singapore harbor.

SEPTEMBER 22

EASTERN FRONT, *CRIMEA*
The Soviet Thirteenth Army crosses

the Dniepr River south of Kiev and bridgeheads gradually emerge along it.

PACIFIC, *PAPUA NEW GUINEA*
Allied land and seaborne offensives begin against the Japanese on the Huon Peninsula.

SEA WAR, *ARCTIC*
A raid by British midget submarines to destroy the German battle squadron at Altenfiord in Norway cripples the battleship *Tirpitz*. The submarines, however, are unable to attack the battlecruiser *Scharnhorst* as it is at sea, and the pocket battleship *Lützow* could not be found. The three midget submarines involved in the attack on the *Tirpitz* are sunk.

SEPTEMBER 22–23

MEDITERRANEAN, *ITALY*
The Eighth Army's 78th Division lands at Bari. British forces then advance to seize Foggia and its valuable airfield five days later.

SEPTEMBER 23

POLITICS, *ITALY*
Benito Mussolini announces the formation of the Italian Social Republic in

northwest Italy. Germany, however, is given control of some northern areas by this "republic."

SEPTEMBER 25

EASTERN FRONT, *SOVIET UNION*
The Soviets recapture Smolensk in their continuing offensive. Germany's Army Group Center is now falling back in some disarray.

OCTOBER 1–8

MEDITERRANEAN, *ITALY*
British troops enter Naples on the 1st, and the US Fifth Army advances northward. Its move north is stopped on the 8th at the Volturno River; all the bridges have been destroyed by the retreating Germans.

OCTOBER 2–11

MEDITERRANEAN, *ITALY*
British commandos land at Termoli on the 2nd and a British brigade arrives nearby on the next night. German forces counterattack but fall back as the British take control of the town by the 11th.

OCTOBER 3–4

MEDITERRANEAN, *AEGEAN SEA*
A force of 1200 German paratroopers capture Kos. Around 900 Allied and 3000 Italian troops are made prisoner. The Germans shoot 90 Italian officers for fighting against their former ally.

OCTOBER 6

MEDITERRANEAN, *AEGEAN*
A German convoy bound for Leros is attacked by two British cruisers and two destroyers. Seven German transports and one escort are sunk. British vessels are also making hazardous sailings without adequate air cover to reinforce their troops on Leros.

OCTOBER 9

EASTERN FRONT, *CAUCASUS*
The Red Army reaches the Kerch Strait. This completes the liberation of the north Caucasus.

▼ *A German sailor struggles to keep his footing on a U-boat during an operation in the Atlantic Ocean.*

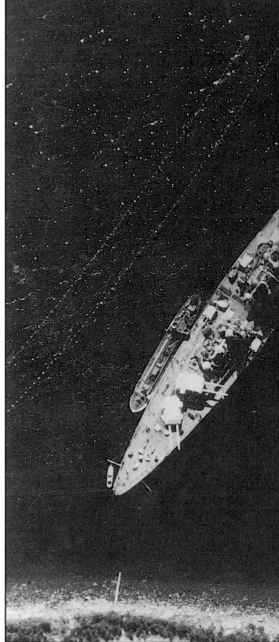

OCTOBER 10–23

EASTERN FRONT, *UKRAINE*
Strong Red Army units continue to strengthen and expand their Dniepr bridgeheads and destroy fiercely defended German positions around Zaporozhye and Melitopol.

OCTOBER 12–22

MEDITERRANEAN, *ITALY*
US forces makes slow progress across the Volturno River and through the mountain terrain in the face of increasingly bad weather. The British Eighth Army begins advancing north across the Trigno River on the 22nd. Field Marshal Albert Kesselring, the German commander-in-chief of Italy since September, has created a strong defensive system along the Garigliano and Sangro Rivers. It is known as the Gustav Line.

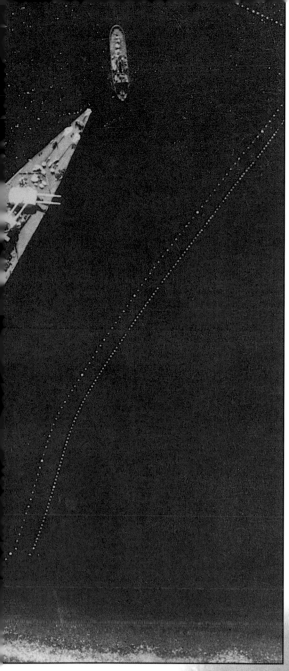

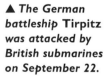

▲ The German battleship **Tirpitz** was attacked by British submarines on September 22.

▼ A British mortar fires on German positions during the fighting north of Naples in early October.

OCTOBER 13

POLITICS, ITALY

Marshal Pietro Badoglio's government, which has some power in southern Italy, declares war on Germany.

OCTOBER 14

AIR WAR, GERMANY

A second raid is made on the Schweinfurt ball-bearings complex by 291 US B-17 Flying Fortress bombers. Sixty aircraft are lost and 140 damaged for little gain. Following this operation, the US 8th Army Air Force halts unescorted daylight raids due to the high losses it has sustained. Daylight bombing raids will be given escorts of long-range fighter aircraft.

▲ Disarmed Italian troops pictured at an internment camp in Bozzano following the German occupation of their country in late September.

OCTOBER 19

POLITICS, ALLIES

Representatives from the main Allied nations attend the Second Moscow Conference in the Soviet Union. Agreements are reached over security for postwar China, the punishment of war criminals, and the establishment of advisory councils to consider the fate of Italy and Europe as a whole.

OCTOBER 21

POLITICS, BRITAIN

Admiral John Cunningham is appointed commander of British naval forces in the Mediterranean after Admiral Andrew Cunningham becomes the First Sea Lord.

◀ *Japanese antiaircraft troops watch for enemy warplanes following the US invasion of the Solomon Islands.*

island is of strategic importance as it offers the Allies airfield sites that can be used for operations against the Japanese base at Rabaul. The island is defended by 40,000 troops and 20,000 sailors. Most of these are concentrated in the south but US forces land farther west at Empress Augusta Bay, where there are fewer defenders.

NOVEMBER 1–2

SEA WAR, *PACIFIC*

A Japanese force of three heavy cruisers, one light cruiser, and six destroyers attempts to disrupt the Bougainville landings at Empress Augusta Bay. A lack of radar and over-complicated maneuvers enable US Task Force 39 to sink a light cruiser and a destroyer. Two heavy cruisers and a destroyer are damaged. Only one of Task Force 39's 12 vessels is damaged by the Japanese.

NOVEMBER 5–11

SEA WAR, *PACIFIC*

US Rear Admiral Frederick C. Sherman's Task Force 38, including the heavy carrier *Saratoga* and light

OCTOBER 25

FAR EAST, *BURMA*

The Burma to Siam rail link is completed by Allied POWs and indigenous forced labor. This Japanese project to build a track through dense jungle forests is achieved at tremendous human cost. A fifth of the 61,000 Allied prisoners on the project die as a result of accidents, abuse, disease, and starvation. This is the largest of Japan's many projects across Asia. The Japanese captors show complete indifference to the sufferings of their captives.

OCTOBER 27–28

PACIFIC, *SOLOMONS*

Landings are made on the Treasury Islands and Choiseul by US and New Zealand forces. These are diversionary

raids for the main Bougainville attack. It succeeds in drawing attention to the Shortland Islands and bases around Buin, southern Bougainville, rather than the US landing area farther west.

OCTOBER 30

EASTERN FRONT, *UKRAINE*

Soviet units reach the northern Crimea and have virtually cleared the Germans from the left bank of the Dniepr.

NOVEMBER 1

PACIFIC, *SOLOMONS*

US forces land on Bougainville; their final objective in the campaign. The

▶ *American troops pose for a photograph in a captured Japanese command post in the Solomons.*

▲ *An American Hellcat takes off from the carrier USS* Essex *during Admiral Frederick Sherman's attack on Rabaul.*

carrier *Princeton*, attacks Rabaul. A surprise attack by 97 aircraft damages eight cruisers and destroyers commanded by Vice Admiral Takeo Kurita. A second air attack by 183 aircraft, launched from the heavy carriers *Bunker Hill* and *Essex*, plus the light carrier *Independence*, hits Rabaul on the 11th. One light cruiser and a destroyer are sunk; five other destroyers and light cruisers are damaged. The Japanese also lose more than 55 aircraft during the raid and their counterattack.

NOVEMBER 6

EASTERN FRONT, *UKRAINE*
The Soviets recapture Kiev. The Seventeenth Army is trapped in the Crimea

as Adolf Hitler orders the region not to be left. Two bridgeheads – at Kiev and southwest of Kremenchug – have been created by the Red Army for the offensive to liberate the western Ukraine.

NOVEMBER 10

MEDITERRANEAN, *AEGEAN SEA*
The island of Kos is now under German control and British destroyers shell the craft anchored in the harbor. Despite the attack, the Germans sail for Leros on the 12th. Shore batteries and infantry counterattacks attempt to halt the invaders. Strong air support

▼ *The US conquest of the Solomons was a superb example of amphibious warfare operations conducted on a vast scale.*

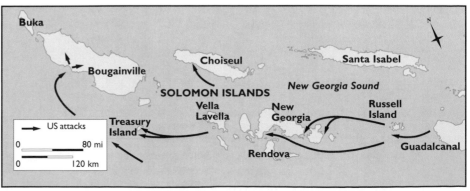

NOVEMBER 15

and an airborne assault help the Germans to stabilize their positions.

NOVEMBER 15

MEDITERRANEAN, *ITALY*

The Supreme Allied Commander in the Mediterranean, General Sir Harold Alexander, orders the Fifteenth Army Group, comprising the US fifth and Eighth Armies, to rest and reform after fighting against determined German delaying tactics. The war in Italy is proving to be very attritional.

SEA WAR, *ARCTIC*

Britain resumes its Arctic convoys.

NOVEMBER 16

MEDITERRANEAN, *AEGEAN SEA*

Germany completes the capture of Leros and defeats the British attempt to seize the Dodecanese. Poor planning and enemy air superiority have led to the failure of the operation. Britain sustains more than 4800 casualties, and loses 20 vessels and 115 aircraft. Germany has 12 merchant ships and 20 landing craft sunk, and suffers 4000 casualties during the short campaign.

▼ *An American soldier fires his Thompson submachine gun against a Japanese position on Cibik Ridge, Bougainville.*

NOVEMBER 18–26

PACIFIC, *SOLOMONS*

At the Battle of Piva Forks on Bougainville, the Japanese desperately try to hold a key strongpoint known as Cibik Ridge, but US troops finally capture the heavily-fortified position.

NOVEMBER 18

AIR WAR, *GERMANY*

A five-month British bomber offensive on Berlin begins. Over 6100 people are killed, 18,400 injured, and vast areas of the city are destroyed. Fifty diversionary raids are made on other cities.

NOVEMBER 20–23

PACIFIC, *GILBERTS*

US Task Force 53 lands 18,600 troops on Tarawa and Betio following several days of preparatory bombardment. Tarawa's network of bunkers, containing some 4800 Japanese defenders, manages to escape destruction.

The landings are hampered by this determined garrison and also because amphibious craft are grounded on the reef around the islands, which means the troops have to wade ashore. This makes them easy targets to hit.

Over 1000 US troops are killed before the island is captured on the 23rd. Of the garrison, only 110 Japanese soldiers survive. Nearby Makin Island is captured by the US 27th Infantry Division during the same operation.

▲ *Following the resumption of Arctic convoys, a depth-charge explodes near a U-boat closing in for an attack.*

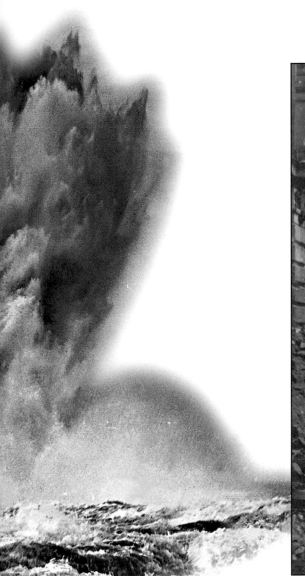

▲ Bomb damage in Berlin – a familiar sight to those who suffered the RAF's five-month campaign against the city.

◄ The Lancaster was an integral part of RAF Bomber Command's arsenal used against the German capital.

NOVEMBER 20–24

MEDITERRANEAN, *ITALY*

The Allies resume the offensive toward Rome but halt at the defenses of the Gustav Line. The British establish a small bridgehead across the Sangro River by the 24th.

NOVEMBER 22–26

POLITICS, *ALLIES*

British Prime Minister Winston Churchill, US President Franklin D. Roosevelt, and China's Chiang Kai-shek meet in Cairo, Egypt. They mainly consider postwar planning for China and Burma. A second conference, between December 4–7, draws up a schedule for the Pacific "island-hopping" campaign.

NOVEMBER 24

SEA WAR, *PACIFIC*
A Japanese submarine sinks the US escort carrier *Liscombe Bay* off Makin Island, claiming 644 lives.

NOVEMBER 25

SEA WAR, *PACIFIC*
At the Battle of Cape St. George, a Japanese destroyer-transport force is attacked by five US destroyers after landing troops at Buka, next to Bougainville. The Japanese lose three vessels during the last surface action in the Solomons.

NOVEMBER 28

POLITICS, *ALLIES*
British Prime Minister Winston Churchill, US President Franklin D. Roosevelt, and the Soviet leader Joseph Stalin meet in Tehran, Iran. Top priority is given to Operation Overlord, the cross-Channel invasion of German-occupied Europe, and a landing in southern France, Operation Anvil, in May 1944. The Soviets have been lobbying for the opening of the Second Front for some time.

DECEMBER 9–26

PACIFIC, SOLOMONS
US advances on Bougainville ensure that air bases can now be opened and missions launched.

DECEMBER 20

PACIFIC, *PAPUA NEW GUINEA*
The Allies achieve supremacy on the Huon Peninsula, although Japanese resistance persists.

DECEMBER 24–29

POLITICS, *ALLIES*
The commanders for the liberation of Europe are announced: General Dwight D. Eisenhower, Supreme Allied Commander; Air Chief Marshal Sir Arthur Tedder, Deputy Supreme Commander; General

Sir Henry Maitland Wilson, Supreme Allied Commander, Mediterranean; Admiral Sir Bertram Ramsay, Allied Naval Commander-in-Chief; Air Chief Marshal Sir Trafford Leigh Mallory, Allied Air Commander-in-Chief; and General Sir Bernard Montgomery, Commander-in-Chief of British Armies.

DECEMBER 25

PACIFIC, *SOLOMONS*
Allied forces land on New Britain and begin advancing to isolate the base of Rabaul from the west.

▲ *Chiang Kai-shek (seated, extreme left), Roosevelt and Churchill at the Cairo Conference in November 1943.*

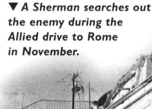

▼ *A Sherman searches out the enemy during the Allied drive to Rome in November.*

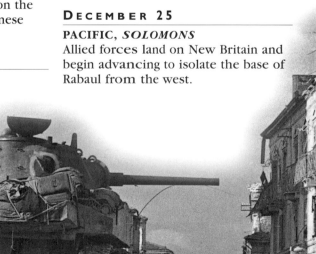

DECEMBER 26

SEA WAR, *ARCTIC*

At the Battle of the North Cape, the German battleship *Scharnhorst* is sunk during an ill-planned operation against convoys JW-55B and RA-55A, which are escorted by the British Home Fleet's battle squadron. The battleship first has its radar and fire control damaged. A running battle follows until the *Scharnhorst* begins to lose speed and is finally sunk by torpedo strikes. Only 36 of *Scharnhorst*'s 1800-strong crew survive.

▲ *Australian troops in typical jungle terrain near Lae, Papua New Guinea, during an offensive against the Japanese.*

▼ *The British battleship HMS* Duke of York, *photographed after participating in the sinking of the* Scharnhorst.

1944

In the Pacific, Japanese defeats at the Battle of the Philippine Sea and around the Mariana Islands, plus losses in Burma, signaled the growing might of the Allies. In Europe, Axis forces suffered reverses and withdrawals in Italy, France, and on the Eastern Front, as the Allies invaded northern France and the Red Army virtually wiped out Army Group Center.

JANUARY 2

POLITICS, *FREE FRENCH*
General Jean de Lattre de Tassigny is appointed commander-in-chief of Free French forces in North Africa.
PACIFIC, *PAPUA NEW GUINEA*
Troops of the US Sixth Army land at Saidor on the north coast of New Guinea as part of Operation Dexterity, cutting off Japanese rearguard forces from their main base at Madang, only 55 miles (88 km) away. The loss of Saidor, a major supply depot, means

▼ *US troops follow a Sherman tank during mopping-up operations on the northern coast of New Guinea.*

EASTERN FRONT, *UKRAINE*

As part of the Red Army's plan to recover the western Ukraine and the Crimea, General Ivan S. Konev's 2nd Ukrainian Front launches an offensive toward Kirovgrad. Despite desperate German resistance, the town falls on the 8th.

JANUARY 9

FAR EAST, *BURMA*

As part of the Allied attempt to break into Burma, the British XV Corps takes the Burmese town of Maungdaw.

JANUARY 10

EASTERN FRONT, *UKRAINE*

General Rodion Y. Malinovsky's 3rd Ukrainian Front launches an offensive toward Apostolovo, but the attack is halted after six days in the face of fierce German resistance.

JANUARY 11

POLITICS, *ITALY*

Count Galeazzo Ciano, the former Italian foreign secretary and Mussolini's son-in-law, is executed by firing squad in Verona. His "crime" was to have voted with other fascists to oust Mussolini in July 1943. Ciano and his wife had been lured to Bavaria in August 1943 following a report that their children were in danger. Having been promised safe passage to Spain, they were handed over to Italy's puppet fascist government.

JANUARY 12–14

ITALY, *CASSINO*

At Cassino, General Alphonse Juin's colonial troops of the French Expeditionary Corps cross the Rapido River on the Fifth Army's

northern sector. Although they fail to take Monte Santa Croce, their success fills the headquarters of the Fifth Army with renewed optimism.

JANUARY 14–27

EASTERN FRONT, *LENINGRAD*

The Soviet Second Shock Army attacks from the Oranienbaum bridgehead, and the Fifty-ninth Army attacks toward Novgorod, in an attempt to break the German blockade of the city. The next day the Forty-second Army attacks from the Pulkovo Heights. On the 19th, the three armies link up near Krasnoe, and two days later German forces in the Petergof and Streina area are wiped out. Fighting continues as the Germans try to stop the Red Army onslaught, but on the 27th a salute of 324 guns announces the end of the German blockade of Leningrad. Some 830,000 civilians have died during the long siege.

JANUARY 17

ITALY, *GUSTAV LINE*

The Allied attempt to break through the Gustav Line – a frontal assault combined with a seaborne hook to the German rear at Anzio – begins. The British X Corps attacks across the Garigliano River and strikes northwest toward the Aurunci Mountains and the Liri Valley. In response, the German commander, General Heinrich von Vietinghoff, transfers two armored divisions to counter this new threat.

that 20,000 Japanese soldiers are now sandwiched between Australian and US forces. Their only escape route is through dense jungle.

JANUARY 3

AIR WAR, *GERMANY*

In a large-scale air raid on Berlin, the RAF loses 27 Lancasters out of 383 aircraft committed, plus 168 crew members. The damage to the German capital is negligible.

JANUARY 4

ESPIONAGE, *EUROPE*

Operation Carpetbagger – regular airborne supply drops to resistance groups in the Netherlands, Belgium, France, and Italy – begins.

JANUARY 5

POLITICS, *POLAND*

The Polish government-in-exile has authorized the Polish underground movement to cooperate with the Red Army only in the event of a resumption of Polish–Soviet relations (the Soviet Union has not yet recognized the London-based Polish government-in-exile).

▶ Algerian troops of General Alphonse Juin's French Expeditionary Corps in action at Monte Cassino, Italy, in the middle of January.

Rome is open. However, although by the evening Lucas has nearly 50,000 men and 3000 vehicles ashore, he orders his forces to dig in to repel any enemy counterattacks. He thus misses the opportunity to strike inland from the beachhead.

JANUARY 24

ITALY, *CASSINO/ANZIO*
At Anzio, Allied patrols venturing inland are halted by increasing German resistance. At Cassino, the US 34th Division finally establishes bridgeheads across the Rapido River to allow the armor to cross. At the other end of the Allied line, French troops make further gains.

JANUARY 26

POLITICS, *ARGENTINA*
Argentina has severed relations with Germany and Japan following the

▲ German paratroopers on their way to attack the Allied bridgehead at Anzio, which had been contained by late January.

JANUARY 20

ITALY, *GUSTAV LINE*
As part of the Allied attack on the Gustav Line, the US II Corps attempts to cross the Rapido River to clear a path for the US 1st Armored Division. The German defenses are strong and the Americans suffer heavy losses.

JANUARY 22

ITALY, *ANZIO*
Troops of the Allied VI Corps make an amphibious landing at Anzio, behind the German lines. Commanded by US General John Lucas, the initial attack is almost unopposed and the road to

▲ The campaign to break through the German defenses to reach Anzio was both long and costly.

◄ A US Marine signals unit in shattered buildings on Kwajalein Atoll, the Marshall Islands, which fell after four days of fighting.

uncovering of a vast Axis spy network in the country.

PACIFIC, *PAPUA NEW GUINEA*
Following several days of fighting, the Australian 18th Brigade takes the key Japanese position of Kankiryo Saddle.

JANUARY 30

PACIFIC, *MARSHALLS*
The American conquest of the Marshall Islands, Operation Flintlock,

Allied attacks
Front line, October 12, 1943
Front line, November 15, 1943
Front line, 15 January, 1944
Front line, 11 May, 1944
Front line, 5 June, 1944

begins with an amphibious assault against Majuro Atoll. The strategy is to concentrate on key islands and their air bases. Once these have been taken, enemy garrisons on lesser islets will be starved into submission. The landing on Majuro was made on one of the atoll's islands, which was undefended.

FEBRUARY 1–4

PACIFIC, *MARSHALLS*
The amphibious assault against the islands of Kwajalein Atoll is launched. Some 40,000 US Marines and infantry land on the islands of Roi, Namur, and Kwajalein. Japanese resistance is fanatical. It takes the Americans two days to secure Roi and Namur at a cost of 737 killed and wounded; four days to conquer Kwajalein for the loss of 372 killed and wounded. Total Japanese losses are 11,612 men killed.

FEBRUARY 4

ITALY, *CASSINO/ANZIO*
Allied attacks edge closer to Monte Cassino, but then fierce German counterattacks stop the advance in its tracks. At Anzio, the Germans, located on the high ground, contain the Allied bridgehead, which now holds more than 70,000 men and 18,000 vehicles.

FEBRUARY 4–24

FAR EAST, *BURMA*
The Japanese launch Operation Ha-Go with their 55th Division, designed to cut off the forward troops of the Allied

▲ *General Joseph Stilwell (right), whose troops were advancing on Myitkyina in early February 1944, with Chinese allies.*

XV Corps and force the Allies back to the Indian border. Initial Japanese attacks are successful and push Allied troops back to a defensive position near Sinzweya called the "Admin Box." The Japanese ring around the position is not broken until the 25th, when the 123rd Brigade fights its way through the Ngakyedauk Pass and reaches the "Admin Box." The failure of Ha-Go is a watershed in the Burma campaign, as Japanese enveloping tactics have failed to produce the expected results.

FEBRUARY 5

FAR EAST, *BURMA*
The 16th Brigade of Orde Wingate's Chindits begins to move south from Ledo, India, toward Indaw in northern Burma. Its mission is threefold: to aid General Joseph Stilwell's advance on Myitkyina by drawing off enemy forces; to create a favourable situation for the Yunnan armies; and to inflict the maximum amount of damage and loss on the Japanese in northern Burma.

FEBRUARY 12

SEA WAR, *FAR EAST*
The Japanese submarine *I-27* sinks the British troopship *Khedive Ismail* with the loss of many lives. The submarine is then sunk by the destroyers *Petard* and *Paladin*.

KEY PERSONALITIES

MARSHAL JOSIP BROZ TITO LEADER OF YUGOSLAVIA

Tito (1892–1980) was nearly 50 years old when World War II broke out. Having seen service in the Russian Revolution and Spanish Civil War, he quickly organized resistance when the Germans invaded Yugoslavia in March 1941. By the fall of that year, he was waging a full-scale guerrilla campaign in Serbia, capturing a number of towns, including Uzice, where he set up an arms factory and printing facilities. He disagreed with the rival Chetnik resistance group and defeated them, but was then driven out of Serbia by the Germans in the first of seven major Axis offensives against the Yugoslavian partisans.

His tactics on the ground consisted of fighting as long as possible, then withdrawing into the hills with his forces, all the while maintaining tight communication and organization as he did so. In May 1943 he was attacked by forces six times greater than his own, lost a quarter of his strength and half his equipment, but still managed to keep his forces together.

In late 1942 Tito began receiving aid from the Western Allies, and the withdrawal of Italy from the war gave him Croatia and vast quantities of Italian weapons. By 1944 he had an army of 250,000 men and women, and on October 20 he took Belgrade. He became the symbol of the country's unity, and was able to establish a postwar communist government.

FEBRUARY 16–17

ITALY, *CASSINO*
The US 34th Division makes a last attempt to capture the German-held monastery. Its attack is halted, however, and the unit is replaced by the 4th Indian and New Zealand Divisions of the British Eighth Army.

FEBRUARY 16–19

ITALY, *ANZIO*
With massive artillery support, 10 German divisions attack the Anzio beachhead in an attempt to wipe it out. By the morning of the 17th, the Germans have created a wedge one mile (1.6 km) deep in the Allied line. However, that afternoon aircraft from the entire Italian front bomb and strafe the German units in an effort to save the beachhead. Allied air attacks, supported by artillery on the ground, eventually force the Germans to retire on the 19th.

FEBRUARY 18–22

PACIFIC, *MARSHALLS*
US forces complete their conquest of

▲ *American Dauntless dive-bombers returning from a strike against Japanese targets in the Marshall Islands.*

the islands with the seizure of Eniwetok Atoll. This combined army and Marine operation is a bloody affair, with 3400 Japanese defenders dying, along with 254 US Marines and 94 army personnel being killed. The Marshalls are the first Japanese prewar territories to fall to the Allies so far in the war.

FEBRUARY 26

EASTERN FRONT, *BALTIC*
The Red Army captures Porkhov and regroups on the Novorzhev and Pustoshka line. In the course of a six-week campaign the Volkhov, Leningrad, and 2nd Baltic Fronts have inflicted a shattering defeat on Germany's Army Group North. They have wiped out three German divisions, routed another 17, and captured 189 tanks and 1800 artillery pieces. In addition, units of local partisans have killed over 21,500 German troops, destroyed 300 bridges, and derailed 136 military trains during a series of wide-ranging attacks.

FEBRUARY 29

PACIFIC, *ADMIRALTIES*
As part of their strategy for isolating the Japanese base at Rabaul, American forces land on the islands, a staging

▼ *A mortar of the US 34th Division shells German-held positions around Cassino.*

KEY PERSONALITIES

GENERAL GEORGE S. PATTON

Something of an innovator in the US Army, Patton (1885–1945) had seen service in World War I and was a firm believer in the tenets of armored warfare. He was given command of the US II Corps in the Torch landings in November 1942, and was then ordered to lead the US Seventh Army in the invasion of Sicily. However, the controversial hitting of shell-shocked soldiers in a field hospital resulted in public censure.

During the campaign in France he led the US Third Army, using it to achieve quick advances to Lorraine and the German frontier. However, he strongly disagreed with Eisenhower's policy of sharing vital military supplies between US forces and Montgomery's British and Commonwealth units. Patton believed that if he had been given more supplies he could have ended the war in 1944. Instead, he fought a bitter battle of attrition on the border and intervened decisively in the Battle of the Bulge. In 1945 he conducted a masterful crossing of the Rhine, which was followed by a whirlwind advance into Czechoslovakia. Patton, the founder of the armored tradition in the US Army, was killed in an motor vehicle accident in December 1945.

post through which the Japanese can reach Rabaul. The fall of the Admiralties will secure the southwest Pacific for the Allies.

MARCH 1

FAR EAST, *BURMA*
The Chindits' 16th Brigade crosses the Chindwin River, as Chinese forces and Merrill's Marauders (a US commando force) under General Joseph Stilwell, advance toward Myitkyina.

MARCH 2

POLITICS, *ALLIES*
The Allies cut off all aid to Turkey due to its government's reluctance to help their war effort.

MARCH 5–11

FAR EAST, *BURMA*
Brigadier Mike Calvert's 77th Brigade of the Chindits begins landing by glider at two selected points code-named "Broadway" and "Piccadilly" in the Kaukkwe Valley, northern Burma. During the first lift, 61 gliders are used, although only 35 reach their target. By the 11th, the whole of Calvert's brigade has been flown in.

MARCH 7

HOME FRONT, *GERMANY*
Members of the Nazi organization for women are making house-to-house calls to recruit females between the ages of 17 and 45 to work "in the service of the community." This is to bolster Germany's depleted labor force.

▼ *Chinese infantry under the overall command of General Joseph Stilwell crossing the Chindwin River in March.*

▲ *Anxious German troops wait for action as the Red Army attacks Army Group North on the Eastern Front.*

MARCH 7–8

FAR EAST, *BURMA/INDIA*
Operation U-Go, the Japanese offensive to drive the Allies back into India by destroying their bases at Imphal and Kohima, begins with moves to sever the Tiddim to Imphal road. The Japanese 33rd Division has orders to cut off the 17th Indian Division at Tiddim and force the British to commit their reserves to rescue it, while the

MARCH 8

▲ *Japanese troops on the attack between Homalin and Thaungdut in their efforts to cut the Imphal to Kohima road.*

▼ *For German workers in 1944 it was a never-ending task of laying new railroad tracks after Allied air raids, in this case after an US 8th Army Air Force attack.*

31st and 15th Divisions are to cross the Chindwin farther north and fall on Imphal and Kohima.

MARCH 8

AIR WAR, *GERMANY*
The US 8th Army Air Force launches a massive daylight precision raid on the

Erker ball-bearing works, Berlin. A total of 590 aircraft mount the raid. There are 75 direct hits on the target, but the Americans lose 37 aircraft. This is the third US raid on Berlin under the escort of P-51 Mustang fighters. It results in the halting of ball-bearing production for some time.

MARCH 11

EASTERN FRONT, *UKRAINE*
General Rodion Malinovsky's 2nd Ukrainian Front reaches the Bug River, brushing aside resistance from the German Eighth Army. The Germans hope to halt the Red Army on this great water barrier.

MARCH 11–12

FAR EAST, *BURMA*
In the Arakan, northern Burma, the Allies recapture Buthidaung and then surround and capture the Japanese fortress at Razabil.

MARCH 15–16

FAR EAST, *BURMA/INDIA*
The Japanese 15th and 31st Divisions cross the Chindwin River between Homalin and Thaungdut and move forward with the intention of cutting the Imphal to Kohima road.

◄ *US B-25 medium bombers on their way to pound German units dug in amid the ruins of Monte Cassino.*

MARCH 18

EASTERN FRONT, *UKRAINE*
The Soviet 2nd Ukrainian Front has reached the Dniester River and seized a large bridgehead at Mogilev Podolsky. This has split the German Army Group South's front in two and has put the Red Army in a position to advance to the Romanian frontier.

MARCH 19

POLITICS, *HUNGARY*
With the Red Army rapidly approaching the Balkans, Hitler has sent troops to occupy the country. Admiral Miklós Horthy, the regent, has been ordered to appoint a pro-Nazi premier, allow the German Army to take over the transport system, and give the SS a free hand in deporting Hungarian Jews to concentration camps.

ITALY, *CASSINO*
A German counterattack against Peak 193 is unsuccessful but has loosened the Allied stranglehold. A New Zealand armored assault against the monastery is destroyed.

MARCH 20–22

ITALY, *CASSINO*
Despite further frontal attacks by New Zealand troops under General Harold Alexander, the German defenders, veterans of the 1st Parachute Division, remain in and around the monastery and repulse all efforts to dislodge

◄ *The remains of the monastery of Monte Cassino.*

MARCH 15–17

ITALY, *CASSINO*
Allied aircraft launch a massive raid against the unoccupied monastery of Monte Cassino (which is later criticized by the Vatican). The New Zealand 2nd Division then launches an assault that takes Peak 193. During the evening the 4th Indian Division attacks and captures Peak 165. All Allied attacks on the 16th are frustrated, but on the 17th a breakthrough by the New Zealanders takes Cassino railroad station. They fail, though, to complete the encirclement of the town itself.

▲ *Waiting for the next Japanese attack: a British machine-gun position at Imphal in late March 1944.*

▲ *Major General Orde Wingate, the brilliant Chindit commander, who was killed in an air crash at Imphal.*

them. On the 22nd, therefore, Alexander halts all frontal assaults.

MARCH 24

FAR EAST, *BURMA*

Major General Orde Wingate, the commander of the Chindits, is killed in a plane crash. A charismatic and controversial figure, Winston Churchill has called him a "man of genius and audacity" following the success of his long-range penetration missions in Burma.

MARCH 28

EASTERN FRONT, *UKRAINE*

As the Germans retreat in haste from the waters of the southern Bug River, Nikolayev falls to the Red Army. The 3rd Ukrainian Front is now developing an assault toward the port of Odessa.

MARCH 29

FAR EAST, *INDIA*

The Japanese 20th Division establishes itself on the Shenam Saddle near

Imphal. Japanese forces have cut the Imphal to Kohima road and begun the siege of Imphal.

MARCH 30

POLITICS, *GERMANY*

Hitler, outraged at the Soviet victories in the Ukraine, has dismissed two of his field marshals – Erich von Manstein and Paul von Kleist – for disregarding his "stand fast" orders. In addition, the Nazi leader believes that the army in the Ukraine has put up weak resistance against the Soviets.

FAR EAST, *BURMA*

The Chindits' 16th Brigade, commanded by Brigadier Bernard Fergusson, retreats following its failure to take the main Japanese supply base at Indaw.

MARCH 30–31

AIR WAR, *GERMANY*

A night raid by the RAF against Nuremberg results in little damage to the city but substantial losses are inflicted on the aircraft involved. The RAF loses 95 out of the

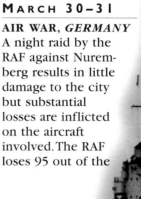

attacking force of 795 bombers, with a further 71 damaged.

APRIL 3

AIR WAR, *NORWAY*
The German battleship *Tirpitz* has been damaged in Altenfiord, Norway, by Royal Navy aircraft flown from the British carriers *Victorious* and *Furious*. *Tirpitz* has been hit 14 times, which means that it will not sail again for several months.

APRIL 4–13

FAR EAST, *INDIA*
The first stage of the Imphal battle has ended. The Japanese have failed to destroy the Allied defense line. The British IV Corps, now concentrated around Imphal, can turn its attention to the destruction of the Japanese. By April 13, the Japanese have been ejected from Nungshigum, one of the hills commanding the Imphal plain, and their 15th Division is being harried down the road to Ukhrul.

APRIL 5

EASTERN FRONT, *UKRAINE*
The Soviet 3rd Ukrainian Front captures Razdelnaya station and cuts the local German forces in two, one of which is forced to withdraw toward Odessa and the other toward Tiraspol.

APRIL 6–11

FAR EAST, *BURMA*
Japanese forces attack the Chindit fortified position at "White City," which is subsequently evacuated.

APRIL 8

EASTERN FRONT, *CRIMEA*
General Fedor I. Tolbukhin's 4th Ukrainian Front (470,000 men, 6000 field guns and mortars, 560 tanks and self-propelled guns, and 1250 combat aircraft) begins the liberation of the

▲ *General Fedor Tolbukhin, whose 4th Ukrainian Front liberated the Crimea and captured Sebastopol in April.*

peninsula. The German and Romanian forces defending the region as part of the Seventeenth Army can muster only 200,000 men, 3600 field guns and mortars, 200 tanks and self-propelled guns, and 150 aircraft.

APRIL 9

EASTERN FRONT, *UKRAINE*
The Soviet 3rd Ukrainian Front reaches the outskirts of Odessa.

APRIL 12

POLITICS, *ROMANIA*
In reply to a Romanian mission regarding the conditions for an armistice between Romania and the Soviet Union, Moscow demands that Romania break with the Germans, that its forces fight alongside the Red Army, and insists on the restoration of the Romanian and Soviet border. It also calls for reparations for damage inflicted on the Soviet Union by Romania, freedom of movement through the country for Soviet and other Allied forces, and the repatriation

◀ *A Swordfish torpedo-bomber returns to HMS Victorious, which took part in an attack on the German battleship Tirpitz.*

of Soviet prisoners. The Romanians reject these conditions and remain with the Axis.

▲ *A US A-20 bomber hits an important rail junction at Busigny in northern France.*

APRIL 15

AIR WAR, *EUROPE*
The US 8th Army Air Force and RAF Bomber Command decide to switch bombing from German urban centers to railroads in Belgium and France to prepare for the forthcoming Allied invasion by preventing German reinforcements reaching the front.

A force of 448 Flying Fortresses and Liberators of the US 15th Army Air Force, escorted by 150 Mustang fighters, also attacks the oil fields at Ploesti and the Romanian capital, Bucharest. During the night the RAF bombs the railroad lines at Turnu Severin in Romania.

APRIL 22

**PACIFIC,
*PAPUA NEW GUINEA***
General Douglas MacArthur, leading a 52,000-strong Allied invasion force, makes an amphibious landing in Hollandia, northern New Guinea. Hollandia will be the base for the next phase of MacArthur's Operation Cartwheel, which is

designed to drive the Japanese from northwest New Guinea.

MAY 3

POLITICS, *JAPAN*
Admiral Soemu Toyoda is appointed commander-in-chief of the Japanese Combined Fleet. He replaces Admiral Mineichi Koga, who has been killed in a plane crash on March 31.

MAY 9

EASTERN FRONT, *CRIMEA*
The Soviet 4th Ukrainian Front liberates the port of Sebastopol. It is a crushing defeat for the German defenders, who have lost 100,000 men killed and captured during the fighting.

◀ *Admiral Soemu Toyoda, the new commander-in-chief of the Japanese Combined Fleet.*

◀ *Mopping up the last pockets of Japanese resistance on the Admiralty Islands – both tedious and dangerous.*

MAY 19

HOME FRONT, *GERMANY*

Following their recapture after a mass breakout from Stalag Luft III near Sagan, Silesia, 50 Allied airmen are shot by the Gestapo. Only three of the escaped prisoners – two Norwegians and a Dutchman – reach England.

MAY 23–31

ITALY, *ANZIO*

Troops of the US VI Corps begin the breakout from the Anzio beachhead in the face of stubborn German resistance. The linkup with troops of the US II Corps occurs on the 25th, four months after the original Anzio landing. Steady gains are made by the Allies, although taking the Adolf Hitler Line, which runs from Terracina on the coast along the Foni to Pico road to Pontecorvo and across the Liri Valley through Aquino and Piedmonte to Monte Cairo, does result in heavy Allied losses. Once again the Germans have proved adept at defense.

▼ *Infantry of the British 4th Division pick their way through shattered streets during the advance to the Rapido River in Italy.*

MAY 11–18

ITALY, *CASSINO*

The Allied 15th Army Group begins its offensive to outflank the monastery. On the 12th, the French Expeditionary Corps takes Monte Faito, but the Polish 5th Division fails to capture Colle Sant'Angelo. On the 13th, the French open the way to Rome, while the US II Corps takes Santa Maria Infante, and the British 4th Division begins to enlarge its bridgehead across the Rapido River.

On the 17th, the Germans evacuate the monastery at Monte Cassino because of the deep breakthroughs by the French Expeditionary Corps and the US II Corps. The next day, the Polish 12th Podolski Regiment storms the ruins of Monte Cassino.

MAY 18

PACIFIC, *ADMIRALTIES*

The last pockets of Japanese resistance on the islands have been crushed. This effectively isolates the main Japanese bases at Rabaul and Kavieng in the southwest Pacific.

On the 25th, the US Fifth Army attacks toward Rome, but is held by the Germans, who have had time to dig in around Valmontone along the Caesar Line. It is not until the night of May 30 – when Major General Fred L. Walker's US 36th Division moves silently up Monte Artemisio and breaks the Valmontone defenses – that the final defensive line barring the entrance to Rome is cut.

MAY 25

BALKANS, *YUGOSLAVIA*
The Germans launch an air, glider, and mortar attack on the partisan head-quarters at Divar, in which Marshal Tito narrowly escapes capture. The attack is believed to have been the plan of SS Major Otto Skorzeny, the officer who rescued Mussolini.

▼ *German paratroopers in Rome on the eve of their evacuation of the city in early June.*

▲ *Soldiers of the US 4th Infantry Division wade ashore under fire at Utah Beach on D-Day, the invasion of northern France.*

MAY 29

PACIFIC, *PAPUA NEW GUINEA*
The first tank battle of the Pacific campaign is fought on Biak Island, off New Guinea, between the Japanese and Americans. It is a US victory.

JUNE 1

FAR EAST, *BURMA*
Brigadier Mike Calvert, commander of the Chindits' 77th Brigade, reaches Lakum near Mogaung.

JUNE 3

FAR EAST, *INDIA*
The 64-day Battle of Kohima ends with the remnants of the Japanese 31st Division withdrawing in good order. It is the lack of supplies, rather than the attacks of the British and Indian forces, which has forced the Japanese to fall back. The fighting at Kohima has been among the most savage of the whole war.

JUNE 3–4

ITALY, *ROME*
Adolf Hitler reluctantly gives Field Marshal Albert Kesselring, the German commander-in-chief in Italy, permission to abandon Rome. Covered by expert rearguard actions of IV Para-chute Corps, the German Fourteenth Army pulls back across the Tiber River. US troops enter the city on the 5th – the first Axis capital to be captured.

JUNE 6

WESTERN FRONT, *FRANCE*

The Allies launch the greatest amphibious operation in history. The statistics for the invasion force are staggering: 50,000 men for the initial assault; over two million men to be shipped to France in all, comprising a total of 39 divisions; 139 major warships used in the assault, with a further 221 smaller combat vessels; over 1000 minesweepers and auxiliary vessels; 4000 landing craft; 805 merchant ships; 59 blockships; 300 miscellaneous small craft; and 11,000 aircraft, including fighters, bombers, transports, and gliders. In addition, the invasion force has the support of over 100,000 members of the French Resistance, who launch hit-and-run attacks on German targets.

D-Day, the Allied invasion of Normandy, code-named Operation Overlord, begins with the assault of three airborne divisions – the US 82nd and 101st on the right flank of the US forces, and the British 6th Airborne on

▲ *German prisoners are led away after their surrender on D-Day.*

◀ *British Horsa gliders litter the fields northeast of Caen on the morning of D-Day – 6 June 1944.*

▼ *After consolidating their beachhead, the Allies built up their forces for the liberation of France. Air superiority, which restricted the movement of German forces, greatly aided their efforts.*

the left flank of the British – while seaborne forces land on five beaches. Utah Beach is the target of the US 4th Infantry Division (part of the US VII Corps); Omaha Beach is the target of the US 1st Infantry Division (part of the US V Corps); Gold Beach is the landing site of the British 50th Infantry Division (part of the British XXX Corps); Juno is the target for the Canadian 3rd Infantry Division (part of the British I Corps); and the British 3rd

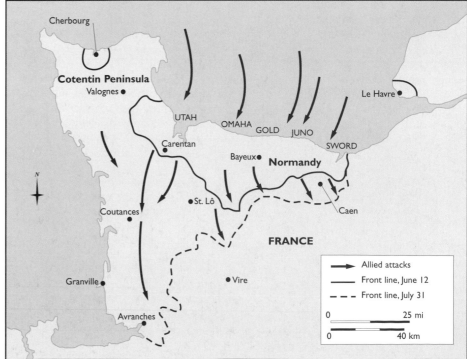

▲ American troops march through bomb-damaged Carentan, the first French city to fall to the invaders after D-Day.

JUNE 9–10

DECISIVE WEAPONS

RESISTANCE

Within those countries and regions overrun by the Germans and Japanese in Word War II, there were those among the various populations who were determined to oppose the occupiers in some way, often at great risk to themselves and their families. This resistance could be active or passive. Passive resistance involved demonstrations, industrial strikes, and slowdowns, the production of underground newspapers and leaflets, and wall slogans. Active resistance involved gathering intelligence, assisting escaped Allied prisoners of war and shot-down aircrews, sabotage, and armed action against occupation forces.

Throughout Europe and the Far East, resistance was never the preserve of any particular political grouping or social class; rather it encompassed a complete cross-section of each country's society.

The dangers of fighting back against occupiers were ever present, and resistance movements were under constant threat from enemy intelligence, collaborators, and informers, with torture and death the usual price of being caught. Ownership of a carrier pigeon, for example, warranted death by firing squad in Europe. In addition, there was often infighting between various resistance groups. In Yugoslavia, the Chetniks and Tito's forces fought each other as well as the Axis occupiers. Nevertheless, with outside help (which was often crucial in keeping the various units going), resistance groups in Europe and the Far East aided the general Allied war effort against the Axis powers.

Jubilant members of the French Resistance near Paris in August 1944, with the Germans in full retreat.

Infantry Division (also part of the British I Corps) is tasked with seizing Sword Beach.

The initial parachute and seaborne landings have mixed results: on Utah resistance is slight and the troops are off the beach by 1200 hours; on Omaha the lack of specialized armor means the Germans can pin down the troops on the beach, with great slaughter; on Gold and Juno the specialized armor of the British and Canadians allow the troops to get off the beaches quickly, and by the afternoon they are probing inland toward Bayeux and Caen; and on Sword the troops are able to link up with airborne units that have been dropped farther inland.

This is fortunate, for it is between Juno and Sword that the Germans make their one major counterattack, comprising a battlegroup of the 21st Panzer Division. However, it is defeated. By the end of the day, at a

▼ *US Marines under fire on the island of Saipan, Marianas, on June 23, 1944. Japanese resistance was, as usual, very fierce.*

cost of 2500 dead, the Allies have a toehold in German-occupied Europe.

JUNE 9–10

EASTERN FRONT, *FINLAND*
The Soviets, in an effort to drive the Finns back to the 1940 frontier and compel them to make peace, launch a major offensive with two armies. The offensive is preceded by a sustained barrage from 5500 guns and 880 rocket-launchers. The attack shatters the Finnish front and, on the 10th, Marshal Karl von Mannerheim, Finland's military leader, orders a retreat to a stronger defensive line.

JUNE 10

WESTERN FRONT, *FRANCE*
The 2nd SS Panzer Division *Das Reich*, moving from its base at Toulouse

to Normandy, has been the constant target of members of the French Resistance. In retaliation, the small town of Oradour-sur-Glane is chosen as the target for a brutal reprisal, one intended to be a lesson to the people of France. The men of the village are herded into barns, the women and children into the church, and the whole town is set on fire. Those who flee are machine-gunned. In total, 642 people are killed, with only 10 able to feign death and escape.

JUNE 11

PACIFIC, *MARIANAS*

US Task Force 58 begins a heavy bombardment of Saipan, Tinian, Guam, Rota, and Pagan prior to an assault on the islands, the occupation of which will allow the US forces operating in the area to

▲ *A Japanese ship under American air attack during the Battle of the Philippine Sea, which fatally wrecked Japanese naval air strength in the Pacific.*

sever the lines of communication to Japan's units operating in the southern Pacific.

JUNE 13

WESTERN FRONT, *FRANCE*
Lieutenant Michael Wittmann, company commander of the SS 501st Heavy Tank Battalion, destroys 27 tanks and armoured vehicles of the British 4th Country of London Yeomanry in a tank battle around the village of Villers-Bocage, Normandy.

PACIFIC, *JAPAN*
The Japanese Combined Fleet is alerted to prepare for Operation A-Go, which is intended to lure the US Pacific Fleet to one of two battle areas – either the Palaus or the Western Carolines – where it can be destroyed. These areas are chosen because they are within range of the greatest possible number of Japanese island air bases, thereby counterbalancing US aircraft carrier superiority.

JUNE 15

PACIFIC, *MARIANAS*
The US Northern Attack Force arrives off Saipan. In response, the Japanese Combined Fleet is ordered to gather. On the island itself, landings are conducted on the west coast by the US 2nd and 4th Marine Divisions.

AIR WAR, *JAPAN*
The iron and steel works at Yahata on the mainland is bombed by B-29s of the US 20th Army Air Force, which is operating from bases in China.

JUNE 16

FAR EAST, *BURMA*
The 22nd Division, part of Lieutenant General Joseph Stilwell's Chinese force, has taken Kamaing, the first of his three objectives – the others being Mogaung and Myitkyina.

JUNE 18

WESTERN FRONT, *FRANCE*
US forces reach the west coast of the Cotentin Peninsula, Normandy, trapping the German garrison in Cherbourg. Hitler has ordered the garrison to fight to the death.

PACIFIC, *MARIANAS*
The warships of US Task Force 58 rendezvous west of Saipan.

JUNE 19–21

PACIFIC, *PHILIPPINE SEA*
On hearing of the US assault on Saipan, the Japanese Combined Fleet, under Admiral Jisaburo Ozawa, puts to sea immediately with five heavy and four light carriers, five battleships, 11 heavy and two light cruisers, and 28 destroyers. The US 5th Fleet, under Admiral Marc Mitscher's tactical command, numbers seven heavy and eight light carriers, eight heavy and 13 light cruisers, and 69 destroyers. Aircraft on either side total 573 Japanese (including 100 based on Guam, Rota, and Yap) and 956 American.

Ozawa's search planes locate the 5th Fleet at daybreak, 300 miles (480 km) from his advance element of four light carriers and 500 miles (800 km) from his main body. Ozawa launches an attack in four waves, while Mitscher, on discovering the enemy aircraft, sends out his interceptors.

Disaster strikes Ozawa immediately, for US submarines sink the carriers *Taiho* and *Shokaku*, and US fighters shoot down many of his aircraft. In the Battle of the Philippine Sea, nicknamed the "Great Marianas Turkey Shoot" by the Americans, the Japanese lose 346 aircraft and two carriers. US losses are 30 aircraft and slight damage to a battleship. Meanwhile, Mitscher's bombers neutralize the Japanese airfields on Guam and Rota.

On the 20th, Mitscher launches 216 aircraft, which sink another carrier and two oil tankers, and seriously damage several other vessels. While the Americans lose 20 aircraft, Ozawa loses another 65, although many US aircraft are forced to ditch into the sea.

Ozawa's costly battle deals a crippling blow to the Japanese naval air arm, not least through the loss of 460 trained combat pilots.

JUNE 20

ITALY, *UMBRIA*
The British XXX Corps opens its attack on the Albert Line, one of a series of German rearguard positions in northern Italy, south of Lake Trasimeno on either side of Chiusi. The fighting is hard; the Germans give ground grudgingly.

JUNE 22

POLITICS, *GERMANY*
Foreign Minister Joachim von Ribbentrop visits Helsinki to try to tie Finland more tightly to Germany.

FAR EAST, *INDIA*
The British 2nd Division reach the defenders of Imphal, but Japanese resistance continues.

▲ *The Red Army liberates another town in Belorussia and its soldiers are welcomed by grateful civilians.*

JUNE 22–26

FAR EAST, *BURMA*
The Chindits' 77th Brigade begins attacking Mogaung from the southeast. Following bitter fighting, it finally falls on the 26th.

JUNE 23

EASTERN FRONT, *BELORUSSIA*
The Red Army launches its Belorussian offensive. Four fronts – 1st Baltic, 1st, 2nd, and 3rd Belorussian, comprising

▼ *Allied troops in the ruins of Valognes during the drive against Cherbourg, which fell on June 29, 1944.*

1.2 million men in all – attack the German divisions of Army Group Center. The Soviets have a four-to-one superiority in tanks and aircraft.

JUNE 26

WESTERN FRONT, *FRANCE*
The British launch Operation Epsom, a drive west of Caen. Troops and tanks of the 15th, 43rd, and 11th Armored Divisions make good initial progress, but are then halted following very heavy losses.

JUNE 29

WESTERN FRONT, *FRANCE*
The port of Cherbourg finally surrenders to forces of the US VII Corps. The cost to the US has been 22,000 casualties, while 39,000 Germans are taken prisoner.

JUNE 30

TECHNOLOGY, *GERMANY*
The Germans have formed the first operational unit equipped with Messerschmitt Me 262 jet fighters.

▲ *Paratroopers belonging to the US 503rd Parachute Infantry Regiment land on Kamirir airstrip, Noemfoor, July 2, 1944.*

The unit will be deployed to France in the near future.
AIR WAR, *BRITAIN*
To date, 2000 German V1 "Flying Bombs" have been launched against England, mostly against London. In response, the British have increased the number of anti-aircraft guns, fighter aircraft, and barrage balloons.

JULY 2

ITALY, *TUSCANY*
The British XIII Corps takes the town of Foiano, northwest of Lake Trasimeno, thereby completing the breakthrough of the German Albert Line.

JULY 4

EASTERN FRONT, *BALTIC*
The Red Army offensive to clear the Baltic states begins. Three Soviet Fronts – 1st, 2nd, and 3rd Baltic – are to be used. The Baltic states are of major importance to Germany, as they are a major source of food and enable the Germans to blockade the Russian fleet and keep supply lanes to Sweden and Finland open.

JULY 7–9

PACIFIC, *MARIANAS*
The Japanese commander on Saipan, General Yoshitsugu Saito, launches a

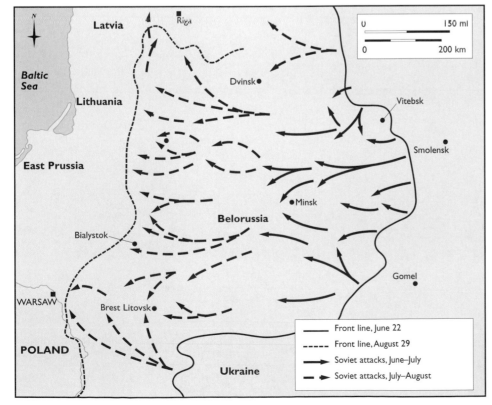

◄ *The Soviet offensive in Belorussia in mid-1944 shattered Army Group Center under a deluge of tanks and men.*

JULY 8

mass charge against the US 27th Infantry Division at Makunsho. Despite losing hundreds of men to US gunfire, the Japanese crash through the American lines. However, they soon lose their momentum and fail. Saito commits suicide and the island is declared secure on the 9th. At least 8000 Japanese defenders and civilians have committed suicide rather than surrender.

JULY 8

POLITICS, *HUNGARY*
With the Red Army fast approaching, Hungary's leader, Admiral Miklós Horthy, orders a halt to the deportation of Hungarian Jews to Auschwitz concentration camp.

JULY 11

POLITICS, *UNITED STATES*
President Franklin D. Roosevelt announces he will run for an unprecedented fourth term in the White House.

EASTERN FRONT, *BELORUSSIA*
The Minsk area falls to the Red Army. The Germans have lost over 70,000 men killed and 35,000 taken prisoner, and their Fourth Army has ceased to exist.

▶ *Same task, different island – flushing out Japanese defenders on Tinian, one of the Mariana Islands, with a pack howitzer.*

▲ *Admiral Miklós Horthy (center), regent of Hungary, who halted the deportation of Hungarian Jews to Auschwitz.*

JULY 15

EASTERN FRONT, *FINLAND*
The battle for the Karelian Isthmus ends with a defensive victory for Finland. Three Soviet armies make excellent early progress, but are unable to achieve the objectives laid down in their orders of June 21. The Soviet military leadership orders its troops in Finland to go over to the defensive on the 11th.

JULY 17

EASTERN FRONT, *UKRAINE*
Units of the Soviet First Guards Tank Army cross the Bug River into Poland.

JULY 18

FAR EAST, *BURMA*
The Japanese high command calls off Operation U-Go.

JULY 18–22

WESTERN FRONT, *FRANCE*
In the face of fanatical resistance, US troops enter St. Lô. The German 352nd Division is destroyed in the process. On the eastern sector of the front, the British and Canadians launch Operation Goodwood, a drive east of Caen to provoke heavier German concentrations in the area. The aim is to wear down German armor to such an extent that it is of no further value to them. The Allies lose over 100 Sherman tanks in the assault. By the 22nd, however, the British have cleared southern Caen.

JULY 19–21

PACIFIC, *MARIANAS*
US battleships begin the pre-invasion bombardment of Asan and Agat beaches on Guam, the most important island in the Marianas group. Two days later, troops of the 3rd Marine Division and 77th Infantry Division begin landing on the island. The Japanese fight back hard.

JULY 20

POLITICS, *GERMANY*
An attempt is made by German officers to assassinate Adolf Hitler. Count Schenk von Stauffenberg, chief-of-staff to General Friedrich Fromm, plants a bomb near Hitler in a conference room at the Nazi leader's East Prussian headquarters at Rastenburg. The bomb explodes at 1242 hours, after von Stauffenberg has left. The bomb fails to kill Hitler and the conspiracy falls apart. Josef Goebbels, Nazi minister for propaganda, acts quickly to convince the Berlin garrison that Hitler is still alive by linking them by telephone. Fromm, to allay suspicions of his involvement in the plot, has von Stauffenberg shot in the evening.

The failure of the plot results in the arrest, torture, and execution of dozens of suspects in the following months. Field Marshal Erwin Rommel is among the most notable of those senior military figures aware of the conspiracy.

JULY 21

POLITICS, *POLAND*
The Soviet-backed Polish Committee of National Liberation is formed.

JULY 23

ITALY, *TUSCANY*
After taking the vital port of Livorno on the 19th, the US 34th Division enters the town of Pisa.

JULY 25

WESTERN FRONT, *FRANCE*
Operation Cobra, the Allied breakout from Normandy, begins. Following a massive aerial bombardment, three infantry divisions of General J. Lawton Collins' US VII Corps open a breach in the German line between Marigny and St. Gilles, allowing the armor to get through. Within five days, the US spearhead reaches Avranches, turning the west flank of the German front.

JULY 25–29

PACIFIC, *MARIANAS*
A Japanese counterattack against the US 3rd Marine Division on Guam is defeated. The Japanese lose 19,500 dead, while US fatalities number 1744. On the 24th, the US 4th Marine Division lands on the island of Tinian.

JULY 27–30

EASTERN FRONT, *UKRAINE*
The Soviet 1st Ukrainian Front liberates Lvov, and goes on to establish

▲ *Hitler shows Mussolini his bomb-damaged conference room following the July assassination attempt.*

▼ *Field Marshal Erwin von Witzleben. Involved in the plot to kill Hitler, he was hanged with piano wire at Ploetzenzee.*

several bridgeheads on the Vistula River by the 30th.

JULY 30

WESTERN FRONT, *FRANCE*
Avranches falls to the US VIII Corps.

AUGUST 1

EASTERN FRONT, *POLAND*
The Warsaw uprising begins. Under the command of Lieutenant General Tadeusz Bor-Komorowski, 38,000 soldiers of the Polish Home Army battle with about the same number of German troops stationed in and around the city. Although the two sides are equal in number, the Germans are superior in weapons and can also call on tank and air support. The uprising is designed to free the city from German control and give the Polish government-in-exile in London some influence over the fate of Poland when the Red Army enters the city.
PACIFIC, *MARIANAS*
The battle for the island of Tinian ends. The entire Japanese garrison of 9000 men has been wiped out.

AUGUST 2

EASTERN FRONT, *POLAND*
The left wing of the Soviet 1st Belorussian Front establishes two bridgeheads across the Vistula River south of Warsaw.

AUGUST 3

FAR EAST, *BURMA*
The Japanese withdraw from Myitkyina following an 11-week blockade by Allied forces.

AUGUST 4

POLITICS, *FINLAND*
Marshal Karl von Mannerheim
succeeds Rysto Ryti as president of the
country. Mannerheim makes it clear to
the Germans that he is not bound by
Ryti's promises to them.

AUGUST 8

POLITICS, *GERMANY*
Eight German officers, including Field
Marshal Erwin von Witzleben, are
hanged at the Ploetzenzee prison in
Berlin for their part in the July Bomb
Plot against Hitler. They are hanged by
piano wire, their last moments
recorded on film for Adolf Hitler's
amusement. All the condemned go to
their deaths with dignity, despite their
callous treatment.

AUGUST 10

PACIFIC, *MARIANAS*
Organized Japanese resistance on
Guam ends, although it is 1960 before
the last Japanese soldier on the island
surrenders.

▲ *US forces in Paris after its liberation.
The German commander of the city chose
to ignore Hitler's order to destroy it.*

▶ *General Mark
Clark, commander
of the US Fifth Army
that took Rome.*

AUGUST 11

WESTERN FRONT, *FRANCE*
Operation Totalize, the
Canadian First Army's offensive toward Falaise, is called
off after failing to meet its
main objectives.

AUGUST 15

POLITICS, *SOVIET UNION*
Moscow announces that the
Polish Committee of National
Liberation is the official
body representing the Polish
nation and that de facto all
negotiations with the émigré
government in London are at
an end.

WESTERN FRONT, *FRANCE*
Units from the US VI Corps and the
French II Corps, together with para-
trooper support, launch the Allied inva-
sion of southern France, code-named
Operation Anvil.

EASTERN FRONT, *UKRAINE*
The Soviet 4th Ukrainian Front,
attacking to seize the passes across the
Carpathian Mountains, makes some
progress but fails to capture the passes
themselves.

AUGUST 19

WESTERN FRONT, *FRANCE*
Allied units have closed the Falaise
pocket two weeks after the Canadian
First Army launched Operation Totalize
to cut off the encircled German troops.
Some 30,000 German soldiers escape
from the pocket across the Seine River,
but an estimated 50,000 are captured
and another 10,000 killed. In the
pocket, which has been continually
strafed and bombed by Allied aircraft,
are hundreds of destroyed and abandoned German vehicles. Canadian,
British, and Polish forces coming from
the north link up with the US First
Army driving from Argentan.

AUGUST 23

POLITICS, *ROMANIA*
King Michael orders his forces to cease
fighting the Allies and has his pro-Axis
premier, Marshal Ion Antonescu,
dismissed. He announces that the
armistice terms have been accepted.

▲ *Members of the Polish Home Army march to battle as German forces squeeze the Polish-held areas in Warsaw.*

WESTERN FRONT, *FRANCE*
The US 36th Division takes Grenoble. General Dwight D. Eisenhower, Supreme Commander of the Allied Expeditionary Force, overrules General Bernard Montgomery, commander of the 21st Army Group, regarding the latter's plea for a concentrated thrust through the Low Countries into northern Germany. Eisenhower decides that after the capture of Antwerp – a port vital to the Allies – there will be an American assault toward the Saar by General George Patton's US Third Army.

AUGUST 25

POLITICS, *ROMANIA*
The former member of the Axis power bloc declares war on Germany.
WESTERN FRONT, *FRANCE*
The commander of the German garrison of Paris, General Dietrich von Choltitz, surrenders the city to Lieutenant Henri Karcher of the French 2nd Armored Division. Choltitz, who has 5000 men, 50 artillery pieces, and a company of tanks under his command, had been ordered by Hitler to ensure that "Paris [does] not fall into the hands of the enemy except as a heap of ruins." Some 500 Resistance members and 127 other civilians are killed in the fighting for the city.

AUGUST 25–26

WESTERN FRONT, *FRANCE*
The British XII and XXX Corps cross the Seine River.
ITALY, *ADRIATIC SECTOR*
The Allied assault on the Gothic Line begins. The German defense line is 200 miles (320 km) long and runs from the valley of the Magra River, south of La Spezia on the west coast, through the Apuan Mountains and the Apennines, ending in the valley of the Foglia River, and reaching the east coast between Pesaro and Cattolica. The assault is conducted by three corps – the British V, Canadian I, and Polish –

▼ *Reconnaissance vehicles of the British Guards Armored Division in Belgium during the Allied advance on Brussels.*

of the Eighth Army. The plan is to seize the Gemmano-Coriano Ridge complex, thereby unlocking the coastal "gate" and allowing Allied armor to break out to the plains of the Po Valley. However, German resistance is fierce.

AUGUST 27

FAR EAST, *BURMA*
The last of the Chindits are evacuated to India.

AUGUST 28

EASTERN FRONT, *POLAND*
The Polish Home Army continues to fight in Warsaw, but German air attacks and artillery fire are so heavy that the Poles have been forced into the sewers. Soviet leader Stalin has refused to help the freedom fighters, and so the Red Army awaits the outcome on the far side of the Vistula River.

AUGUST 30

EASTERN FRONT, *SLOVAKIA*
Elements of the armed forces and partisans in the Nazi puppet state stage an uprising against their German overlords as the Red Army approaches the country's eastern border.

AUGUST 31

WESTERN FRONT, *FRANCE*
The US Third Army spearheads an advance toward the Meuse River as the British XXX Corps secures all the main bridges over the Somme near Amiens.

SEPTEMBER 1–3

WESTERN FRONT, *FRANCE/BELGIUM*
The British Guards and 11th Armored Divisions, both part of the British XXX

SEPTEMBER 2

Corps, reach Arras and Aubigny. The Canadian II Corps, part of the Canadian First Army, liberates Dieppe.
 On the 2nd, XXX Corps is instructed to slow its advance and await a projected paratroop drop. With the cancellation of the drop, the advance resumes again. The 32nd and 5th Brigades of the Guards Armored Division begin a race for Brussels, which is won by the 32nd Brigade on the 3rd. On the same day, the British XII Corps is bogged down in fighting around the town of Béthune.

SEPTEMBER 2

POLITICS, *FINLAND*
Finland accepts the preliminary conditions for a peace treaty with the Soviet Union and breaks off diplomatic relations with Germany. The Soviet Union then agrees to an armistice.
EASTERN FRONT, *BULGARIA*
The Red Army reaches the Bulgarian border.

SEPTEMBER 3

WESTERN FRONT, *FRANCE/BELGIUM*
The US First Army takes Tournai and three German corps are crushed. The British Second Army liberates Brussels.

SEPTEMBER 4

WESTERN FRONT, *BELGIUM*
The British Second Army liberates the port of Antwerp.

ITALY, *ADRIATIC SECTOR*
The British Eighth Army fails to breach the Gemmano–Coriano Ridge on the Gothic Line. The ridge is the pivot point of the German Tenth Army's second line of defense, and as such it is strongly held, particularly by anti-tank weapons. An attack by the British 2nd Armored Brigade, for example, is defeated easily, with the British losing over half their tanks.

▼ *British Eighth Army artillery shells German strongpoints on the Gothic Line in Italy. But the initial assaults failed.*

▲ *Those Allied troops who liberated Brussels experienced something akin to a Roman triumph on the streets of the city.*

SEPTEMBER 5

WESTERN FRONT, *FRANCE*
US Third Army spearheads cross the Meuse River. General Karl von Rundstedt is made Commander-in-Chief West by Hitler with orders to counterattack the Allies and split their armies apart. However, his resources for such an undertaking are scant.
EASTERN FRONT, *BULGARIA*
After declaring war on the country, Red Army units invade rapidly and reach Turnu Severin. The Soviet Union's leadership is planning to occupy the entire Balkans.

SEPTEMBER 8

POLITICS, *BULGARIA*
Bulgaria declares war on Germany.
AIR WAR, *MANCHURIA*
China-based B-29 Superfortress bombers make their first daylight raid against Japanese industrial targets at Anshan.

SEPTEMBER 8–13

WESTERN FRONT, *BELGIUM/HOLLAND*
The British 50th Division crosses the Albert Canal at Gheel. On the 10th, the British Guards Armored Division advances to De Groot.

Three days later, the British 15th Division crosses the Meuse–Escaut Canal.

SEPTEMBER 8–25

EASTERN FRONT, *SLOVAKIA*

The Soviet 1st and 4th Ukrainian Fronts begin their attacks on the Dukla Pass, the key to the Carpathian Mountain barrier separating the Red Army from eastern Slovakia. It will take the Soviets until the end of November to clear the Carpathians.

SEPTEMBER 10–14

EASTERN FRONT, *POLAND*

Despite Stalin's refusal to aid the hard-pressed Warsaw insurgents, units of Marshal Konstantin Rokossovsky's 1st Belorussian Front attack Praga, the east bank quarter of the city. Fighting is savage, and it is not until the 14th that the area is freed from German control.

SEPTEMBER 15

EASTERN FRONT, *POLAND*

Units of the Soviet-raised First Polish Army cross the Vistula River and seize bridgeheads in Warsaw.

AIR WAR, *NORWAY*

Lancasters from 9 and 617 Squadrons of the RAF attack Germany's only remaining battleship – the *Tirpitz* – in Altenfiord. However, little damage is done, chiefly due to the effectiveness of the German smokescreens.

▲ *British paratroopers in action near Arnhem. The enemy is close, as indicated by the acute angle of the mortar tube.*

▼ *Allied vehicles rumble across the bridge at Nijmegen, Holland, during the disastrous Operation Market Garden.*

SEPTEMBER 17

WESTERN FRONT, *HOLLAND*

Operation Market Garden, General Bernard Montgomery's plan for an armored and airborne thrust across Holland to outflank the German defenses, begins. The British 1st Airborne Division lands near Arnhem, the US 101st Airborne Division near Eindhoven, the US 82nd Airborne Division near Grave and Nijmegen, while the British XXX Corps advances from the Dutch border. The 82nd lands without difficulty and takes the Maas and Maas–Waal Canal bridges, but then encounters heavy resistance at Nijmegen. The 101st Division also takes its bridges, but the British paratroopers discover their way to Arnhem is blocked by German units. Only one battalion, under Lieutenant Colonel John Frost, manages to reach the bridge, where it is quickly cut off.

SEPTEMBER 19–21

WESTERN FRONT, *HOLLAND*

Forward elements of the British XXX Corps reach US paratroopers at Eindhoven, but at Arnhem all attempts to break through to the troops fail. On the 20th, the bridge at Nijmegen is captured by a combined force drawn from the US 82nd Airborne Division and the British XXX Corps. The next day, the British troops at Arnhem are

▲ A PIAT antitank weapon waits for enemy armor on the outskirts of Arnhem as the Germans close in on the British.

Canadian II Corps; its garrison of 20,000 men is taken into captivity.

SEPTEMBER 22–25

WESTERN FRONT, *HOLLAND*
Outside Arnhem, the British XXX Corps' advance is slowed by German resistance. The Polish Brigade drops south of the Neder Rijn near Driel. On the 23rd, attempts by the Poles and advance troops of XXX Corps to cross the river are driven back, and so the evacuation of the surviving paratroopers begins two days later, leaving 2500 of their dead comrades behind.

SEPTEMBER 23

AIR WAR, *GERMANY*
The RAF makes a night precision raid on the Dortmund to Ems Canal, the inland waterway that links the Ruhr with other industrial centers. A total of 141 aircraft are involved, the canal is breached, and a section drained. The RAF loses 14 bombers.

SEPTEMBER 23–30

WESTERN FRONT, *FRANCE*
The Canadian 3rd Division invests the port of Calais, which is defended by

overwhelmed. The remainder form a defensive perimeter on the northern bank of the Neder Rijn, around the village of Oosterbeek.

SEPTEMBER 21

POLITICS, *YUGOSLAVIA*
The partisan chief Marshal Tito meets the Soviet leader Joseph Stalin. They reach agreement on the "temporary entry of the Red Army into Yugoslavia."
ITALY, *ADRIATIC SECTOR*
The Eighth Army takes Rimini after a week of heavy fighting. Since the beginning of its offensive against the Gothic Line, it has lost 14,000 men killed, wounded, and missing, plus 200 tanks. The Italian campaign has not lived up to being the "soft underbelly of Europe." A more accurate description would be "tough old gut."

SEPTEMBER 22

WESTERN FRONT, *FRANCE*
Boulogne surrenders to the

▼ Sherman tanks of the British Eighth Army on the move near Rimini during the grim battle of attrition against the Gothic Line.

▲ Beaten but defiant, these British paratroopers are led into captivity at the end of Market Garden – 2500 of their comrades were killed in the operation.

7500 men. Following heavy artillery and bomber attacks, and the use of specialized armor, Calais surrenders on the 30th.

OCTOBER 2

EASTERN FRONT, *POLAND*
After a bitter two-month battle, the last Poles in Warsaw surrender. The Germans evacuate the entire remaining population and begin the systematic destruction of anything left standing. Polish deaths number 150,000, while the German commander, SS General Erich von dem Bach-Zelewski, claims he has lost 26,000 men.

OCTOBER 3

AIR WAR, *BRITAIN*
The German bombardment of Britain with V2 long-range heavy rockets has resumed from new launch sites dotted across Holland.

▶ A British paratrooper in cover on the outskirts of Oosterbeek. The failure of XXX Corps to cross the Neder Rijn doomed the airborne operation.

OCTOBER 4

MEDITERRANEAN, *GREECE*

Determined to prevent a communist takeover in Greece, Winston Churchill launches Operation Manna. British troops land at Patrai in the Peloponnese as German forces pull back.

OCTOBER 9

WESTERN FRONT, *BELGIUM*

Although the Allies captured Antwerp on September 4, they have not been able to use the great port because there are German units on both sides of the Scheldt estuary. Therefore, the Canadian First Army commences operations to eradicate the enemy presence in this area.

PACIFIC, *IWO JIMA*

Admiral Chester W. Nimitz, commander of all Allied forces in the Central Pacific, informs Lieutenant General Holland M. "Howling Mad" Smith, one of the leading exponents of amphibious warfare and commander of all US Marines in the Pacific, that the island of Iwo Jima will be his next target and that Smith will lead

▲ Landing craft and vehicles of the Canadian First Army engaged in clearing the Scheldt estuary near Antwerp.

▼ A German V2 rocket is readied for launch from a site in Holland. The only way to reduce the damage caused by these weapons was to bomb their launch sites and their construction factories.

the invasion with three US Marine divisions. The island is within bombing range of the Japanese mainland.

OCTOBER 10-29

EASTERN FRONT, *HUNGARY*
A massive tank battle rages around Drebrecan between two panzer divisions of Germany's Army Group Southern Ukraine, commanded by General Johannes Friessneer. The German forces have cut off three Soviet tank corps of Marshal Rodion Malinovsky's 2nd Ukrainian Front. The Soviets lose many tanks in the initial German attacks, but fresh Soviet units tip the scales against the Germans, who do not have the forces to fight attritional battles. Farther south, the German Army Group E leaves Greece.

OCTOBER 11-19

BALKANS, *YUGOSLAVIA*
The Red Army joins with the Yugoslavian First Army in the drive to Belgrade, which is abandoned by the Germans on the 19th.

OCTOBER 14

POLITICS, *GERMANY*
Field Marshal Erwin Rommel commits suicide with poison. Implicated in the July assassination plot against Hitler, he has killed himself, under pressure, to save his family from arrest. He is to be given a state funeral as part of the charade to maintain the illusion that he was an uncompromising Nazi.

▲ *A knocked-out Joseph Stalin tank at Drebrecan, the site of a massive tank battle and a German defeat.*

▼ *General Douglas MacArthur (second from left) wades ashore in the Philippines, keeping his promise "I shall return."*

OCTOBER 20

BALKANS, *YUGOSLAVIA*
The 1st Proletarian Division of Marshal Tito's Army of Liberation captures Belgrade.

PACIFIC, *PHILIPPINES*
As the US Sixth Army lands on Leyte Island, General Douglas MacArthur wades ashore and keeps a promise he made two years earlier: "I shall return." By the evening 10,000 US troops are dug in around Leyte's capital, Tacloban, and Dulag to the south.

OCTOBER 21

WESTERN FRONT, *GERMANY*
The city of Aachen surrenders to US forces following a 10-day siege.

OCTOBER 23-26

PACIFIC, *PHILIPPINES*
Following the US landings on Leyte, the Japanese put in motion their Sho Plan, in which a part of the Combined Fleet is used to decoy the US carrier force while the remainder concentrates against the landing area and attempts to destroy the amphibious armada. The resulting naval battle of Leyte Gulf has four phases: the Battle of the Sibuyan Sea, the Battle of the Surigao Strait, the Battle of Samar, and

DECISIVE WEAPONS

KAMIKAZE

Kamikaze, meaning "Divine Wind," was a suicide tactic employed by the Japanese military to destroy US military shipping by crashing explosive-filled aircraft into vessels. The cult of the kamikazes was influenced by the Bushido code of conduct based on spiritualism under the influence of Buddhism, which emphasized both bravery and conscience.

The Battle of Leyte Gulf in October 1944 saw the beginning of the Kamikaze Corps, and at the end of the war Japan had over 5000 aircraft ready for suicide missions. Kamikaze pilots endeavored to hit the deck of their target to cause maximum damage (against carriers the best point of aim was the central elevator). The overall military effect of the kamikazes was limited: during the Okinawa battles, for example, of the 1900 suicide sorties made, only 14 percent were effective.

The damaged hangar of USS Sangamon *following a kamikaze attack by just one aircraft.*

the Battle of Cape Engano. The result is that the Japanese Combined Fleet is finished as a fighting force, not least because its losses in trained pilots are irreplaceable. It loses 500 aircraft, four carriers, three battleships, six heavy and four light cruisers, 11 destroyers, and a submarine, while every other ship engaged is damaged. US losses are 200 aircraft, one light carrier, two escort carriers, two destroyers, and one destroyer-escort.

OCTOBER 31

EASTERN FRONT, *BALTIC*
The Soviet 1st Baltic Front isolates the remnants of Army Group North in the Courland Peninsula.

NOVEMBER 7

ESPIONAGE, *JAPAN*
The Japanese hang the spy Richard Sorge at Sugamo Prison, Tokyo. He has been working for eight years as the Tokyo correspondent for a German newspaper, and during this time has sent the Soviet Union detailed information concerning German and Japanese plans, including the attack on the Soviet Union in 1941.

NOVEMBER 8

WESTERN FRONT, *BELGIUM*
The Canadian First Army completes the clearing of the Scheldt estuary. It takes 41,000 prisoners during the operation at a cost of 12,873 men killed, wounded, and missing.

NOVEMBER 9

WESTERN FRONT, *FRANCE*
General George Patton's US Third Army (500,000 men and 500 tanks) crosses the Moselle River on a broad front toward the heart of the Reich.

▲ *The US Navy bombards the island of Iwo Jima to soften up the defenses prior to an amphibious landing.*

NOVEMBER 11–12

PACIFIC, *IWO JIMA*
The US Navy bombards the Japanese-held island for the first time.

NOVEMBER 12

AIR WAR, *NORWAY*
RAF Lancaster bombers from 9 and 617 Squadrons sink the German battleship *Tirpitz* in Altenfiord, killing 1100 of its crew when the ship capsizes.

NOVEMBER 24

AIR WAR, *JAPAN*
American B-29 Superfortress bombers mount their first raid against Tokyo from the Mariana Islands.

DECEMBER 4

FAR EAST, *BURMA*
General William Slim, commander of the British Fourteenth Army, begins the destruction of Japanese forces in Burma. The British IV and XXXIII Corps begin the offensive, heading for the Japanese airfields at Yeu and Shwebo. The Japanese Fifteenth Army, commanded by General Shihachi

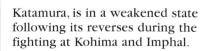

Katamura, is in a weakened state following its reverses during the fighting at Kohima and Imphal.

DECEMBER 5–7

PACIFIC, *PHILIPPINES*
The final US offensive on Leyte begins with a drive by the X Corps into the northern Ormoc Valley, with simultaneous assaults by the XIV Corps in central and southwestern Leyte. On the 7th, the 77th Division lands virtually unopposed below Ormoc. Japanese forces are pressed into the Ormoc Valley, and are under intense artillery and aerial attack.

HOME FRONT, *GERMANY*
The Nazi women's leader, Gertrud Scholtz-Klink, appeals for all women over 18 to volunteer for service in the army and air force to release men for the front.

DECEMBER 8

PACIFIC, *IWO JIMA*
The US Air Force begins a 72-day bombardment of Iwo Jima, the longest and heaviest of the Pacific war, to pave the way for an amphibious assault.

DECEMBER 15

PACIFIC, *PHILIPPINES*
As part of General Douglas MacArthur's second phase of the invasion of the Philippines, the US 24th Division lands on the island of Mindoro.

FAR EAST, *BURMA*
The British 19th and 36th Divisions meet at Indaw, and set up a continuous front against the Japanese in northern Burma.

▲ *After spending most of the war in Norwegian coastal waters, the* Tirpitz *was finally sunk on November 12.*

▶ *British troops of IV Corps move against the Japanese Fifteenth Army after Kohima and Imphal.*

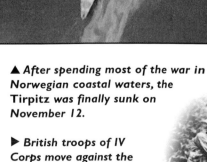

DECEMBER 16–22

▲ *A barrage of rockets is unleashed against enemy beach defenses as the first wave of US assault units heads for Mindoro Island in the Philippines.*

DECEMBER 16–22

WESTERN FRONT, *ARDENNES*
Hitler launches Operation Watch on the Rhine, his attempt to break through the US VIII Corps on the Ardennes front, reach the Meuse River, and capture Antwerp, thereby splitting the Allies in two. The German units – 200,000 men – form Army Group B under the overall command of Field Marshal Gerd von Rundstedt. This force comprises the Sixth SS Panzer Army, Fifth Panzer Army, and Seventh Army. US forces total 80,000 men.

Surprise is total and there is dense cloud and fog, which negates Allied air superiority, but the Germans fail to take the towns of St. Vith and Bastogne immediately, which narrows their attack front. On the 17th, troops of SS Lieutenant Colonel Joachim Peiper's battlegroup murder 71 American prisoners of war at Malmédy in Belgium, leaving their bodies in a field.

By the 22nd, the Americans, having lost 8000 of 22,000 men at St. Vith, pull back from the town, but the men of the 28th Infantry, 10th, and 101st Airborne Divisions continue to hold out stubbornly in Bastogne against one infantry and two panzer divisions. On the same day the Germans mount their last attempt to reach the Meuse.

As part of their sabotage operations, the Germans are using English-speaking commandos dressed in US uniforms to spread confusion, especially at road junctions and on bridges. However, measures have been taken to defeat these infiltrators, many of whom are later shot as spies.

DECEMBER 20

MEDITERRANEAN, *GREECE*
British tanks and armored cars have lifted the siege of Kifissia RAF base by ELAS rebels (the National Liberation Army – the military wing of the country's communist party).

DECEMBER 24

AIR WAR, *BELGIUM*
The first jet bomber operation takes

162

south of the German "bulge" into the Ardennes. The US Third Army's 4th Armored Division relieves Bastogne as Hitler is informed by his generals that Antwerp can no longer be reached by his forces. The only hope of salvaging any sort of victory in the Ardennes is to swing the Fifth and Sixth Panzer Armies north to cross the Meuse west of Liège and come in behind Aachen. However, this presupposes the capture of Bastogne and an attack from the north to link with the panzers – both are increasingly unlikely.

DECEMBER 30

WESTERN FRONT, *ARDENNES*
At Bastogne, General George Patton, his forces swollen to six divisions, resumes his attack northeast toward Houffalize. At the same time, General Hasso von Manteuffel, commander of the German Fifth Panzer Army, launches another major attempt to cut the corridor into Bastogne and take the town. The fighting is intense, but Patton's forces stand firm and defeat the German attack.

DECEMBER 31

POLITICS, *HUNGARY*
The Provisional National Government of Hungary, set up under Soviet control in the city of Drebrecan, declares war on Germany.

▲ *Aided by secrecy and poor weather, the initial assaults of the German Ardennes offensive met with success.*

▼ *Abandoned German Panther and Panzer IV tanks in the Ardennes in late December. Shortages of fuel, stubborn defense, and Allied air attacks contributed to the failure of the offensive.*

place when twin-engined German Arado 234B bombers raid a factory and marshaling yards. The raid is led by Captain Dieter Lukesch.

DECEMBER 26

WESTERN FRONT, *ARDENNES*
The US First and Third Armies launch counterattacks against the north and

1945

In this final year of the war, Germany and Japan were defeated by a relentless tide of aircraft, tanks, ships, and men. Their cities were devastated by fleets of bombers, their armies were encircled and then annihilated, and their merchant and naval fleets were either sunk or trapped in port. There was no match for the economic might of the United States and the numerical superiority of the Soviet Union. Atomic bombs finally ended the war against Japan.

JANUARY 1

EASTERN FRONT,
CZECHOSLOVAKIA
The Soviet 2nd and 4th Ukrainian Fronts begin an offensive against the German Army Group Center in Czecho-slovakia. The German-held area contains the last foreign industrial resources under the control of the Third Reich. The Soviet fronts between them have 853,000 men, 9986 guns, 590 tanks, and 1400 combat aircraft. German forces total 550,000 men, 5000 guns, and 700 combat aircraft. Despite German fortifi-cations and resistance, the Red Army makes good progress.

JANUARY 1–21

WESTERN FRONT, *FRANCE*
In a follow up to the attack in the Ardennes sector, General Johannes von Blaskowitz's Army Group G attacks the US Seventh Army in Alsace and Lorraine, forming the so-called Colmar Pocket. The Americans retreat, although General Dwight D. Eisen-hower, commander-in-chief of Allied forces in Europe, orders Strasbourg to be held after the leader of the Free French, General Charles de Gaulle, expresses concern that the loss of the city would affect French morale. The fighting

▶ Chinese soldiers of the Northern Combat Area Command march to the front in northern Burma.

▲ *US troops and vehicles in Bastogne, which resisted all German assaults in December 1944 and January 1945.*

▼ *The US 7th Fleet prior to the assault on Luzon. The Consolidated Catalinas are from the Air-Sea Rescue Squadron.*

JANUARY 3–4

PACIFIC, *RYUKYUS*

The US 3rd Fleet attacks Japanese targets on Formosa, destroying 100 enemy aircraft.

JANUARY 3–16

WESTERN FRONT, *ARDENNES*

The last German attack against Bastogne is defeated. The Allied counterattack begins: on the northern flank the US First Army attacks the northern sector of the "bulge," while the southern sector is assaulted by the US Third Army. In the "bulge" itself, Hitler orders a German withdrawal to Houffalize on the 8th. However, in the face of overwhelming Allied superiority in men and hardware the Germans are forced to retreat farther east, and the US First and Third Armies link up at Houffalize on the 16th.

JANUARY 4

FAR EAST, *BURMA*

Units of General William Slim's British Fourteenth Army make an unopposed landing on the island of Akyab, securing the port and the airfield.

JANUARY 4–6

PACIFIC, *PHILIPPINES*

Prior to the landings on Luzon, the Japanese launch a series of kamikaze attacks on ships of the US 7th Fleet. Over 1000 Americans and Australians are killed in the suicide attacks, a minesweeper is sunk, and more than 30 other vessels are damaged.

JANUARY 5

AIR WAR, *BELGIUM/HOLLAND*

The Luftwaffe launches Operation Bodenplatte in support of the

is bitter. It costs the US 15,600 casualties, and the Germans, 25,000.

JANUARY 1–27

FAR EAST, *BURMA*

The Chinese units of Lieutenant General Daniel Sultan's Northern Combat Area Command and Marshal Wei Lihuang's Y Force link up in northern Burma in the face of significant resistance from the Japanese 56th Division.

JANUARY 2

TECHNOLOGY, *UNITED STATES*

An American Sikorsky helicopter is used in convoy escort duties for the first time.

▲ *Following their unopposed landing, troops of the US Sixth Army examine a knocked-out Japanese tank on Luzon.*

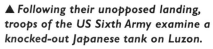

Ardennes offensive with 1035 fighters and bombers attacking Allied airfields in Belgium and southern Holland. The Germans destroy 156 Allied aircraft but lose 277 of their own, losses the Luftwaffe cannot make good. It is the last major German air attack.

JANUARY 7

EASTERN FRONT, *HUNGARY*
German forces capture Esztergom, northwest of Budapest, a Nazi National Redoubt, in their attempt to relieve the garrison in the capital.

JANUARY 9

PACIFIC, *PHILIPPINES*
Preceded by a heavy bombardment, units of the US Sixth Army, commanded by Lieutenant General Walter Krueger, make unopposed amphibious landings on Luzon.

JANUARY 10-February 10

EASTERN FRONT,
CZECHOSLOVAKIA
With the Red Army on their soil, Czech partisans begin to attack German units and supply lines.

JANUARY 12-17

EASTERN FRONT, *POLAND*
The Red Army begins its Vistula–Oder offensive. Soviet forces total over two million men: Marshal Georgi Zhukov's 1st Belorussian Front, Marshal Ivan Konev's 1st Ukrainian Front, and General Ivan Petrov's 4th Ukrainian Front. In addition, Marshal Konstantin Rokossovsky's 2nd Belorussian Front and General Ivan Chernyakhovsky's 3rd Belorussian Front are providing tactical and strategic cooperation. The Soviets make excellent progress, and by the 17th, Zhukov's Second Guards Tank Army has reached Sochaczew. To the north, the 1st Baltic, 2nd Belorussian, and 3rd Belorussian Fronts launch an offensive into East Prussia on the 13th.

JANUARY 14

FAR EAST, *BURMA*
The 19th Division, part of Lieutenant General William Slim's British Fourteenth Army, crosses the Irrawaddy River at Kyaukmyaung but is then violently attacked by Japanese troops holding the line of the waterway. Forced back by hordes of infantry with fixed bayonets, the division manages to hold the bridgehead in the face of the fierce onslaught.

JANUARY 15-26

WESTERN FRONT, *GERMANY*
After the containment of the German Ardennes offensive, the Allies launch a large counterattack against the Germans. In the north, Field Marshal Bernard Montgomery's British 21st Army Group presses into the Roermond area, while farther south General Omar Bradley's US 12th Army Group approaches the upper Roer River.

JANUARY 16

FAR EAST, *BURMA*
In the north of the country, General Daniel Sultan's Chinese New First Army occupies Namhkan. The last Japanese positions threatening the Burma Road have been eradicated.

JANUARY 18-27

EASTERN FRONT, *HUNGARY*
The German IV SS Panzer Corps launches an

▶ *One of the hundreds of Japanese soldiers killed in and around the Irrawaddy River, Burma.*

KEY PERSONALITIES

MARSHAL GEORGI ZHUKOV

Georgi Zhukov (1896–1974) was born into a peasant family and conscripted into the Imperial Russian Army in 1915. After fighting in World War I, he joined the Red Army in October 1918. He studied at the Frunze Military Academy (1928–31), and in 1938 was appointed deputy commander of the Belorussian Military District. Apparently earmarked for execution in the Stalinist purges, he escaped with his life due to an administrative error.

Zhukov's generalship skills first came to the fore in 1939, when he led the Soviet 1st Army Group to a decisive victory over the Japanese at the Khalka River (the so-called "Nomonhan Incident" over a disputed frontier in Manchuria). Following the German invasion of the Soviet Union in June 1941, Zhukov held a variety of staff positions and field commands, repulsing the enemy from Moscow in late 1941, having a hand in the great Soviet victories at Stalingrad and Kursk, and capturing Berlin in 1945. The victory at Stalingrad was particularly impressive, as the German Sixth Army had more men than Zhukov's forces. He used his units to achieve a crushing superiority over weaker Romanian armies along the front on both flanks of the Sixth Army. Once they had been smashed, he cut off the German forces in the Stalingrad area.

Zhukov was a forceful commander who possessed outstanding tactical and strategic ability – qualities that made his superiors view him as a potential threat. The fact that as a general he never lost a single battle is testament to his attributes as a military leader.

offensive to relieve Budapest. In the face of Soviet resistance, it reaches the Vali River on the 22nd, only 15 miles (24 km) southwest of the city. However, the momentum of the attack had been halted by the 25th, and two days later the Red Army counterattacks with 12 rifle divisions and strong armored support, effectively ending the German Budapest relief operation.

JANUARY 18–FEBRUARY 3

FAR EAST, *BURMA*
A vicious battle develops at Namhpakka between the Japanese 56th Division, which is

▲ *As the Red Army steamroller gathers momentum, Estonian coastguards fire a salute to welcome the Soviets.*

retreating to Lashio, and the American Mars Brigade.

JANUARY 19

EASTERN FRONT, *POLAND*
Following heavy fighting, units of the 1st Ukrainian Front liberate Cracow, the former capital of Poland. The German Third and Fourth Panzer Armies are now isolated in East Prussia, and the German front is falling apart in the face of immense pressure.

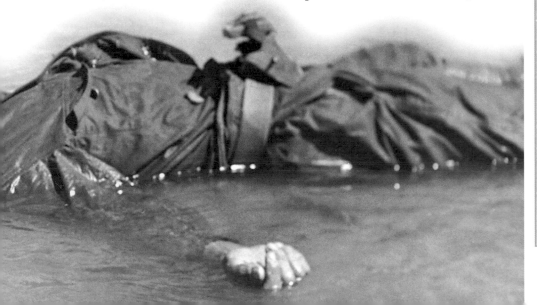

JANUARY 21

JANUARY 21

FAR EAST, *BURMA*

The island of Ramree is invaded by the British 71st Brigade. Japanese resistance is virtually non-existent, although it stiffens as Allied troops push farther inland. The island is not cleared until the middle of February, by which time General William Slim has an invaluable base for future long-range operations against Rangoon.

JANUARY 23

EASTERN FRONT, *EAST PRUSSIA*

The Soviet 2nd Belorussian Front cuts all road and rail crossings across the Vistula River, isolating German units on the east bank.

EASTERN FRONT, *POLAND*

The Soviet Second Guards Tank Army, part of the 1st Belorussian Front, storms the fortified town of Bromberg, an important strongpoint in the German Poznan Line.

JANUARY 27

EASTERN FRONT, *POLAND*

The Red Army liberates the Nazi death camp at Auschwitz. The SS has evacuated the camp nine days previously, taking 20,000 weak inmates with them. Those left number a few hundred disease-ridden inmates in the camp's hospital block.

FAR EAST, *BURMA*

Units of the Allied Y Force, pushing across the Shweli River at Wanting,

▼ *British troops carry a wounded comrade to a dressing station near Myitson, Burma.*

reopen the Burma Road supply route into China.

JANUARY 28

WESTERN FRONT, *ARDENNES*

The last vestiges of the German "bulge" in the Ardennes are wiped out. The total cost to the Germans in manpower for their Ardennes offensive has been 100,000 killed, wounded, and captured. The Americans have lost 81,000 killed, wounded, or captured, and the British 1400. Both sides have lost heavily in hardware – up to 800 tanks on each side. The Germans have also lost around 1000 aircraft.

▲ *German prisoners taken during the Ardennes offensive. The Wehrmacht lost over 100,000 men and 800 precious tanks.*

However, whereas the Americans can make good their losses in just a few weeks, for the Germans the military losses are irreplaceable.

JANUARY 28–FEBRUARY 1

WESTERN FRONT, *ARDENNES*

Two corps of General Courtney Hodges' US First Army and one from General George Patton's US Third Army try to penetrate the German defenses

northeast of St. Vith, which lies astride the Losheim Gap. Snow and ice inhibit progress, and the Germans manage to fight back hard, thereby slowing the rate of the US advance.

▼ *As fighting rages in and around Manila, the capital of the Philippines, refugees pour out of the city. This bridge was built by US engineers.*

JANUARY 29

PACIFIC, *PHILIPPINES*
Major General Charles Hall's US XI Corps lands unopposed on the west coast of Luzon just to the north of the Bataan Peninsula.

JANUARY 30

EASTERN FRONT, *GERMANY*
The left wing of the 1st Ukrainian Front has reached the Oder River and some of its units have set up bridge-heads on the west bank. This ends one of the greatest strategic operations of the whole war.

The Red Army has advanced 355 miles (568 km), liberated all of Poland and a large part of Czechoslovakia, reached the Oder on a broad front, and is only 100 miles (160 km) from Berlin. In its offensive, it has inflicted losses of 500,000 dead, wounded, or captured on the Germans, and captured 1300 aircraft, 1400 tanks, and over 14,000 guns of all calibers.

JANUARY 31

PACIFIC, *PHILIPPINES*
Elements of the US 11th Airborne Division go ashore at Nasugbu Bay against light Japanese resistance. The US troops land just 50 miles (80 km) southwest of the capital Manila, which is their ultimate objective.

▲ *The destruction in Manila after the city fell to the US XIV Corps. The whole of the Japanese garrison was wiped out.*

JANUARY 31–FEBRUARY 21

FAR EAST, *BURMA*
The British 36th Division effects a crossing of the Shweli River at Myitson following a savage battle against the Japanese. The division's success threatens the Japanese northern approaches to the Mandalay Plain.

FEBRUARY 1

EASTERN FRONT, *EAST PRUSSIA*
The trapped German Fourth Army attempts to reach German-held Elbing but is halted by a Soviet counterattack.

FEBRUARY 3–MARCH 3

PACIFIC, *PHILIPPINES*
The US XIV Corps begins its attack against Manila, which is defended by 17,000 Japanese troops under Rear Admiral Sanji Iwabuchi. The garrison, after destroying the city (the "Rape of Manila"), is wiped out. US casualties total 1000 dead and 5500 wounded; 100,000 Filipino citizens are killed.

FEBRUARY 4–11

POLITICS, *ALLIES*
Marshal Joseph Stalin, President Franklin D. Roosevelt, and Prime

▲ *The "Big Three" at the Yalta Confer-ence, where the postwar division of Germany and Austria was agreed.*

Minister Winston Churchill meet at the Yalta Conference in the Crimea to discuss postwar Europe. The "Big Three" decide that Germany will be divided into four zones, administered by Britain, France, the United States, and the Soviet Union. An Allied Control Commission will be set up in Berlin, and Austria will also be divided into

four zones. The capital, Vienna, will be in the Soviet zone and will also have a four-power administration. The Soviet Union will declare war on Japan two months after the war in Europe has ended, while changes to Poland's borders will allow the Soviet Union to annex former Polish areas.

FEBRUARY 5

WESTERN FRONT, *FRANCE*
The German bridgehead on the west bank of the Rhine, south of Strasbourg

around the town of Colmar – the Colmar Pocket – is split by units of the French First Army attacking from the south and elements of the US Seventh Army advancing from the north. The elimination of the pocket is essential to the crossing of the Rhine.

FEBRUARY 8–24

EASTERN FRONT, *GERMANY*
Marshal Ivan Konev's 1st Ukrainian Front begins its offensive to disrupt German plans and establish an impregnable defense line along the southern Oder. By the 24th his forces have advanced 75 miles (120 km) and seized Lower Silesia, in addition to freeing 91,300 Soviet citizens and 22,500 other foreigners from German imprisonment.

FEBRUARY 9

WESTERN FRONT, *FRANCE*
Following Allied pressure against the Colmar Pocket, Field Marshal Gerd von Rundstedt, German commander-in-chief in the West, convinces Hitler to pull back the Nineteenth Army across the Rhine. The west bank of the river south of Strasbourg is now free of German troops.

FEBRUARY 10

EASTERN FRONT, *POLAND*
The Soviet 2nd Belorussian Front launches an offensive in the region of Grudziadz and Sepolno but runs into determined resistance from the German Second Army. Soviet progress is very slow.

◄ *German rockets scream through the air as the Second Army tries to halt the Soviet 2nd Belorussian Front in Poland.*

▼ *Women help clear rubble from the ruins of the Catholic cathedral in Dresden after the Allied air raids against the city.*

suburbs. The bombing triggers the worst firestorm of the war, in which at least 50,000 people are killed. The raid is controversial, as the city has negligible strategic value, is virtually undefended, and is crammed with refugees. The next morning, the city is bombed again by 400 aircraft of the US 8th Army Air Force.

FEBRUARY 14

EASTERN FRONT, *EAST PRUSSIA*

As a result of the Red Army's advance, over half of the 2.3 million population of East Prussia have fled west. Some have been taken out by boat, although most have walked or made their way by horse and wagon. Thousands have died from either cold or exhaustion, or in Soviet air and artillery attacks.

FEBRUARY 16–28

PACIFIC, *PHILIPPINES*

US forces begin to clear the Japanese from the entrance to Manila Bay, Luzon. The peninsula of Bataan falls relatively easily, though Corregidor proves a harder nut to crack. The assault begins on the 16th with a battalion of US paratroopers dropping on the southwest heights of the island. Simultaneously, an amphibious assault by a battalion of infantry takes place on the southern shore. By the evening of the 26th, almost the whole island is in US hands. It is declared secure on the 28th. The Japanese garrison refuses to surrender, and is virtually wiped out in the fighting.

FEBRUARY 11

EASTERN FRONT, *HUNGARY*

The trapped Axis garrison in Budapest attempts to break through the Soviet lines. However, of the nearly 30,000 Germans and Hungarians, fewer than 700 are able to escape.

FEBRUARY 13–14

AIR WAR, *GERMANY*

The RAF mounts a night raid on Dresden. The 805 bombers inflict massive damage on the city's old town and inner

▲ *Boeing B-17 Flying Fortress bombers of the US 8th Army Air Force unleash death and destruction on Dresden.*

▼ *American paratroopers in action on Corregidor during the operations to clear the entrance to Manila Bay.*

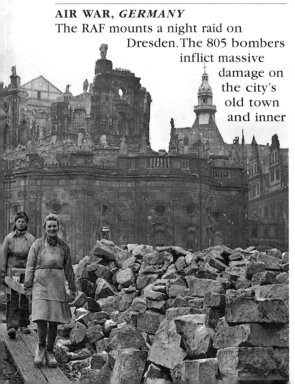

FEBRUARY 16

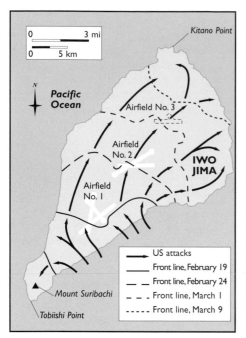

▲ *US Marines head for the beaches of Iwo Jima and one of the bloodiest battles in their Pacific War. Conquering the island required the destruction of the garrison.*

▲ *The conquest of Iwo Jima was a tough battle, especially the agonizing drive to the north against a fanatical enemy.*

FEBRUARY 16

PACIFIC, *IWO JIMA*

The US Navy begins a three-day concentrated bombardment of Iwo Jima. The island has to be taken for four reasons: the unescorted US bombers flying from the Marianas to Japan are suffering heavy losses, and, therefore, airfields closer to Japan are needed for fighter escorts; Iwo Jima has two air bases and is only three hours' flying time from Tokyo; Iwo

Jima is prewar Japanese territory, whose loss would be a severe blow to the homeland; and it is a key link in the air defenses of the Marianas.

FEBRUARY 17

PACIFIC, *IWO JIMA*

Under the command of Lieutenant General Holland M. Smith, the US 4th and 5th Marine Divisions land. Resistance is at first light, but then the attackers are hit by intense artillery and small-arms fire from the 21,000-man Japanese garrison. However, despite casualties, the Americans have 30,000 men on the island by the end of the day.

FEBRUARY 21

WESTERN FRONT, *GERMANY*

The Canadian First Army takes Goch, which ends Operation Veritable, an offensive from the Nijmegen area between the Rhine and the Maas Rivers.

FAR EAST, *BURMA*

General William Slim's British Fourteenth Army begins the reconquest of

▶ *Troops of Slim's army wade across the Irrawaddy in the drive toward Mandalay.*

◀ *Lieutenant General Holland M. Smith, who commanded the US forces on Iwo Jima.*

central Burma. Breaking out of the Irrawaddy bridgeheads, columns are directed to Mandalay, Burma's second city, and the important rail and road communications center at Meiktila.

In northern Burma, the British 36th Division breaks through Japanese positions at Myitson after a vicious three-week battle. Japanese forces are now on the retreat in the area.

FEBRUARY 23

WESTERN FRONT, *GERMANY*

The US First and Ninth Armies launch Operation Grenade, the crossing of the Roer River, and head to the Rhine. Preceded by a barrage from over 1000

that only those states that declare war before March 1 will be invited to a conference in San Francisco on the proposed postwar United Nations.

WESTERN FRONT, *GERMANY*

The US First Army begins its drive to the Rhine River, spearheaded by the VII Corps.

PACIFIC, *PHILIPPINES*

A regiment of the US 41st Division captures the island of Palawan.

MARCH 1

EASTERN FRONT, *GERMANY*

Marshal Georgi Zhukov's 1st Belorussian Front begins an offensive to destroy the German Third Panzer Army – which has 203,000 men, 700 tanks, 2500 guns, and 100 coastal artillery and fixed anti-aircraft guns – as part of the Red Army's effort to secure its flanks prior to the assault on Berlin itself.

MARCH 3

WESTERN FRONT, *FRANCE*

In snow and freezing rain, General George Patton unleashes his US Third Army over the Kyll River toward the

guns, four infantry divisions cross the river in the face of sporadic resistance. German reserves have been committed to halt Operation Veritable farther north. By the end of the day, 28 infantry battalions have crossed the river.

PACIFIC, *IWO JIMA*

US Marines raise the American flag on the summit of Mount Suribachi in the south of the island. The US Marines now have to turn north to clear the rest of the island.

FEBRUARY 25

PACIFIC, *IWO JIMA*

As the fighting on Iwo Jima becomes more intense, the US 3rd Marine Division is committed to the battle.

FEBRUARY 28

POLITICS, *SAUDI ARABIA*

Following the example of Syria on the 26th, Saudi Arabia declares war on Germany. The rush to join the Allies in part stems from the announcement

▼ *General George Patton's US Third Army on the move toward the Rhine River at the beginning of March.*

MARCH 4

Rhine. The attack is spearheaded by the VIII and XII Corps, which make good progress.

EASTERN FRONT, *GERMANY*
In an effort to try to recapture the lost defenses on the Oder River, the German Fourth Panzer Army counterattacks from the Lauban area toward Glogau. However, strong Soviet entrenched positions stop the attack in its tracks.

▲ *A US B-29 Superfortress bomber near Tokyo, having flown from Iwo Jima.*

FAR EAST, *BURMA*
General David Cowan's 17th Indian Division and 255th Indian Tank Brigade take the communications center of Meiktila after heavy fighting.

MARCH 4

PACIFIC, *IWO JIMA*
The first US B-29 Superfortress bomber lands on the island.

MARCH 6

EASTERN FRONT, *HUNGARY*
The Germans launch Operation Spring Awakening, designed to secure the Nagykanizsa oil fields, retake Budapest, and win a prestigious victory on the Eastern Front. The Sixth SS Panzer and Second Panzer Armies make good initial progress despite very poor weather conditions.

MARCH 7

POLITICS, *YUGOSLAVIA*
Marshal Tito forms a provisional government in which he accepts representatives of the former royalist government-in-exile. This is a temporary measure, as he intends to retain full control of the government for the Communist Party, which he believes the population will accept without question as a result of partisan successes during the war.

WESTERN FRONT, *GERMANY*
Units of the US First Army capture the Ludendorff bridge over the Rhine River at Remagen. The bridge, having withstood bombs, demolition, heavy usage, and artillery shells, collapses into the river 10 days later.

MARCH 10

WESTERN FRONT, *GERMANY*
Field Marshal Bernard Montgomery's 21st Army Group completes the conquest of the area west of the Rhine River. The group has lost 22,934 casualties, although the Germans have suffered casualties totaling 90,000 men defending the area immediately west of the Ruhr.

AIR WAR, *JAPAN*
The first American fire raid on Japan, against Tokyo, burns out over 16 square miles (25.6 sq km) of the city and kills 100,000 people.

MARCH 14

WESTERN FRONT, *GERMANY*
General George Patton's US Third Army crosses the lower Moselle River to cut behind the German Siegfried Line defensive system.

MARCH 16

EASTERN FRONT, *HUNGARY*
Marshal Fedor Tolbukhin's 3rd Ukrainian Front commences the Red Army's counterattack against Operation Spring Awakening on the front between Lake Velencei and Bicske. The German IV SS Panzer Corps holds in the face of overwhelming superiority in tanks and men, but the Hungarian Third Army on the left collapses.

PACIFIC, *IWO JIMA*
The island of Iwo Jima is declared secure by the Americans following 26 days of combat. They have lost 6821 soldiers and sailors dead, while of the 21,000 Japanese garrison, only 1083 are taken prisoner. The rest have been killed or have committed suicide.

Japanese evacuate the fort on the 19th – Mandalay is in British hands.

MARCH 18

PACIFIC, *PHILIPPINES*

In the island-hopping campaign in the theater, the US 40th Division lands on Panay, secures it, and then moves on to clear nearby Guimaras Island.

MARCH 20

EASTERN FRONT, *GERMANY*

Units of the 1st Belorussian Front storm Altdamm. There are now no German positions on the east bank of the northern Oder River.

MARCH 22–31

WESTERN FRONT, *GERMANY*

The Allied crossings of the Rhine River begin. The 5th Division of the US Third Army crosses the Rhine near Nierstein and Oppenheim and establishes bridgeheads on the east bank. By the end of the 23rd, the whole of the division is over the river. German resistance is negligible.

Field Marshal Bernard Montgomery's 21st Army Group (1.25 million men) begins crossing the river on the 23rd, when the British 51st (Highland)

▲ *Paratroopers of the British 6th Airborne Division dropping on the east bank of the Rhine on 23 March, 1945.*

▼ *The Rhine was a formidable barrier, but crossing it was largely a logistical rather than a military problem for the Allies.*

MARCH 17–19

FAR EAST, *BURMA*

The battle for Mandalay begins. The main Japanese garrison is situated in Fort Dufferin, which is pounded incessantly by British artillery. Following an intensive aerial bombardment, the

▼ *Prisoners taken by the Allies in their Rhine operations. Many Germans were now offering only token resistance.*

▲ *The US II Amphibious Corps pours ashore on Okinawa. By the end of the first day, 50,000 troops had been landed.*

Division and the Canadian 3rd Division cross near Rees and Emmerich. On the 24th, the US 87th Division crosses at Boppard and the 89th at St. Goer, while farther north the British 6th and the US 17th Airborne Divisions land east of the Rhine and link up with advancing British forces.

German units, exhausted and depleted by the fierce battles west of the river, are only able to offer token resistance. By the end of the month the Algerian 3rd Division of General de Lattre de Tassigny's French First Army has crossed the river – every Allied army now has troops on the east bank of the Rhine.

MARCH 24

FAR EAST, *BURMA*
The Allied Chinese New First Army links up with the Chinese 50th Division near Hsipaw, thus bringing the campaign in northern Burma to an end.

MARCH 25–28

EASTERN FRONT, *HUNGARY*
The Soviet 2nd Ukrainian Front starts its attack across the Hron River and along the north bank of the Danube. Hungarian troops begin deserting their German allies in droves, while German commanders report a loss of confidence among their own men. By the

28th, the Red Army has reached the Austrian border in the Köszeg–Szombathely area.

MARCH 30

EASTERN FRONT, *POLAND*
Danzig is captured by the Red Army, along with 10,000 German prisoners and 45 submarines in the harbor.

APRIL 1

PACIFIC, *OKINAWA*
Operation Iceberg, the US invasion of the island, commences. Admiral Chester W. Nimitz, commander-in-chief Pacific Fleet and Pacific Ocean areas, has assigned Vice Admiral Richmond Turner as commander of the amphibious forces and Vice Admiral Marc Mitscher as commander of the fast carrier forces. The US Tenth Army is led by Lieutenant General Simon B. Buckner, and comprises 183,000 men.

The island, only 325 miles (520 km) from Japan, has two airfields on the western side and two partially-protected bays on the east coast – an excellent springboard for the proposed invasion of the Japanese mainland.

The amphibious landing by the US II Amphibious Corps and XXIV Corps is virtually unopposed. The Japanese commander, Major General Mitsuru

▶ *The conquest of islands close to Japan meant US fighters, such as these Mustangs, could escort the bombers on their missions to the Japanese homelands.*

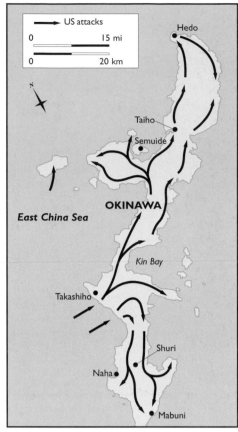

▲ *After the initial US Army and Marine thrust across Okinawa, the 6th Marine Division cleared the north of the island.*

◄ *The Japanese battleship Yamato under air attack. Its sinking signaled the end of the Japanese surface fleet.*

Ushijima, has withdrawn his 80,000 men behind Shuri, where he has built a major defensive line.

APRIL 2–3

WESTERN FRONT, *GERMANY*

Units of the US First and Third Armies meet at Lippstadt to complete the

encirclement of the economically-important Ruhr region.

APRIL 4

WESTERN FRONT, *HOLLAND*

Field Marshal Bernard Montgomery's 21st Army Group begins its offensive to liberate Holland and sweep across northern Germany. As food stocks in Holland are low, this operation is important as the Dutch postwar political attitude toward the Allies will depend on the speed of liberation.

APRIL 5

POLITICS, *CZECHOSLOVAKIA*

At Kosice, the National Front government of Czechs and Slovaks announces its program and proclaims the democratic principles of the Czech Republic. Stating that the liberation of the country is the first priority, it calls on the population to undertake a broad and active struggle against the Germans.

APRIL 7

SEA WAR, *PACIFIC*

The *Yamato*, the world's largest battle-ship, is sunk at sea by US warplanes while making its way to attack US forces on Okinawa. The battleship is on a suicide mission, with just enough fuel to reach the island.

AIR WAR, *JAPAN*

Some 108 P-51s take off from Iwo Jima to escort B-29 bombers heading for Japan. They are the first US land-based fighters to reach mainland Japan.

APRIL 9

PACIFIC, *OKINAWA*

The US XXIV Corps begins to attack the Shuri defenses on Okinawa. Japanese resistance is heavy and the Americans can make no headway.

APRIL 9–10

ITALY, *ARGENTA GAP*

The final campaign in Italy begins as the US Fifth and British Eighth Armies commence their fight for control of the Po Valley. The plan of Field Marshal Harold Alexander, commander-in-chief of Allied forces in Italy, is for the Eighth Army to attack westward through the Argenta Gap, while the Fifth Army strikes north, west of Bologna, thereby trapping German Army Group C between the two.

On the night of April 9, after a massive aerial bombardment and five artillery bombardments, the offensive opens with the Indian 8th and New Zealand 2nd Divisions attacking toward Lugo across the Senino River. By dawn on the 10th, Allied tanks are crossing the Senino River over three bridges, with Allied aircraft overhead providing effective support to the operation.

APRIL 10

FAR EAST, *BURMA*

General William Slim's British Four-teenth Army commences an offensive to capture Rangoon. It is a race against time to take the city before the monsoons begin in mid-May. He must

▼ *The funeral procession of US President Franklin D. Roosevelt, who died with victory in Europe a matter of days away.*

DECISIVE WEAPONS

ATOMIC BOMBS

The science behind the atomic bomb is relatively simple: a neutral neutron particle hits the nucleus of a uranium atom, which splits into two fragments: a krypton atom and a Barium atom. The reaction also releases an enormous burst of energy. One or two fresh neutrons are released, some of which find other nuclear targets and repeat the process. Each splitting or "fission" causes more – the chain reaction. A rapid chain reaction becomes a nuclear explosion. However, uranium has several isotopes, and the trick is to find a way of isolating the uranium isotope U-235, which has the highest energy factor for the development of nuclear power.

The atomic bomb dropped on Hiroshima, "Little Boy," was a "gun-type" weapon, shooting a piece of subcritical U-235 into another, cup-shaped piece to create the supercritical mass – and the nuclear explosion. The bomb used against Nagasaki – "Fat Man" – used the implosion method, with a ring of 64 detonators shooting segments of plutonium together to obtain the supercritical mass. The costs were huge: the Manhattan Project, the secret US project led by J. Robert Oppenheimer that developed the atomic bomb, cost the US government $2 billion.

also stop the Japanese forming a defensive line north of Rangoon and halting his advance.

APRIL 11

WESTERN FRONT, *GERMANY*
The US Ninth Army arrives at the Elbe River near Magdeburg. An increasing number of German towns are surrendering without a fight, while Hitler's armies fighting in western Germany are disintegrating.

APRIL 12

POLITICS, *UNITED STATES*
President Franklin D. Roosevelt dies of a cerebral haemorrhage in Warm Springs, Georgia. Vice President Harry S. Truman takes over the position of president, and one of his first decisions is to cancel a plan to launch old, pilotless aircraft packed with explosives against industrial targets in Germany following Prime Minister Winston Churchill's concern that it may provoke retaliation against London.

APRIL 13

EASTERN FRONT, *AUSTRIA*
The Red Army liberates Vienna.

APRIL 14

POLITICS, *ALLIES*
General Dwight D. Eisenhower, Supreme Commander of Allied Armies in the West, informs the Combined Chiefs-of-Staff that the Allied thrust against Berlin takes second place to the securing of the northern (Norway and Denmark) and southern (south Germany and Austria) Allied flanks. The British chiefs-of-staff are dissatisfied, but acknowledge Eisenhower's reasoning, and approve his plans on the 18th.

ITALY, *ARGENTA GAP*
The offensive by the US Fifth Army in northern Italy begins. Preceded by a bombardment by 500 ground-attack aircraft, the US 1st Armored, US 10th Mountain, and Brazilian 1st Divisions attack between Vergato and Montese, and make good progress.

APRIL 16

EASTERN FRONT, *GERMANY*
The Soviet offensive to capture Berlin commences. The Soviet plan has three parts: a breakthrough on the Oder and Neisse Rivers; the fragmentation and isolation of German units in and around Berlin; and the annihilation of said units, capture of the city, and an advance to the Elbe River.

The Red Army forces involved are the 2nd Belorussian and 1st Ukrainian Fronts, the Long Range Force, the Dniepr Flotilla, and two Polish armies – a total of 2.5 million men, 41,600 guns and mortars, 6250 tanks and self-propelled guns, and 7500 combat aircraft. German forces consist of the Third Panzer and Ninth Armies of Army Group Vistula; the Fourth Panzer and Seventeenth Armies of Army Group Center; a host of *Volkssturm* ("home guard"), security and police detachments in Berlin itself; and a reserve of eight divisions – a total of

▼ *US Private Paul Drop stands guard over thousands of German prisoners taken in the Ruhr Pocket in April 1945.*

▲ *The Hohenzollern Bridge over the Rhine River near Cologne, demolished by retreating German forces in April 1945.*

▲ *A US truck races past the corpse of a German soldier during the Allied drive to liberate Holland.*

one million men, 10,400 guns and mortars, 1500 tanks or assault guns, and 3300 combat aircraft.

ITALY, *ARGENTA GAP*
The 78th and 56th Divisions of the British Eighth Army overcome the Fossa Marina, a canal running northeast from Argenta into

Lake Comacchio, with a combination of land and amphibious assaults. The German line has been fractured, and the Allies are through the Argenta Gap.

APRIL 17

PACIFIC, *PHILIPPINES*
Elements of the US X Corps land on Mindanao.

APRIL 18

WESTERN FRONT, *GERMANY*
All German resistance in the Ruhr industrial area ceases; 370,000 prisoners fall into Allied hands.

WESTERN FRONT, *HOLLAND*
The Canadian I Corps, encountering sporadic resistance, has reached Harderwijk, thus isolating German forces in the west of the country.

APRIL 20

WESTERN FRONT, *GERMANY*
Nuremberg, the shrine of National Socialism in southern Germany, falls to the US Third Army after a five-day battle. The city had been defended by two German divisions, Luftwaffe and

▼ *The taking of Berlin, Hitler's capital, was the climax of the Red Army's war.*

→	Soviet attacks
——	Front line, April 16
-----	Front line, April 18
– · –	Front line, April 25
– –	Front line, May 8

0 ____ 50 mi
0 ____ 80 km

Volkssturm battalions, and ringed by anti-aircraft guns, and the German commander had vowed to Hitler that he and his men would fight to the bitter end.

EASTERN FRONT, *GERMANY*
Marshal Georgi Zhukov's 1st Belorussian Front has smashed German resistance on the Oder River and is advancing toward Berlin. The Soviet troops have had to overcome three defensive belts, each consisting of two or three layers of troops.

APRIL 22

EASTERN FRONT, *GERMANY*
The Soviet high command has ordered Marshals Georgi Zhukov and Ivan Konev to complete the encirclement of German forces in the forests southeast of Berlin by April 24 to prevent them breaking through to the city to increase the strength of its garrison. This move will also close the Red Army ring to the west of Berlin to prevent the escape of enemy units from the capital of the Third Reich. Adolf Hitler, spurning a chance to flee to Bavaria, decides to stay in the city and supervise its defense.

ITALY, *ARGENTA GAP*
The South African 6th Armored and British 6th Armored Divisions meet at Finale, north of the Reno River. The Germans are in head-long retreat from the Argenta Gap toward the Po River, leaving most of their guns, tanks, and transport behind.

▲ *The last reserves: a Berlin woman learns how to use an antitank weapon in the final days of the war.*

▶ *Soviet troops close in on "Fortress Berlin." German resistance alternated between the fanatical and token.*

APRIL 23

WESTERN FRONT, *GERMANY*
The last German defenders in the Harz Mountains are captured. Farther north, the British Second Army enters the outskirts of Hamburg.

APRIL 25–27

EASTERN FRONT, *GERMANY*
Marshal Georgi Zhukov's 1st Belorussian Front and Marshal Ivan Konev's 1st Ukrainian Front complete the encirclement of Berlin, trapping its defenders. The assault on the

▶ *As the Battle of Berlin rages, British troops mop up the last pockets of resistance in north Germany.*

city begins on the 26th, preceded by heavy air strikes and artillery bombardments, with attacks from all sides simultaneously. By the 27th, "Fortress Berlin" has been reduced to an east-to-west belt 10 miles (16 km) long by three miles (5 km) wide. German forces within the city are affected by widespread desertions and suicides.

APRIL 28

POLITICS, *HOLLAND*
The first meeting between Allied and German representatives takes place in western Holland. The Reichskommissar for the Netherlands, Artur von Seyss-Inquart, has offered the Allies the freedom to import food and coal into German-occupied western Holland to alleviate the plight of the civilian population if they will halt their forces to the east. This leads to a cessation of hostilities and saves the country from the ravages of further fighting.

POLITICS, *ITALY*
Mussolini's puppet fascist state collapses along with German resistance in the north of the country. Attempting to flee to Austria, Il Duce and his mistress Claretta Petacci are captured by partisans. On the orders of the Committee of National Liberation, Walter Audisio, a communist member of the Volunteer Freedom Corps, shoots them both. Their mutilated bodies are later hung up in the Piazzale Loreto, Milan.

EASTERN FRONT, *GERMANY*
Soviet troops begin the assault on the Reichstag by attacking across the Moltke Bridge. The Germans launch furious counterattacks, and at the strongpoints of the Ministry of the Interior (defended by SS troops) and the Kroll Opera resistance is fierce.

APRIL 29

POLITICS, *GERMANY*
Adolf Hitler, now confined to the "Führerbunker" behind the Reichs Chancellery, orders Colonel General Ritter von Greim to leave Berlin and arrest Heinrich Himmler, head of the SS, for his attempts to seek peace with the Allies. Greim had been appointed commander-in-chief of the Luftwaffe on the 23rd following Hermann Goering's attempt to negotiate with the Allies on his behalf. Hitler publishes his "Political Testament," in which he blames international Jewry for the outbreak of the war. He nominates Admiral Karl Doenitz as his successor, and marries his long-time mistress, Eva Braun.

POLITICS, *ITALY*
As a result of behind-the-scenes dealings between Karl Wolff, senior commander of the SS and police in Italy, and Allen Dulles, head of the American Office of Strategic Services (OSS) in Switzerland, Wolff and General Heinrich von Vietinghoff, German commander-in-chief in Italy, sign the instrument of unconditional surrender in northern Italy, to come into affect on May 2. The Swiss, the Allies, and many Germans and Italians in Italy have been concerned about a drawn-out campaign in Hitler's "Alpine Fortress," and the probable destruction of north Italy's industry as a result of Hitler's scorched earth policy.

▼ *Soviet rocket-launchers blast German positions in Potsdam railroad station in the final days of the Battle of Berlin.*

▲ *Hitler and his mistress Eva Braun, whom he married in Berlin just prior to their mutual suicide at the end of April.*

EASTERN FRONT, *GERMANY*
The trapped German force around Frankfurt-an-der-Oder attempts to break out of its pocket to reach Berlin. This results in three days of savage fighting in which it is annihilated. Of its original strength of 200,000 men, 60,000 are killed, and 120,000 taken prisoner. Only small groups succeed in slipping through Soviet lines.

HOME FRONT, *HOLLAND*
The RAF begins dropping food supplies to alleviate the plight of the country's starving civilians.

APRIL 30

POLITICS, *GERMANY*
Adolf Hitler and Eva Braun commit suicide in the Führerbunker in Berlin. Hitler shoots himself, while Braun takes poison. Their bodies are later cremated by the SS.

MAY 1

POLITICS, *GERMANY*
General Krebs, chief of the General Staff of the Army High Command, initiates cease-fire negotiations with the Soviets on behalf of the Nazi leadership in Berlin (Martin Bormann, Nazi Party Minister, and Josef Goebbels, Reichskommissar for Defense of the Capital). The Soviets demand unconditional surrender and the fighting in the capital and elsewhere continues.

FAR EAST, *BURMA*
In the early hours, the 2nd Gurkha Parachute Battalion makes an airborne drop to secure Elephant Point, southeast of Rangoon, to enable Allied amphibious forces to enter the Rangoon River unopposed from the sea. After a brief fight the site is secured.

MAY 2

WESTERN FRONT, *GERMANY*
The British 6th Airborne Division of the 21st Army Group moves into Wismar, just in time to prevent the Red Army entering Schleswig-Holstein.

EASTERN FRONT, *GERMANY*
Following a savage three-day battle, in which half the 5000-strong garrison has been killed, the Reichstag in Berlin falls to the Red Army and the Hammer and Sickle is raised above the shell-scarred parliament building.

General Helmuth Weidling, commandant of Berlin, surrenders the city and its remaining troops to Marshal Georgi Zhukov. Taking the city has cost the Soviets 300,000 men killed, wounded, or missing, over 2000

▶ The Hammer and Sickle flies over Berlin, signaling the fall of the city to the Red Army and the end of the Third Reich.

tanks and self-propelled guns, and over 500 aircraft. The Germans have lost one million men killed, wounded, or taken prisoner.

FAR EAST, *BURMA*
The Indian 20th Division captures the town of Prome, thus severing the Japanese line of retreat from the Arakan. In the south, the Indian 26th Division makes an amphibious landing along the Rangoon River.

MAY 3

FAR EAST, *BURMA*
Following 38 months of Japanese occupation, Rangoon falls to the Allies without a fight. The city's infrastructure is in tatters, with buildings extensively damaged by bombing.

MAY 3–4

POLITICS, *GERMANY*
The whole of the northwest of the country is under British control. Admiral Karl Doenitz sends Admiral Hans von Friedeburg to Field Marshal Bernard Montgomery's headquarters at Lüneburg to discuss surrender terms. On the 4th, the German delegation signs the instrument of surrender – covering German forces in

Holland, northwest Germany, the German islands, Schleswig-Holstein, and Denmark – to come into effect at 0800 hours on May 5.

MAY 4–5

POLITICS, *DENMARK*
Some 20,000 members of the Danish Resistance movement, organized under the central leadership of the Freedom Council, come out of hiding and take over the key points in the country. Soon, they are in control of Denmark. The first Allies arrive on the 5th.

MAY 5

EASTERN FRONT, *CZECHOSLOVAKIA*
With the Red Army getting nearer, Czech nationalists begin the Prague uprising. By the end of the day, there are 2000 barricades in the city, and all the important bridges over the Vltava River have been seized. Field Marshal Ferdinand Schörner, commander of the German Army Group Center, has ordered units to the city to crush the rebellion.

MAY 7

POLITICS, *GERMANY*
General Alfred Jodl, acting on behalf of the German government, signs the act of surrender to the Allies of all German forces

◄ *A grim-faced Admiral Hans von Friedeburg and Field Marshal Bernard Montgomery finalize the German surrender.*

realizing that the situation is hopeless, commits ritual suicide in the early hours of the morning in a cave near Mabuni. The 82-day battle, which has seen the extensive use of Japanese kamikaze attacks, has claimed the lives of 110,000 Japanese military personnel. US Navy losses amount to 9731, of whom 4907 are killed, while the Tenth Army has suffered 7613 men killed or missing, and 31,807 wounded. There have also been over 26,000 noncombatant casualties, mostly Japanese civilians, many of whom have committed suicide.

JULY 3–11

FAR EAST, *BURMA*

The remnants of the Japanese Thirty-third Army – 6000 men – attack Allied positions at Waw from the Pegu Yomas. The aim is to threaten and, if possible, to cut the British Twelfth Army's rail and road links to Rangoon, and also draw some of its units away from the center, thus making possible the movement of the Japanese Twenty-eighth Army east between Toungoo and Nyaunglebin. However, in the face

▼ *Czech nationalists fight German troops in Prague behind one of the 2000 barricades erected by the insurgents.*

still in the field. Hostilities are to cease by midnight on May 8 at the latest. In Norway the German garrison of 350,000 men capitulates to the Allies. The German Army Group South surrenders to the US Third Army in Austria.

MAY 9–10

EASTERN FRONT, *CZECHOSLOVAKIA*

Prague is liberated by the Red Army with the help of the partisans. By the evening, Soviet troops have sealed off all avenues of escape west for Army Group Center. German troops, seeing the hopelessness of their situation, begin to surrender in their thousands. On the 10th, the 1st Ukrainian Front makes contact with the US Third Army on the Chemnitz–Rokycany line.

MAY 15

BALKANS, *YUGOSLAVIA*

The last German troops fighting in the country surrender.

MAY 29

PACIFIC, *OKINAWA*

The US 1st Marine Division takes Shuri after hard fighting. To date the Americans have suffered 20,000 casualties trying to take the Japanese-held island.

JUNE 1

FAR EAST, *BURMA*

Having broken and scattered all Japanese opposition in Burma, General William Slim's British Four-teenth Army is mopping up the 70,000 widely-dispersed enemy troops in the country. The Japanese Twenty-eighth Army, having been forced to retreat east to avoid starvation, has been shattered by the XXXIII Corps at the Kama bridgehead. It is now nothing more than an ill-armed rabble.

JUNE 22

PACIFIC, *OKINAWA*

All Japanese resistance on the island ends. The Japanese commander, Lieutenant General Mitsuru Ushijima,

of heavy ground and air resistance, all Japanese efforts to take Waw cease by the 11th.

JULY 12

POLITICS, *JAPAN*

War leader Shigenori Togo instructs the Japanese ambassador in Moscow to inform the authorities that the emperor wants the war to cease. To this end, Prince Konoye is to be sent as a special envoy to the Soviet Union, with authority from the emperor to discuss Soviet and Japanese relations, including the future of Japanese-occupied Manchuria. However, Togo has repeatedly stressed that the Allied demand for unconditional surrender leaves his government with no choice but to continue fighting.

Indeed, the Allies are laying plans to invade the Japanese mainland. Its is proposed that the first landings, code-named Operation Olympic, will take place in November. The second, Operation Coronet, is scheduled for March 1946. The US planners expect to suffer severe casualties. However, neither operation will take place.

JULY 16

TECHNOLOGY, *UNITED STATES*
The world's first atomic bomb is

▼ The Soviet offensive in Manchuria was a superb example of an all-arms mobile operation on a vast scale.

exploded at Alamogordo, New Mexico. The secret work to develop the weapon is code-named the Manhattan Project. A specialized bomber unit, the 509th Composite Group, is training to attack Japan with atomic bombs.

JULY 17–AUGUST 2

POLITICS, *ALLIES*
The Potsdam Conference takes place in Germany. The "Big Three" – US President Harry Truman, Soviet leader Marshal Joseph Stalin, and British Prime Minister Clement Attlee (who had defeated Churchill in a general election on July 5) – meet to discuss postwar policy. Japan

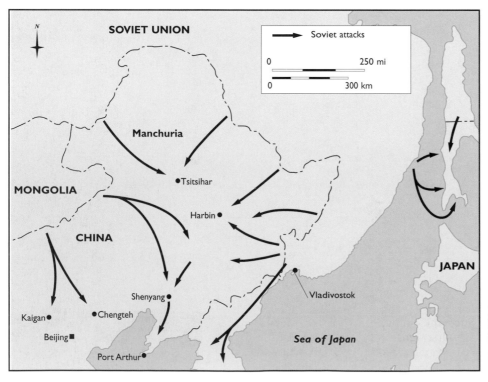

is informed that an immediate surrender would result in the continued existence of its nation, although not its empire. War criminals will be prosecuted and there will be a temporary occupation. The proclamation also makes it clear that continued resistance will lead to the "utter devastation of the Japanese home-land." This is a veiled reference to the use of atomic weapons against Japan.

JULY 19

FAR EAST, *BURMA*
The Japanese Twenty-eighth Army attempts to break out of the Pegu Yomas east across the Sittang River. Forewarned, the Indian 17th Division's guns cut down the Japanese in their hundreds, while many others drown in the river. The breakout is a shambles, and signals the end of the army.

JULY 26

PACIFIC, *PHILIPPINES*
Following an amphibious landing at Sarangani Bay on the 12th, Japanese resistance on Mindanao is overcome.

JULY 28

POLITICS, *JAPAN*
Prime Minister Kantaro Suzuki announces that both he and his cabinet will ignore the recent Allied Potsdam Proclamation.

▼ *Sailors and officials on the deck of the* USS Missouri *witness the Japanese sign surrender documents in Tokyo Bay.*

AUGUST 4

FAR EAST, *BURMA*
The last remnants of the Japanese Twenty-eighth Army are killed. The Allies have lost just 96 men killed.

AUGUST 6

AIR WAR, *JAPAN*
The B-29 Superfortress *Enola Gay* drops an atomic bomb on the Japanese city of Hiroshima, killing 70,000 and injuring the same number.

AUGUST 9

FAR EAST, *MANCHURIA*
A massive Soviet offensive by 1.5 million men begins against the Japanese Kwantung Army. The swiftest campaign in the Red Army's history has begun.

AIR WAR, *JAPAN*
A second US atomic bomb is dropped on Nagasaki, following Tokyo's non-compliance with an ultimatum that further bombs would be dropped unless there was an immediate surrender. The bomb kills 35,000 people and injures a further 60,000.

AUGUST 10

POLITICS, *JAPAN*
Following a conference, during which the emperor voices his support for an immediate acceptance of the Potsdam Proclamation, Japan announces its will-ingness to surrender unconditionally.

AUGUST 15

POLITICS, *JAPAN*
Emperor Hirohito broadcasts to the Japanese people for the first tine calling on them to respond loyally to his command to surrender.

AUGUST 23

FAR EAST, *MANCHURIA*
The campaign in Manchuria ends in total Soviet victory. The Japanese have lost over 80,000 dead and 594,000 taken prisoner. Soviet losses are 8000 men killed and 22,000 wounded.

SEPTEMBER 2

POLITICS, *ALLIES*
Aboard the battleship *Missouri* in Tokyo Bay, Foreign Minister Mamoru Shigemitsu and General Yoshijiro Umezo sign the Instrument of Surrender. General Douglas MacArthur, Supreme Commander for the Allied Powers, signs on behalf of all the nations at war with Japan. World War II is finally over.

KEY MOMENTS

COUNTING THE COST
World War II was probably the most destructive conflict in the history of mankind. Of the major belligerents, the Soviet Union suffered the most casualties, with an estimated 7.5 million military dead. The Nazis' racial policies and general disre-gard for the population of the Soviet Union resulted in an estimated 15 million Russian civilian deaths. Germany, having plunged the world into conflict, paid a huge price, its armed forces suffering 2.8 million fatalities and a further 7.2 million wounded. On the home front, a total of 500,000 Germans lost their lives. Japan suffered 1.5 million military dead in the war, and 300,000 civil-ians died during the US bombing campaign of the Japanese homeland. Italy had 77,000 military deaths and upward of 40,000 civilian fatalities.

The Western Allied nations lost far fewer men than the Soviet Union: the United States 292,000; Great Britain 397,762; and France 210,600. US civilian deaths were negligible, while Great Britain suffered 65,000 civilian deaths; France 108,000.

In total, the military dead during the war is estimated to be 15 million, and civilian deaths are estimated at 34 million, including some six million Jews murdered in the various Nazi extermination camps.

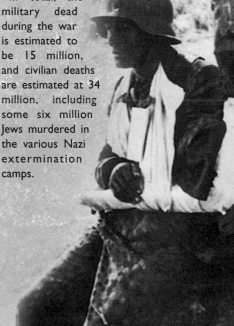

AFTERMATH

The end of World War II ushered in the Nuclear Age, and the political and military strategy of all nations was influenced by the confrontation between the two major nuclear powers: the United States and the Soviet Union. Both countries had achieved superpower status simultaneously, having done so amid the ruins left by World War II.

They were afraid of each other, and they represented incompatible systems: capitalism and communism. The most important strategic fact of life for each was the existence and power of the other. The friction that resulted from this confrontation was called the Cold War, and was to have a profound affect on the postwar world.

THE COLD WAR

In the postwar period, the most important confrontation was the Cold War between the superpowers. Following the inconclusive Potsdam Conference, Stalin decided to consolidate communist control over Eastern Europe, which was occupied by one million Red Army troops. The process was gradual, and the 1945 and 1946 elections in the

region were relatively free. However, by 1947 Soviet-dominated governments had been set up in Hungary, Poland, Bulgaria, and Romania (and in Czechoslovakia in February 1948) – only Yugoslavia retained some independence. Moreover, so-called "national communist" leaders, such as Wladyslaw Gomulka in Poland, were removed, thus assuring full Soviet control.

▼ Berlin in ruins after the war. Germany's infrastructure was all but destroyed during the fighting.

◄ *A torn and twisted railroad bridge – just one example of Europe's wrecked communications network.*

since 1911 a strong regime controlled all Chinese territory, and had plans (already tested in some areas) for the regeneration of the economy and the transformation of the country. With the establishment of an industrial infrastructure, a growing petroleum sector, and a nuclear capability, China quickly became a major power in Asia.

In February 1950 China signed a Treaty of Friendship with the Soviet Union, thus creating a supposed "monolithic" structure of world communism. One tangible result of this was massive Chinese involvement in the Korean War (1950–53), which was countered by US and other Western military forces on the Korean Peninsula. Fortunately for the West, the ideological differences and conflicting ambitions of the Soviet Union and China rapidly created major splits in their alliance.

When civil war and an attempted communist coup in Greece took place in December 1947, and the Soviet Union attempted to freeze out the Western sectors of Berlin and incorporate the whole city into the German Democratic Republic in April 1948, the United States reacted with vigor, and began a policy to "contain" the Soviet Union by a series of alliances and bases, such as the North Atlantic Treaty Organization (NATO) and the South-East Asia Treaty Organization (SEATO). By 1959, the United States had over 1400 foreign bases. Fortunately, overt hostilities between the two superpowers never took place.

The victory of Mao Zhe-dong in the Chinese Civil War in 1949 created the People's Republic of China. When the communists came to power they inherited a bankrupt economy: hyper-inflation had destroyed the currency, the banking system, and urban business. Industrial plant was in ruins, and much of the rail system was inoperative. However, for the first time

▶ *The "Big Three" nations fell out after the end of the war.*

THE UNITED NATIONS

The term "United Nations" was originally used during World War II to denote those countries that were allied against the Axis powers of Germany, Italy, and Japan. The earliest attempt to permanently establish the United Nations was a conference at Dumbarton Oaks, Washington D.C., where representatives of the "Big Four" (the United States, Great Britain, the Soviet Union, and China) met from August 21 to October 7, 1944, to draft preliminary proposals.

These proposals for the postwar world were discussed in more detail at the Yalta Conference in February 1945, and the decisions reached at that venue formed the basis of negotiations at the United Nations Conference held in San Francisco two months later. The resultant Charter of the United Nations was signed by 50 states in June and came into force on October 24, 1945.

The basic aims of the United Nations are the maintenance of international peace and security, the development of friendly relations between states based on the principles of equal rights in law and self-determination, and the encouragement of international cooperation to solve international social, economic, cultural, and humanitarian problems.

position to revitalize the world economy. The manifestation of this revitalization was the Marshall Plan (April 1948–December 1951), designed to rehabilitate the economies of 17 European nations in order to create stable conditions in which democratic institutions could survive. The aims suited US foreign policy, as it was feared that poverty, unemployment, and dislocation would reinforce the popular appeal of communism.

Aid was initially offered to almost all European nations, including those under the military occupation of the Soviet Union. However, the plan was rejected by Stalin in January 1949 and the Soviet Union and its dependencies established the Council of Mutual Economic Assistance (Comecon) in response. This left the following countries to participate in the plan: Austria, Belgium, Denmark, France, Great

▶ *French tanks and an armored personnel carrier in Indochina in 1948.*

▼ *Unloading food supplies during the 1948 Berlin blockade – an example of Soviet brinkmanship during the Cold War.*

The Cold War's main front, however, was not in Asia but in Europe, with the dividing line running through the center of the continent, and through the center of Berlin. Europe itself was politically disorganised and economically shattered. In European Russia and much of Eastern Europe, where the tides of war had ebbed and flowed, a vast wilderness had been created that was barren of everything save people. Agricultural production was in dire straits, compounded by the breakdown of the communications network, and output of coal, steel, and iron was reduced drastically compared to prewar levels. The sheer enormity of the physical damage would have prevented a rapid return to peacetime conditions anyway, but the partition of Europe into US and Soviet spheres of influence further aggravated the problem.

THE MARSHALL PLAN
Only the United States, with its surplus of production and materials, was in a

for in mid-1945 Germany had no running railroads, no postal service and in many areas no gas, electricity, or water. But US aid (also given to Japan) stimulated production and revitalized the economy. One of the benefits was a social democratic Federal Republic of Germany, which joined its former enemy France to create a bloc which promoted peace and development in Central Europe.

DECOLONIZATION

The reverberations of the changes in Europe were felt in Africa and the Middle East, where nationalism developed rapidly after World War II. In Africa, the experience of African soldiers in overseas theaters, the examples of nationalist movements in India and Indonesia, plus the influx of Allied personnel into African countries, from whom native Africans learned new skills and new attitudes, made the end of colonialism inevitable. There was a new generation of nationalist leaders, such as Jomo Kenyatta, founder of the Kenya African Union.

By the end of 1960 all the former colonies of French West and French Equatorial Africa were politically independent, and Britain and Belgium had read the signs of the times and had granted their colonies independence. Only Portugal and the white settlers in Algeria, Rhodesia, and South Africa held out, although the tide of change would eventually sweep them away. A new age had dawned out of the ashes and horrors of World War II.

Britain, Greece, Iceland, Ireland, Italy, Luxembourg, the Netherlands, Norway, Portugal, Sweden, Switzerland, Turkey, and western Germany. The US distributed some $13 billion worth of economic aid, which helped to restore industrial and agricultural production, establish financial stability, and expand trade. The European states set up the Committee of European Economic Cooperation to coordinate participation, which was later replaced by the permanent Organization for European Economic Cooperation (OEEC).

The Marshall Plan was very successful, with some states experiencing a rise in their gross national products of between 15 and 25 percent in this period. In addition, the plan contributed greatly to the rapid renewal of the Western European industries.

The Marshall Plan also facilitated the integration of western Germany into Europe's political and economic infrastructure, paving the way for the Federal Republic of Germany (created in 1949) to play an active role in the European Coal and Steel Community and NATO. This was indeed remarkable,

▶ *A "hot war" during the Cold War. British troops fire at Chinese forces during the Korean War with a Bofors Gun.*

Entries in **bold** refer to major battles or offensives; page
numbers in *italics* refer to picture captions.

INDEX & ACKNOWLEDGMENTS

ACKNOWLEDGMENTS

Robert Hunt Library, pages: 1, 2–3, 4–5, 7(top and bottom), 8(bottom), 8–9(top), 9(bottom), 11(both), 12(top and bottom), 13(bottom left and right), 14–15(top), 15(top center and bottom), 16, 17(all three), 18(bottom), 18–19(top), 19(top), 20(bottom left), 21(bottom), 22–23(all four), 24(top), 25(both), 26(both), 28(all three), 29(all three), 30(top right), 31(both), 32(bottom left and right), 33(both), 34(bottom), 35(all three), 36(top left and right), 38–39(top and bottom), 40(both), 41(bottom right), 42(bottom), 43(bottom right), 44(bottom), 44–45(top), 45(bottom right), 46(top), 47(all three), 48(top), 50(bottom), 52(top left and bottom), 54–55(all four), 56–57(top), 57(bottom), 58(top and bottom), 58–59(center), 60–61(top), 62(top), 62–63(top and bottom), 65(both), 66–67(all three), 68–69(top and bottom), 70–71(all four), 72, 73(top and bottom left), 74(top), 75(top), 76(top and bottom), 76–77, 78(both), 81(both), 82(bottom), 82–83(top), 83(bottom), 84(bottom), 85(both), 86(both), 90–91(bottom), 92(top), 92–93(bottom), 94, 99, 100–01(bottom), 104(bottom), 107(top), 108(center right and bottom), 109(bottom), 110–11(bottom), 111(bottom), 112(both), 114(bottom), 115(bottom), 118(both), 120(both), 122(both), 123(top), 126(top), 128–129(top), 129(top), 135(both), 138(top), 141(top), 142(bottom) 142–43(top), 144(top and bottom), 147(top), 148(top), 150(top), 153(top), 155(both), 156(top), 159(both), 162–63(top and bottom), 166(top), 166–67(bottom), 167(top), 170(top and bottom), 171(top), 170–71(top), 172(bottom left and right), 173(top), 174–75(bottom), 177(top), 178(bottom), 180(top), 180–81(top), 181(top and bottom), 182, 183(bottom), 184(top), 184–85(bottom), 185(bottom).186, 187(bottom), 188(bottom), 188–89(top).
Robert Hunt Library/Australian War Memorial, pages: 77(top), 91(top).
Robert Hunt Library/Bundesarchiv, pages: 10, 12–13(top), 20(top), 24(bottom), 26(top), 28(top), 41(bottom left), 43(bottom left), 44(top), 51(top), 53(bottom), 59(both), 74(bottom), 98(bottom), 98–99(top), 105(bottom), 109(center), 113(top), 117(top), 119 134(top), 151(bottom).
Robert Hunt Library/ECPA, pages: 19(bottom), 21(top), 26(bottom).
Robert Hunt Library/Imperial War Museum, London, pages: 6–7(center), 14, 30(top left),

32(top), 34(top), 36(bottom), 37(both), 42(top), 45(bottom left), 46(center), 48(bottom and center right), 49(both), 51(bottom), 52–53(bottom), 60(bottom), 60–61(bottom), 63(top), 64(top), 69(top right), 80(bottom), 84(top), 87(bottom), 88(top), 88–89(bottom), 89(top), 90(bottom), 95(bottom), 97(bottom), 105(top), 106(both), 113(bottom), 114(top), 115(top), 116(bottom), 116–17(bottom), 121, 122–23(bottom), 124–25(top), 126(bottom), 128(bottom), 129(bottom), 130–31(all four), 132–33(top), 134(bottom), 137(bottom right), 138(bottom), 138–39(top), 139(bottom), 140(top left and right), 142(top), 143(bottom), 144–45(bottom), 145(top), 146(bottom), 151(top), 152(bottom), 153(bottom), 154(both), 156(bottom), 157(both), 158(both), 161(both), 162(top left), 164, 166–67(bottom), 168(bottom), 175(bottom right), 177(bottom), 179(top), 180(bottom), 183(bottom), 189(bottom).
Robert Hunt Library/National Maritime Museum, London, page: 56(bottom).
Robert Hunt Library/SADO, Brussels, pages: 73(bottom right), 80(top), 83(top), 88(center), 101(top), 103(bottom), 109(top),124(bottom).
Robert Hunt Library/SIPHO, Brussels, pages: 30(bottom), 51(center left), 64(bottom), 79(bottom), 103(top), 107(bottom), 108(top), 110(bottom), 116(top), 137(top).
Robert Hunt Library/US Air Force, pages: 110–11(top), 174(top), 176–77(bottom).
Robert Hunt Library/US Army, pages: 75(bottom), 79(top), 132(bottom), 137(bottom left), 146(top), 148(top), 149(top), 152(top), 165(both), 168(top), 168–69(top), 169(top), 171(bottom), 175(top), 178–79(bottom and top), 187(top).
Robert Hunt Library/US Information Agency, page: 136(top).
Robert Hunt Library/US Marine Corps, pages: 102, 126–27(bottom), 127(top), 134(bottom), 146–47(bottom), 150(bottom), 172–73(top).
Robert Hunt Library/US National Archives, pages: 20(bottom), 87(top), 90(top).
Robert Hunt Library/US Navy, pages: 38–39(top), 93(bottom), 95(top), 97(top), 136(bottom), 140–41(bottom), 160(both), 176(top).
Robert Hunt Library/US Office of War Information, pages: 100–101(top).
Robert Hunt Library/YIVO Institute for Jewish Research, pages: 96(top), 104(top).